About This Book

Why is this topic important?

It is almost impossible to underestimate the knowledge gap that will be caused by the retirement of the baby boomer generation. Scientists, CEOs, senior faculty members, nuclear technicians, doctors, lawyers, sales managers, seasoned trainers, and other highly skilled individuals are not walking out the door; they are running out. Simultaneously, a new generation of employees, dubbed gamers, are entering the workforce with a different focus, mentality, and learning style from any previous generation—a mentality forged by playing video games, communicating with handheld gadgets, and Internet surfing.

The knowledge of the departing boomers must be successfully transferred to the incoming gamers. The consequences of inaction or failure are high. But what methods work, and how? Why is knowledge transfer needed? What technology is already in place for this transfer? What organizational commitment is required? Are there examples to follow? *Gadgets, Games, and Gizmos for Learning* answers those questions and more. It serves as a resource providing learning and development professionals, executives, academics, and organizational leaders with the information they need to address this growing issue in a practical and sustainable way.

What can you achieve with this book?

This book provides you with practical and innovative solutions to the impending boomer-to-gamer knowledge transfer problem. It describes how gamer values—such as the use of cheat codes, the love of gadgets, the need to play games, and the desire to be constantly connected—can be leveraged as methods for moving knowledge from the heads of the boomers to the minds of the gamers or, in some cases, to their gadgets and gizmos. As a result, you will not just be helping your organization survive this transitional time period; you will help it profit and thrive.

How is this book organized?

The first chapter of the book introduces several concepts critical to the remainder of the work: the impending boomer retirement wave, boomer traits, and their current control over the workplace. It also defines gamers and describes their traits and the influence that technology and video games have had on them. Finally, it describes the need for innovative methods of transferring knowledge from boomers to gamers.

Each subsequent chapter in the book describes a trait, value, belief, or habit of gamers and how it can be used effectively to transfer knowledge from the boomers to the gamers. The final three chapters discuss how to integrate the knowledge transfer process into an organization, how to sell the concept of gadgets and games to business skeptics, and personal action items a reader, boomer, or gamer can take to understand the other side.

About Pfeiffer

Pfeiffer serves the professional development and hands-on resource needs of training and human resource practitioners and gives them products to do their jobs better. We deliver proven ideas and solutions from experts in HR development and HR management, and we offer effective and customizable tools to improve workplace performance. From novice to seasoned professional, Pfeiffer is the source you can trust to make yourself and your organization more successful.

Essential Knowledge Pfeiffer produces insightful, practical, and comprehensive materials on topics that matter the most to training and HR professionals. Our Essential Knowledge resources translate the expertise of seasoned professionals into practical, how-to guidance on critical workplace issues and problems. These resources are supported by case studies, worksheets, and job aids and are frequently supplemented with CD-ROMs, websites, and other means of making the content easier to read, understand, and use.

Essential Tools Pfeiffer's Essential Tools resources save time and expense by offering proven, ready-to-use materials—including exercises, activities, games, instruments, and assessments—for use during a training or team-learning event. These resources are frequently offered in looseleaf or CD-ROM format to facilitate copying and customization of the material.

Pfeiffer also recognizes the remarkable power of new technologies in expanding the reach and effectiveness of training. While e-hype has often created whizbang solutions in search of a problem, we are dedicated to bringing convenience and enhancements to proven training solutions. All our e-tools comply with rigorous functionality standards. The most appropriate technology wrapped around essential content yields the perfect solution for today's on-the-go trainers and human resource professionals.

Pfeiffer
www.pfeiffer.com

Essential resources for training and HR professionals

GADGETS, GAMES, AND GIZMOS FOR LEARNING

Pfeiffer™

GADGETS, GAMES, AND GIZMOS FOR LEARNING

Tools and Techniques for Transferring Know-How from Boomers to Gamers

Karl M. Kapp

Foreword by John Beck

BICENTENNIAL
1807
WILEY
2007
BICENTENNIAL

John Wiley & Sons, Inc.

Published by Pfeiffer
An Imprint of Wiley
989 Market Street, San Francisco, CA 94103–1741
www.pfeiffer.com

For additional copies/bulk purchases of this book in the U.S. please contact 800–274–4434.

Pfeiffer books and products are available through most bookstores. To contact Pfeiffer directly call our Customer Care Department within the U.S. at 800–274–4434, outside the U.S. at 317–572–3985, fax 317–572–4002, or visit www.pfeiffer.com.

Pfeiffer also publishes its books in a variety of electronic formats. Some content that appears in print may not be available in electronic books.

Library of Congress Cataloging-in-Publication Data

Kapp, Karl M., 1967-
  Gadgets, games, and gizmos for learning: tools and techniques for transferring know-how from boomers to gamers/Karl M. Kapp; foreword by John Beck.
     p. cm.
  Includes bibliographical references and index.
  ISBN-13: 978-0-7879-8654-4 (cloth)
  ISBN-10: 0-7879-8654-2 (cloth)
1. Employees—Training of—Technological innovations. 2. Video gamers as businesspeople. 3. Knowledge management. I. Title.
  HF5549.5.T7K274 2007
  658.3'124—dc22

                                                        2006101889

Acquiring Editor: Lisa Shannon
Director of Development: Kathleen Dolan Davies
Developmental Editor: Susan Rachmeler
Production Editor: Rachel Anderson

Editor: Beverly Miller
Manufacturing Supervisor: Becky Carreño
Editorial Assistants: Caitlin Clarke and Marisa Kelley
Illustrations: Kristin Longenecker and Lotus Art

Printed in the United States of America

Printing   10 9 8 7 6 5 4 3 2 1

Contents

List of Figures and Tables

Figures

Tables

Foreword

WHEN MITCHELL WADE and I sat down to conduct research for *Got Game: How the Gamer Generation Is Reshaping Business Forever,* we never imagined the results we would uncover. We, like many other boomers, had overlooked the force that video games had become. We still viewed them as a niche item that teenagers played to pass the time. Although we expected the research to reveal some differences between gamers and nongamers, what we found was amazing. Quite frankly, we were blown away.

In a survey of twenty-five hundred professionals, we found that those who reported playing more video games when they were young reacted to business situations differently from those who did not—in fact, very differently. Weaned on video games, we call this phenomenon the *gamer generation.*

The gamer generation has grown up in the video game world of immersion, unlimited do-overs, and instant feedback. The result is that they have verifiably different mind-sets, attitudes, and behaviors regarding business, education, and culture from those who did not grow up playing video games.

As a boomer myself, I didn't grow up playing that many video games. I remember desperately wanting *Pong* as a Christmas present when I was a boy. My parents told me that it was too expensive. (I have lived with those emotional scars ever since!) So my coauthor (who has similar emotional scars) and I definitely cannot claim we were part of the gamer generation. Then when the results from our survey came in and were surprisingly positive, they changed my attitude of how I would deal with my kids and their electronic game habits. It also changed how I saw the role of gamers in the workplace.

For one thing, our research revealed that gamers learn differently from boomers. During the boomer generation's matriculation, kindergarten teachers expected children to show up knowing their colors, numbers, and some basic words. Now, gamers not only know the basics but also show up at kindergarten as budding strategists, having already learned problem-solving strategies from electronic children's games like Scholastic's *I'm Ready for Kindergarten: Hugley's Sleepover,* THQ's *Scooby-Doo: Knight of 100 Frights,* and Sound Source Interactive's *The Land Before Time: Math Adventure,* not to mention hundreds of similar games. The expectation of instructors who expect the old industrial age style of teaching to endure in this new environment is as quaint as expecting society to go back to black and white television. It's just not going to happen.

Playing electronic games has created a learning style for the gamers that:

- Aggressively ignores formal instruction.

- Leans heavily toward trial and error (the Reset button is only a click away).

- Encourages exploration and interactive adventures.

- Includes learning from peers but little learning from boomers.

- Is consumed in very small bits, exactly when the learner wants and usually right before it is needed.

Gamers have learned to manipulate electronic information in games, on the Internet, and through electronic gadgets. These gamers are definitely gadget oriented. They think about them, they care about them, and they learn from a very young age to know when a new controller is out or when the next version of a game platform is released. Gadgets and video games are part of their ethos in ways that boomers can maybe appreciate but never fully comprehend. This new relationship with technology will remain with our society forever.

Businesses need to act quickly and decisively to help these gamers, with their new and aggressive self-learning style, to assimilate into the boomer-controlled workplace. Boomers need tools and methods to effectively transfer their knowledge to this new generation—a generation they barely understand.

In lectures and speeches that we have delivered since the publication of *Got Game,* we have made it clear to organizations—business, nonprofit, and governmental—that work and learning systems need to be adapted to this gamer generation. We are regularly surprised by how many boomer executives recognize that there is a disconnect between them and their younger employees, but how few have realized that one of the sources of that generation gap is really the hours upon hours upon hours of video game play that these youngsters logged before entering the workforce. Those who don't recognize games as the source of a gap say that it is the Internet that differentiates them.

And while gamers are facile with the Internet, boomers have almost universally adopted the Internet (at least for e-mail and search functions). But boomers don't know the first thing about games: they don't know the titles, they don't know the metaphors, and in most cases they can't even manipulate a controller. And very important, they didn't grow up with games.

We argue in our book that the way gamer generation minds work is different from those who haven't grown up playing video games. Basic neural pathways in the brain form in our brains until the early teenage years. (The hardening of these neural pathways is exactly why we can naturally learn a new language before that age and have to connect it to a language we already know after we hit about age fifteen.) We believe that those who grow up on games have different models about how the world works, how to succeed, how to learn, how to teach, and how to work together.

What we try to impress on all of the executives with whom we work is that it is simply not enough to become aware that this generation exists. It is important that organizations begin to change the way they interact with employees. As Kapp explains in this book, tapping into the technologies and mind-sets that are second-hand to the gamer generation is ultimately the only way to transfer the knowledge of the boomers to the minds of the gamers.

Any professional concerned about the future workforce will be interested in the ideas and concepts contained in this book—concepts that explain how the boomer generation can transfer its vast knowledge to the gamer generation.

If you are an executive, *Gadgets, Games, and Gizmos for Learning* will open your eyes to the need to establish an infrastructure for transferring knowledge from your existing workforce to these gamers. If you are a manager, this book provides practical examples of how to oversee this emerging workforce. If you are a frontline supervisor, you will learn how you can take simple but effective steps to move some of the knowledge from your older workers to these up-and-comers. If you are working side-by-side with gamers, you'll understand a little bit more about what makes them tick and how you can work together to accomplish goals. If you are a gamer just entering the workforce, you'll learn strategies for understanding how boomers think and relate to you.

As video games become an even bigger influence on our culture and our economy, we all will need to pay attention to the ins and outs of what gamers are thinking both today and tomorrow. There is no doubt that it is a combination of gadgets, games, and gizmos that will lead the way to bridging this new generation gap.

February 2007   John Beck

Preface

"**F**UN."

"Awesome."

"It was so great, I couldn't put it down."

"We have to share this with our friends."

These were the comments I kept hearing from my basement as my two boys played their new video game. New games always translate into neighborhood kids congregating in our basement and investing hours and hours of time trying to reach, and ultimately defeat, the final level. Collaboration, shared vision, working together to achieve a common goal, fun, excitement, and high levels of energy all accompany a new video game's entry into our house.

Meanwhile, back in the office, clients and fellow faculty members kept complaining about boring e-learning, irrelevant training programs, archaic teaching styles, and the increasing pressure to transfer knowledge to new employees or students quickly and effectively. "What is wrong with these kids? Why can't they learn? These kids don't read, and they're always watching TV, listening to music, and working on the computer—all at the same time."

Many of my clients also expressed concern about the impending massive retirement of baby boomers: "We need to capture the knowledge of these boomers before it is too late. What do we do? How do we capture the knowledge and then train the newbies quickly and completely? Why aren't our current methods working?" Trying to find answers to these questions kept me awake at night.

One of those sleepless nights, I found myself watching a televised poker tournament at 2:00 A.M. Through half-open eyes, I noticed twenty-one year olds playing against fifty-five year olds, the grand masters of poker, and winning. How could that be? Why were these young guys, kids really, winning? How could they hold their own against such experienced and knowledgeable players?

Then the announcer, as if reading my mind, provided the answer: "One of the reasons relatively unknown poker players can defeat thirty-year poker veterans is because of online poker." What? Did I hear him correctly: online poker? What do you mean? How is that like "real" poker? Before he could fully explain, he was interrupted by a commercial.

I was fully awake when he returned. The announcer explained that online poker allows a gambler to play as many as eight hands at once against unseen but real opponents. The experience of playing so many hands over and over again while receiving almost instant feedback on good or bad bluffs allows twenty-one year olds to gain as much experience in two years as someone who has been playing poker all his life.

Wow! It hit me. Maybe this generation of kids, my kids, my gamer kids, has a different expectation for learning, an expectation built on a framework of video games providing instant feedback and constant interaction. A framework augmented by constant access to gadgets and a comfort level with technology that boomers and Generation Xers can only imagine.

My boys are obviously able to learn enough to progress through video games at a fairly rapid pace. They have fought with *Donkey Kong,* built roller coasters, commanded armies, outwitted bad guys as *James Bond,* and helped

Link rescue the princess. Kids are learning skills from these games and apply-ing those skills over and over again in other games to achieve success.

In addition, they are techno-savvy. My boys know more about the func-tions of my personal digital assistant than I do. They multitask effortlessly and talk about strategy, economic trade-offs, and online bartering as if they were seasoned M.B.A.s. They pace back and forth with a cell phone like a stock-broker and exchange knowledge and information with each other in huge online communities. Maybe the problem isn't with the kids at all. Maybe it's with us. Maybe it is with our clumsy attempts at knowledge transfer.

That sleepless night resulted in many more, but for entirely different rea-sons. I realized that baby boomers are trying to use an old paradigm to trans-fer knowledge to a new generation, and our traditional methods, hundreds of years old, have begun to crumble. I was fascinated (my wife would say obsessed) with the search for new and innovative methods for knowledge trans-fer, and I found them. They exist in creative efforts in large and small compa-nies, academic institutions playing with the latest in Web technology, and the gadgets, games, and gizmos of this upcoming generation—the gamers.

The result of my late-night insight and subsequent research is this book. It contains techniques and recommendations, gleaned from colleagues, pro-fessional acquaintances, and people in all kinds of fields, transferring all types of knowledge. *Gadgets, Games, and Gizmos for Learning* attempts nothing less than a recasting of existing knowledge transfer and computer systems into tools that can be used to transfer knowledge from the experienced boomers to the incoming gamers. It seeks to create an understanding between two groups who have a critical need to communicate with each other for the sur-vival and success of many organizations.

I hope that future corporate and academic knowledge transfer efforts will elicit the same terms I hear from my basement when a new game is brought home: "Fun." "Awesome." "It was so great, I couldn't put it down." "We have to share this with our colleagues."

February 2007   Karl M. Kapp
Danville, Pennsylvania   www.gadgetsgamesandgizmos.com

To DOROTHY S. KAPP, the best grandmother two gamers could ever have, and to Nathan and Nicholas, the greatest gamers I know

Acknowledgments

WRITING A BOOK is a process with many people to thank for helping bring it to life. First thanks go to Nathan and Nicholas, the gamers who inspired this work and who challenge me on a daily basis to transfer knowledge to them in meaningful ways.

Thank you to my many consulting clients, business associates, former students, and colleagues who made time in their busy schedules to contribute to this book or track down permissions for me: Laura Porter from Sprint Nextel, who provided the fastest permission turnaround known to humankind; Patrick Larkin of Johnson & Johnson, an alumnus of Bloomsburg University; Audrey Kuna, another alumna and founder of her own company, Get Thinking; Greg Walsh of Black and Decker, an alumnus and one of the most creative people I know; David Manning, president of Performance Development Group (PDG), not an alumnus but still a great guy; Richard Mesch, the director of simulations and special projects at PDG; and Tomas Ramirez at Bristol-Myers Squibb. Other Bloomsburg alumni I'd like to thank are

R. Lynn Hummel, an instructional technology specialist at a vocational school in Lewistown, Pennsylvania; Lucas Blair, game player extraordinaire and master of *World of Warcraft;* and Eric Poole, associate director of online M.B.A. programs at Drexel University's LeBow School of Business.

I also extend thanks to David Dunlap of Coccinella Development, who created a fantastic simulation for learning a language through the creative use of a game engine; Andrew Howe, the client service director at AXIOM; Marty Siederer, senior director of training and customer service for the Leukemia & Lymphoma Society; Mark Sylvester, CEO and cofounder of introNetworks; Bjorn Billhardt, CEO of Enspire Learning; and Stephen Robinson of Enspire Learning for tracking down permissions and contributing screen captures.

More thanks go to Amanda Lannert, president and corporate evangelist of Jellyvision; Alison Stone-Briggs, the associate director of the Corporate Institute at Bloomsburg University and my cohort in many corporate-focused activities; Shelia Dove-Jones, professor of special education in the Department of Exceptionality Programs at Bloomsburg University; and Kirk Cantor, professor of plastics and polymer technology at the Pennsylvania College of Technology.

Thanks to Jack Hughes, CEO and founder of TopCoder; Jeff Liable of TopCoder; David Gardiner, licensing manager for Army Game Project; Matthew Adlai-Gail, innovation officer at EduNeering; Chris Carro for his help with understanding the public relations side of the game industry; Gordon Synder Jr., executive director and principal investigator of the National Center for Telecommunications Technologies; and Brian Palagallo at Paramount for his help with permissions.

Special thanks go to John Beck, who got me interested in the academic side of the topic of games and gamers, and Don Deieso, president and CEO of EduNeering, who continually challenges me with new ideas and perspectives on learning, knowledge, and business. Also a wink and a nod to Bonni Scepkowski and Heath Miller of Stellar Meetings and Events.

Thanks to all of my students and former students who contribute to my learning in so many ways and a special thank-you to those whose work appeared in this book: Vince Basile, Yanru Wang, Brian Smith, Justin Moranski, Bill and Ronnie Noone, Regina Bobak, Richard Peck, Frank Brophy, Adrienne Marquette, David Cerreta, Nick Pastore, Ula Konczewska, and Norm Verbeck.

Special thanks to faculty and staff at Bloomsburg University's Institute for Interactive Technologies who contributed in some way to the creation of the book: Kelly Woltornist, Helmut Doll, Celina Byers, Pam Berman, Robyn Defelice, Eric Milks, Mary Nicholson, Karen Swartz, Beth Holmes, Tammy Matthews-Hunter, Michael Phillips, Sara Kliamovich, and Lara Beth Winschuh.

Thank you to Marc Rosenberg for allowing me to take him to lunch and to quiz him on the many aspects of publishing with Pfeiffer. And a thank-you to Kevin Kruse and Clark Aldrich for their help in guiding me to Lisa Shannon. Also, special thanks to the team at Pfeiffer, including Lisa Shannon, who helped the idea to become a manuscript, Caitlin Clarke, Susan Rachmeler, and Bev Miller, who I only know through copyedits. As well as Rachel Anderson, who many times helped me navigate the editing process.

Also, a big thank-you to my three formal reviewers, Mark Oehlert, Michael Qaissaunee, and Bill Herman—two of whom, Mike and Mark, later became contributors. Mark, also thanks for the telephone conversation and insightful ideas. And thanks to Joey L. Monaco, who provided an informal review that was right on the money and kept the book grounded.

A huge thank-you to Kristen Longenecker for the wonderful artwork and cartoons that adorn so many pages of this book. They add value to and a bit of professional whimsy (if there is such a thing) to the topic.

Also, a thank-you to anyone I may have missed. So many people have helped, and any omission is purely an accident.

And finally, a grateful thank-you to my wife, Nancy, who had to put up with a husband who kept claiming that buying and playing video games and cool electronic gadgets was "research."

GADGETS, GAMES, AND GIZMOS FOR LEARNING

Crossing the Chasm

SITTING ALONE IN A DARK and dreary basement is a male creature bathed in a flickering bright light. Occasionally this strange beast emits a sound of defeat, screeching as if its life were ending. At other times, the creature lets out a cry of sheer joy, leaping up and down as if it had just conquered the world.

This is the somewhat skewed image most baby boomers (or boomers) have of someone who plays a lot of video games (Figure 1.1). It is the image of a lonely teenage boy sitting in his parents' basement hours on end and socializing with a game. He thrives on playing in an environment of extreme violence and debauchery. Parents, teachers, and other concerned citizens often mumble or even yell, "Video games rot brains! You'll never grow up to be anything if you play video games all day."

Nothing could be further from the truth.

A growing body of research has begun to reveal that video and computer games have tremendous educational value. It turns out that many of the traits,

Figure 1.1. A Boomer's Somewhat Skewed Image of a Typical Video Game Player.

Source: Reprinted with permission of the artist, Kristin Longenecker.

habits, beliefs, and actions that teenagers and young adults pick up playing electronic games and working with handheld gadgets will help them as they enter the ever-changing global workforce.

In fact, these very traits will forever alter the makeup of businesses, educational institutions, and government agencies. Boomers will be forced to adjust to the characteristics of the gamers, and gamers will need to learn the rules of the boomers. As this generational transition occurs, it is fraught with the usual strife between the work ethic and beliefs of the incoming generation and the institutions and parameters of the ruling generation.

And the timing couldn't be worse.

As gamers enter the workforce, boomers are leaving in droves and taking with them decades of knowledge, experience, and know-how. These independent, career-driven boomers have collectively transformed economies and driven productivity to unprecedented levels. They have lived through and shaped one of the most prosperous and dangerous times in history, and now they are leaving.

It is almost impossible to underestimate the knowledge gap that will be caused by the retirement of the boomers, a retirement wave that is already underway. In the next five years, approximately 40 percent of the skilled labor force will retire.[1] In the next ten years, the entire boomer generation will be over fifty years old.[2]

As the boomers leave and gamers enter, there needs to be an unprecedented transfer of knowledge, information, and data from one generation to the other. The transfer needs to be smooth and effective, or corporations, academic institutions, and government agencies will experience tremendous setbacks in productivity, profitability, quality, and even safety.

In his book *Lost Knowledge,* David DeLong tells a frightening story of a nuclear weapons designer retiring from the Los Alamos National Laboratory after thirty years of loyal service. Usually the retirement of one person is not that big of a deal. However, this retirement is of particular importance: the employee's exit leaves no one left in the lab who understands the design of missiles built between the 1950s and 1960s. "So what?" you might ask. "These missiles are no longer used, are they?"[3] In fact, they are deployed in military bases all over the world. The weapon designer's knowledge of nuclear missiles has to be transferred accurately and effectively to the next generation. Lives are at risk.

In a less dramatic example, one organization had to shut down its most successful production line for a month because a retiree left with key knowledge she didn't even know she possessed.[4] She was the only one who knew the proper method of placing a circuit board onto a customized soldering bench. Although the company thought to give her a gold watch as she retired, no one thought about the need to train a replacement. It was a simple job, after all; the new employee would just follow the written standard operating procedure (SOP) for circuit board placement.

Unfortunately, the SOP was wrong: the documentation had the placement of the board upside down. The retiree knew the SOP was wrong because she had discovered it years ago. And once she discovered the difference, she never used the SOP, and just placed the board in the correct position. She didn't even think about it. Her replacement followed the SOP to the letter, and millions of dollars of circuit boards had to be scrapped. The retired employee solved the problem when the company, four weeks later, decided to call her back to see if she could solve the problem. It took her ten minutes.

Where Is Everybody Going?

One of the biggest, most difficult issues facing organizations over the next ten years is knowledge transfer. In less hectic times, the knowledge transfer from the outgoing generation to the incoming generation took place slowly and at a pace easily digestible by organizations and institutions. This time the pace is blistering. Boomers are ready to retire now. Even if they don't fully retire from the workforce, they will be retiring from their current positions.

Muddying the water is the fact that the incoming gamers have grown up in a vastly different world than the boomers did. Gamers have different ideas about connectivity, reporting hierarchies, learning, and communication, all forged while playing games, manipulating gadgets, and surfing the Web.

Organizations that successfully transfer business acumen and hard-earned experiences to the incoming gamer generation will see tremendous leaps in productivity, quality, and profitability. Organizations that cannot transfer knowledge will experience dire results.

Going, Going . . .

The numbers are staggering. There are between 64 and 77 million boomers, roughly 28 percent of the total U.S. population and 40 percent of the workforce.[5] The sheer size of the post–World War II boomer generation has shaped everything it has encountered.

In the 1950s and 1960s, when the number of children ages five to fourteen increased by more than 40 percent, the sales of potato chips skyrocketed. Auto sales rose as the boomers reached driving age. When the boomers move on, what they once embraced tends to languish like the Hula Hoop or the large number of primary schools built in the 1960s.[6]

Over the years, the boomers have "built up a tremendous amount of knowledge about how things work, how to get things done, and who to go to when problems arise. In some cases, this practical knowledge will be extremely hard to replace because it has been developed in an era of unprecedented technological and scientific advances."[7] The knowledge is starting to walk out the door and will soon be sprinting toward the exits.

The leading edge of the boomer generation began turning sixty in January 2006. According to the Bureau of Labor Statistics approximately 35 million boomers will retire between 2000 and 2020 and another 23 million will retire during the following ten years.[8]

Boomers are ready to retire for a number of reasons: changing interests, a desire to make a difference, spending more time with the family, playing more golf, and concerns about their health. Although boomers claim that they want to rewrite retirement rules and stay employed until later in their sixties, research indicates that most will call it quits earlier than they think.[9] While nearly half of baby boomers expect to work past age sixty-five, only 13 percent of current retirees actually work until that age.[10]

Many retire because they see themselves as not healthy enough or feel too old to work.[11] As of 2005, only 60 percent of sixty year olds, 32 percent of sixty-five year olds, and 19 percent of seventy year olds were employed. The average retirement age in the United States is fifty-nine.[12] A survey of London accountants found that one in ten did not envision working past age fifty.[13] There is a strong possibility that boomers will not work for as long as they are predicting (or hoping).

Even if boomers do stay employed, chances are it will be in a new job. They will become independent consultants or switch to another line of work. Although 71 percent of workers ages forty-five to fifty-six plan to work into their retirement years, 35 percent of that group plan to work part time for interest or enjoyment, 11 percent expect to start their own business, and 7 percent plan to retire from their current jobs but work full time at something else.[14] So even if boomers do not leave the workplace en masse, they will most likely be leaving your organization, taking with them a vast amount of knowledge and possibly costing your company dearly if you don't prepare now.

Broad Impact. No segment of the economy will escape unscathed. The U.S. Defense Department's civilian workforce of 675,000 is expected to lose 506,250 people by 2010. One-third of all secondary schoolteachers in the United States are expected to retire by that time as well. The oil and gas industry can expect to lose more than 60 percent of its employees by 2010, as will the aviation industry.[15]

In the automobile manufacturing sector, the estimated cost of retiring boomers is between $50 and $100 million.[16] This high cost reflects the expense of recruiting new employees, training those employees, and, most critical, lost productivity. The experienced boomers are taking a lot of know-how with them. According to Kim Hill of the Center for Automotive Research in Ann Arbor, Michigan, "The looming skilled labor shortage is the single most important issue the U.S. automobile industry will be facing in the next five to ten years."[17]

The manufacturing sector is in particularly bad shape; many manufacturing companies have eliminated their apprenticeship programs. Trade and vocational schools are mistakenly viewed as places to send troubled students. There have been well-publicized layoffs and plant closures. All of the signals are leading gamers to fear that manufacturing jobs are dead ends.[18] The manufacturing industry will not be able to transfer knowledge to new employees if new employees don't enter into the field. In fact, many old-economy jobs are not seen as desirable by the gamer generation, and the recruitment of gamers is going to be a hot issue in those fields.

While manufacturing seems to have it bad, other studies indicate it is not in the worst shape. Examine the energy, health care, and government sectors for the really alarming data.[19] Half the U.S. government's civilian workforce is eligible to retire within four years. With these types of retirements, there could be a labor shortage of over 5 million skilled workers between 2010 and 2012, because only 25 percent of U.S. companies surveyed indicated they were ready for such a mass exodus. A staggering 31 percent indicated that they have not even thought about the problem.[20]

International Trend. The problem is not confined to the United States. In Europe, the pool of workers ages thirty-four to forty-four is expected to shrink by 19 percent in the United Kingdom, 27 percent in Germany, and 9 percent in Italy.[21] The Ford Motor Company expects the number of workers older than fifty years old to double in its European plants by 2010.[22] Across Europe, baby boomers are already starting to retire, although the first of the European boomers won't reach age sixty-five until 2011. Many of Europe's state-funded pension systems encourage early retirement. Currently, 85.5 percent of adults in France quit work by age sixty, and only 1.3 percent work beyond sixty-five. In Italy, 62 percent of adults call it quits by age fifty-five.[23]

In Japan, the number of people between ages fifteen and sixty-four is expected to decline an average of 740,000 a year for the next ten years; already seventeen out of every one hundred people are over age sixty-five, and this ratio will become thirty out of a hundred in fifteen years.[24] Japan's large neighbor, China, will have over 265 million sixty-five year olds by 2020.[25]

Traits of Boomers

The workplace the boomers are leaving behind is one of their own creation. Although boomers are retiring, they are still very much in control of many institutions, from for-profit companies, to academic institutions, to political leadership. The events and the social setting in which the boomers grew up influences how they act, interact, and react to social and professional situations. Boomers have been classified as having the following characteristics:[26]

- Individualistic
- Driven
- Loyal
- Idealistic
- Skeptical

Individualistic

Boomers value independence and work hard to do their own thing. The skeptics call them the "Me" generation because of the intense focus boomers have on themselves and their own wants and needs. Boomers pioneered the concept of customized products and services. They stand in line waiting to order a grande double espresso with a shot of caramel syrup or one of the other staggering number of coffee options available at Starbucks. Boomers have driven food companies to offer more and more specialized items. Arby's sold only one kind of roast beef sandwich when it was founded in 1964. It now sells thirty different sandwiches. Dryer's Grand Ice Cream offered 34 flavors in 1977; now it offers over 250.[27] The boomers want to do their own thing, even if it means scrapping some of the institutions of their parents. In fact, nearly 50 percent of all U.S. marriages now end in divorce partly as a result of the desire of boomers to "go their own way."[28]

Driven

The drive of this generation is evident in their early commitment to social causes and their later commitment to work and fulfilling their own dreams. This generation invented the term *workaholic*. To boomers, work and life become intertwined in a drive for that elusive sense of success. They applaud the achievement of individuals and strive for the recognition and trappings that come from obtaining success. This generation created the concept of quality time, meaning that if you spend a little bit of high-value time with your kids, it is the equivalent of spending a lot of "regular" time with them. In this generation, both parents tend to work. Boomers take their intense drive and work ethic with them into profit-driven activities as well as leisurely pursuits.

Loyal

Boomers are loyal. Their loyalty to brand names like Coca-Cola, Harley Davidson, and Disney is legendary. Boomers have been known to tattoo logos of these brands on their bodies. They have intense loyalty to the past and to such rock groups as the Rolling Stones who have been touring for decades. Some pundits see this as a refusal to grow old, while others see the loyalty to corporations and to each other as a positive trait. They respect face-to-face meetings and build loyalty through physically meeting with others and establishing face time with peers. Boomers work well in a team setting controlled by an outside authority like a manager or a boss. They respect and are loyal to their work and social teams. They hang together in times of strife and pressure.

Idealistic

Although not every boomer was at Woodstock, lived in a commune, or participated in a college sit-in, they do generally have a tendency toward idealism and spirituality. They have a certain expectation of how society and organizations should function. This generation saw leaders like Martin Luther King Jr. make a difference and organizations like the Peace Corps come to life. They witnessed the United States putting a man on the moon. Boomers marched for civil rights and launched the feminist and gay rights movements. They believe in crusades, ideals, and working tirelessly to see those ideals come to fruition. The group Mothers Against Drunk Driving (MADD) was founded by a boomer in the 1980s.

Skeptical

But this generation also witnessed the shooting of President John F. Kennedy, the assassination of Martin Luther King Jr., and the shooting of Robert Kennedy on television. This is the same generation that followed the Grateful Dead, flaunted rock and roll in the face of their parents, shouted the phrase, "Don't trust anyone over thirty," protested every type of institution from universities to the government, and then graduated from college and went to work for J. P. Morgan, Arthur Andersen, and Coopers & Lybrand—some of the stodgiest institutions in the country.

Decades later, the founder of MADD disagrees with the direction of the organization and has become a lobbyist for the American Beverage Institute.[29] According to its Web site, the institute is dedicated to the protection of "responsible on-premise consumption of adult beverages" (read "promotes drinking").[30]

Boomers witnessed the Vietnam War on television and watched Richard Nixon lie about Watergate. They have been victims of the largest layoffs in history. They have seen ten, twenty, even twenty-five years of service ignored in the search for bigger corporate profits. It's no wonder boomers are skeptical of authority. Paradoxically these skeptical boomers are also now the authority. This dual sentiment is adeptly expressed in a television commercial for the telecommunications company Sprint. In the commercial flaunting the virtue of a wireless calling plan, a somewhat melancholy boomer is telling his underling how he is avoiding paying for unwanted minutes through his new calling plan.

He says, "I can talk when and how I want, it's my little way of . . . sticking it to the man."

The younger man looks at him quizzically and says, "But you *are* the man."

"I know," the boomer replies.

"So you're . . . sticking it to yourself?"

"Maybe?"[31]

Boomer Workplace Ethos

Boomer mentality and traits have dominated the corporate landscape. For one, the drive toward individualism tied the boomers' identities to their work. They defined their job, and their job defined them. They did more with less while simultaneously attempting to have it all. Failure was never an option. Climbing the corporate ladder was an honorable endeavor. They wanted the benefits of a career and the peaceful family life of their parents. Remember the woman from the Enjoli perfume commercial with a baby and briefcase in one hand and a frying pan in the other? She could "bring home the bacon, fry it up in the pan," and still be romantic when her husband arrived home from work. She was a boomer.

The boomer work ethic was based on the need to be successful coupled with the desire to buy more and more material goods, which were being created in increasingly large numbers. Boomers believed working hard should have its rewards. When they wanted something, they wanted it now. The credit card industry soared as the boomers grew up and embraced the concept of buy now, pay later.

Having a career meant making a commitment to an employer. Whatever effort was needed to get the job done, the boomers would do it—staying after 5:00 P.M. or making a personal sacrifice. If it was perceived as good for the boomer and their employer, they made it happen. Consequently, boomers worked longer hours than their parents—sometimes sixty or seventy, or even eighty, hours a week. Personal needs were often put aside in an attempt to be loyal to the company and achieve results.

Boomers needed to be seen at work. Advancement was earned by putting in plenty of face time with the boss. The processes of doing the work and being seen at the physical place of employment were important. Telecommuting never really took off with the boomers because they needed to be seen. Out of sight equaled out of mind.

Chances are that every boomer has struggled with some type of new technology while working on a project. Boomers faced emerging technologies at every turn in their careers: desktop computers, fax machines, cell phones, and the Internet. They witnessed the space race and the transition from black and white to color to high-definition television. This was especially tough for boomers, because their formative educational experiences were devoid of technology. They did not have computers in the classroom or even calculators in many cases. Even their first years on the job did not involve much technology. It wasn't until late in their careers that computers began to dominate the workplace. As management maven Tom Peters observes, "The modern computer has been with us for more than half a century. But it was arguably a member of the supporting cast, not a prime determinant of enterprise strategy, until the early- or mid-1990s."[32]

The boomers are digital immigrants.[33] They have had to work hard to learn to live with technology and its associated array of gadgets.[34] Although boomers have adapted to the technology, it is still not something they are 100 percent comfortable with. Many fondly look back to a time when there was no information overload and technology didn't change every year.

To help control their for-profit and nonprofit organizations, boomers adopted a team-based command-and-control structure. They wanted teams to accomplish tasks, but the team reported to one manager or boss in a traditional hierarchical structure. Divisions and departments would work with each other, but cross-functional teams were slow to come about. Functional silos were developed, and areas within the company would often do well individually, though at the expense of the entire company. For example, a purchasing department in a large manufacturing company buys lots of raw materials because of a good deal from a vendor. This large amount of inventory drives up costs for the material control department, which is then blamed for having too much inventory, and the production department grumbles because they have to work around the excess inventory. However, at the end of the day, the purchasing department is rewarded for keeping purchasing costs low.

Departments do not cooperate with each other. To solve any problem, the employees inform their manager, who in turn takes the matter up with the manager of the other department. The process is slow and inefficient, but proper reporting lines must be followed or heads roll.

This generation built elaborate hierarchical structures and corporate ladders that clearly indicated who reported to whom within the organization. Reporting and promotional paths were clear. If you spent enough time with a particular organization, kept your nose clean, and did good work, you would naturally move up the corporate ladder. These hierarchies were effective for many years until disruptive technologies and globalization made them too slow and unresponsive to react to the changing marketplace.

Unfortunately, many companies run by boomers were slow to respond, and boomers who had worked faithfully for one employer for years found themselves suddenly out of work. This reinforced the skepticism of the boomers and rocked their perception of who they were. Even if they personally didn't live through a layoff, they inevitably had friends who did.

This has caused a number of boomers to exit the "rat race" and seek volunteer work or to start their own companies. The idealism that once defined the generation is drawing boomers toward more socially conscious endeavors as they begin to exit the workplace and seek calmer lives.

Defining a Gamer: Four Levels

Waiting in the wings for the big boomer retirement are about 90 million people who are part of the gamer generation.[35] The leading edge of this generation began playing video games in earnest in the early 1980s at the same time as the emergence of the video game *Pac-Man*. It is no coincidence.

A short time later, Tim Berners-Lee took the Internet (a network of computers that could transfer files but had no graphics or hyperlinks) to the next level. His creations enabled the World Wide Web complete with hyperlinks and graphics. MS Windows was born in the 1980s, bringing with it a widespread acceptance of a graphical user interface and a thing called a "mouse." People now had access to computer games.

On the video game front, the Atari 2600, Mattel's Intellivision, and Coleco's ColecoVision game consoles were introduced. Anyone with a television could now play arcade-style games. While it may have taken the modern computer over a half a century before it began to have an impact on organizations' strategic thinking, the influence of video games was already affecting the workplace. The convergence of these technological events is shaping the gamers and introducing them to skills and behaviors unlike those of any previous generation.

Definition of *Video Game*

The term *video game* is used in this book to encompass all types of electronic games—games with screens. The definition of *video game* includes handheld games like the PSP and the seemingly ubiquitous GameBoy series. It includes what are known as console games, which are better known by the major brand names of Xbox, PlayStation, and Nintendo. The definition covers PC games and games that can be played on the Internet. Most games can be played across the various platforms, and the primary traits that gamers learn while playing on the different types of game interfaces are similar. So for the sake of readability, unless needed for clarification, the term *video game* will be used to describe any of the game delivery platforms.

Ready or Not . . . Here They Come

A *gamer* is someone who has grown up in the generation influenced and shaped by video games and technology. Those who have grown up during the time when many people within their generation were playing video games are gamers. Even if the person did not own a console or a PC on which to play games, chances are he or she played the video games at a friend's house, at the arcade, or even at school.

This broad definition is not based on whether the person is currently playing video games. Many kids have grown up playing video games and then moved on to other pursuits as they got older (although many have not; a typical gamer is about thirty years old). Kids who played video games during their formative years or were involved in the popular culture that hyped and discussed the attributes of video games have been shaped by video games, whether they know it or not.

In much the same way, baby boomers were shaped by the culture of television even if every boomer did not have a television at home. For the boomers, cultural references, opinions of leaders, and the influence of others were shaped by the introduction and widespread adoption of television. The same is true of the gamers, who were shaped by video games.

As video games evolved, they placed different demands on the players and began to have differing levels of influence on the cognitive processing of those players. The level of complexity, realism, and cognitive engagement of video games has changed dramatically over the past few decades (Figure 1.2). Kids playing video games in the early 1980s played considerably different games from kids in the year 2007. The influence of games on learning style, expectations, and business acumen is just now becoming visible. As today's gamers start to enter the workforce, the differences will be even more profound and accelerated.

Looking at the evolution of games and gamers, there is a breakdown of four distinct categories. The categories are based on birth year and what games were available when the person hit his or her prime gaming years, which start at about age ten, although that age seems to be dropping (Table 1.1).

Figure 1.2. Game and Console Evolution Chart.

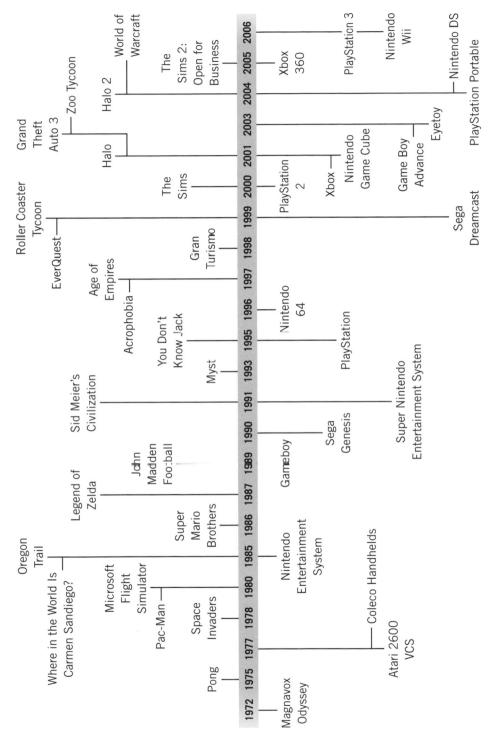

Source: Author.

Table 1.1. Levels of Gamers.

	Gamer 1.0	**Gamer 2.0**	**Gamer 3.0**	**Gamer 4.0**
Birth Years	1960–1970	1971–1980	1981–1990	1991–2000
Gaming Years	1970–1980	1981–1990	1991–2000	2001–2010
Defining games	*Pong*	*Pac-Man, Space Invaders, Battlezone, Super Mario Brothers, Tetris*	*Myst, Zelda, Manic Manson, The Secret of Monkey Island, Tomb Raider, Diablo, EverQuest, Super Mario 64*	*SimCity, The Sims, Halo, World of Warcraft, America's Army, Grand Theft Auto 3*
Level of interactivity	Extremely low	Low	Moderate	Immersive
Degree of realism	Extremely low	Very low	Low to moderate	High to extremely high
Degree of cognitive processing	Low	Low	Moderate	High
Thought process	How do I hit this ball to return it to the other player? Can I bounce the ball off the wall to fool my opponent? What pattern do I need to memorize?	Do I move to the right or the left? How do I avoid or jump over that obstacle? Can I jump up to that platform? How can I jump to the platform? What changes to the pattern will I encounter at this level?	Where do I look to find the hidden pieces? What do I need to complete my quest? Should I talk to that person? What visual clues have I encountered? How can I relate the items I am collecting to the goals I am trying to accomplish?	What variables do I need to balance to ensure that I keep my people happy? Can I find someone to trade the items I have for a more valuable item? What would be a fair trade? What is the trade-off between these three choices? What strategy is the most effective for this type of

Table 1.1. Levels of Gamers *(continued)*.

	Gamer 1.0	Gamer 2.0	Gamer 3.0	Gamer 4.0
				situation? How can I get a team together to defeat this boss?
Player collaboration level	None	Low	Minimal	High

Gamer 1.0. This was the first segment of the gamer generation to experience video games, and their experience was limited in scope. They were born between 1960 and 1970 and overlap the tail end of the boomer generation. At about age ten, in the 1970s and early 1980s, these kids started playing basic electronic games, which were mostly limited to *Pong* and arcade games. One video game system available in 1972 was the Magnavox Odyssey. It included overlays that had to be placed on the television screen to help with the aesthetics of the various games because the electronic graphics were so crude.

The level of interactivity and realism in these games was extremely low. The player didn't need to do much cognitive processing (thinking) to play the games successfully. Players could not collaborate with each other through the game. The only collaboration they had was to shout instructions to each other across the room. Most games were single player or, if they were multiple players, were limited to two players working against each other.

The process of playing these types of games started to change the mind-set of these individuals in a subtle way. They learned to look for and respond to predictable patterns that presented themselves in the game. They also learned that entertainment could be actively consumed versus passively received, as it was with television. Still, these early games were considered just another pastime. Parents viewed and could understand these games. They didn't always understand the appeal, but they knew what was happening.

Gamer 2.0. Gamers 2.0 are kids born between 1971 and 1980, whose primary game-playing years were from the 1980s to the 1990s. When they hit the primary gaming age, they were playing *Pac-Man, Gauntlet,* and *Dragon's Lair* in the arcades; *Space Invaders, Combat,* and *Breakout* at home on the Atari 2600 VCS; and *Oregon Trail* and *Where in the World Is Carmen Sandiego?* at school.

These were the first kids to experience *Super Mario Brothers,* which forged a path many other games followed. These games had improved graphics from the days of *Pong* but were still two-dimensional and cartoonish. Players did need to think a little more as they worked their way through the world of Mario, but it was mostly jumping over obstacles or figuring out how to defeat a boss at the end of a level. Most of the games of the time were not free form but were hard-wired and followed precise patterns. Some *Pac-Man* masters knew the patterns so well they could defeat the game without looking at the screen.

To combat this practiced ability to anticipate the predictable patterns and keep gamers playing, game developers added multiple levels to games and created the goal of beating the entire game instead of just obtaining the high score. Players had to think about patterns and predict what to do next, and then apply some of that learned knowledge to the next level. Each level built on the learning of the previous level and then expanded what the player needed to learn.

In schools, Gamers 2.0 were also challenged with *Oregon Trail,* an educational adventure game with text-based messages and instructions that forced players to think through various problems to devise a solution. Even if a Gamer 2.0 never played *Oregon Trail,* the influence of the game was huge. Many other similar games were developed to try to capitalize on the fact that learning and fun could be combined together in the form of a video game. After *Oregon Trail,* the link between video games and learning became clear. It also became a goal of many future game developers, educators, and corporate trainers.

On the entertainment front, these Gamers 2.0 were confronted for the first time with a game that was more exploratory or discovery based, *The Legend of Zelda.* In this two-dimensional game, the player assumed the role of Link, a blonde-haired hero who had to find the eight lost pieces of the Triforce of

Wisdom and save the princess. This game was different from its predecessors: whereas most previous video games were one-shot experiences, offering no continuity from one gaming session to the next, *The Legend of Zelda* introduced a backup system to record player progress. When it came time to keep playing your quest, you simply selected the correct file and continued.[36]

Shigeru Miyamoto, the creator of *The Legend of Zelda* and *Donkey Kong* and other famous Nintendo games, stated that the first *Legend* was created to allow players to explore freely; he wanted to make a game where the player becomes more creative by playing the game. He has been quoted as saying, "I tried to make a game where the next move the player is supposed to take is not already determined. Each player has to decide the route he or she thinks is best and take the best possible action . . . players themselves can grow."[37]

This era also include the introduction of the famous puzzle game *Tetris,* which had a massive appeal to both male and female players. It involved trying to position geometrical shapes in the right place to complete a solid row of blocks. Once the row was complete, it would disappear. The object was to not let the blocks reach the top of the screen.

Gauntlet hit the arcades in 1985. This multiplayer role-play game allowed up to four players to keep playing as long as they kept depositing quarters in the game. The game was so popular that in some arcades, operators limited the number of coins a player could play at one time.[38]

These types of games began having an impact on players' thinking processes outside the gaming environment, especially with some of the problem solving that was required. The Gamer 2.0 grew up expecting instant feedback and to be the hero. These traits were beginning to be learned, but the unrealistic nature of the games and the lack of immersion didn't provide a tremendous difference between those who played these types of games frequently and those who did not. In addition, video games were still in their infancy and were not as widely available as they would soon become.

These games were now a little more complicated than hitting a digital ball or shooting digital aliens. It was becoming more difficult for a casual observer to walk by the television or PC and figure out what was going on. Parents really needed to sit down and watch the game to figure it out.

Gamer 3.0. This is the first group that had a chance to play in worlds approximating three dimensions and providing an increased degree of realism. Gamers 3.0 were born between 1981 and 1990 and played games in their formative years from 1991 to 2000. Anyone who has ever played video or nonvideo games was always able to get lost or immersed in a game (think of how immersive an intense poker or chess game can be). The addition of realistic graphics to the video gaming world added a visual dimension that transported players to another world in a way that was not previously possible.

Gamers 3.0 were introduced to the highly interactive adventure game *Myst,* where they entered a mysterious world of linking books and had to solve puzzles and find clues to determine the outcome of the game—all from the first-person perspective. The player didn't watch a character move through the game world; he or she actually moved through the game world and saw the world as if there. The *Myst* Web site describes the experience: players "journey to an island world surrealistically tinged with mystery. Only your wits and imagination will serve to stay the course and unlock the ancient betrayal of ages past."[39]

Gamers 3.0 had more realism than 1.0 or 2.0 Gamers: they had increased adventures, more difficult challenges, and a deeper level of involvement with the video games. This was mainly due to the release of more powerful game consoles. The PlayStation and the Nintendo 64 were both introduced during this time frame with improved, realistic graphics. One game that took full advantage of the Nintendo 64 platform was *Super Mario 64,* which provided a rich three-dimensional world.

Players could embark on a pirate adventure with the game *Secret of Monkey Island.* They could work together in *Madden Football,* which released a new version practically every year, or join forces with friends online in *Diablo,* an online role-play game that had a multiplayer mode, allowing up to four people to work together to fight creatures or trade goods. The online play was enabled by a system called Battle.net, an online service started in 1997 by Blizzard Entertainment as a way of allowing players to interact with each other over the Internet. In 1999, *EverQuest,* a three-dimensional fantasy massively multiplayer online role-play game (MMORPG) game was released. It went on to become one of the most popular MMORPGs ever.

Players who didn't want to collaborate with friends could battle them to the death in *Mortal Combat* and score extra points by finishing them off with a fatality, an extremely graphic killing of an opponent after defeating them. It involved tearing or ripping off a part of the opponent's body. *Mortal Combat* was one of the first games with digitized motion-captured graphics, a feature that raised the bar on future graphic expectations.

Games like *Doom, Tomb Raider, Resident Evil,* and *Metal Gear Solid* ushered in the era of cinematic flair for video games. Cinematic camera angles were used to increase suspense and drama. These games included a new level of exploration, allowing players to have more freedom than ever before within the game world.

The impact outside the gaming environment was huge. Kids were learning that they could have rich, interactive experiences while playing games. They could get lost in a realistic world and be a hero in their own adventures. They could collaborate with each other to achieve success and define how they interacted within the world of the game.

Parents needed to sit down and play these games to understand what was happening. It was not possible to observe the game and grasp it.

Gamer 4.0. This group hasn't yet entered the workforce, but when they do, they'll have a huge impact. These are the kids flooding the schools and causing all types of problems. They find it hard to sit still in lectures when they are used to instant feedback and constant stimulation. These kids, born between 1991 and 2000, are just now moving toward the end of their formative gaming years. They have been gods, ruling the lives of simulated beings in *The Sims 2,* they have been the first-person hero in dozens of *Halo* and *Halo 2* levels, they have mastered city planning in *SimCity,* and they have played as Scooby-Doo, Jimmy Neutron, and other cartoon characters on game consoles, handheld games, and the Internet at www.cartoonnetwork.com. And before that, they played as Blue or Dora the Explorer on www.nickjr.com.

These kids have their own cell phones, personal digital assistants, and laptop computers. They play games that are deeply involved and collaborate online in MMORPGs, such as *World of Warcraft, Runescape,* and *America's Army.* They have their own online economies, trade for goods, and strategize in business and commerce. These kids experience the open-ended sandbox game play of *Grand Theft Auto 3,* a game that, if you can look past the violence, allows an unprecedented freedom to go anywhere at any time. It has a completely nonlinear format where players can literally play the game any way they want. These are the serious gamers.

Online Trading

Runescape is an MMORPG. It is like a huge online world where you interact with other players doing trades, talking, or helping each other with quests. You can level up your character in many different ways. One of the ways you can level up is in woodcutting skill. Leveling up helps you get more abilities: the higher the woodcutting skill, the more trees you can cut. For example, if your woodcutting level is 30, you can cut willows. But if your woodcutting level is only 15, then you can cut only oak trees.

One day I was making a deal with a person named Dungmonkey38: he said if I cut him fifteen thousand willows, I could get Full Rune, which is really good armor. I thought that fifteen thousand was a lot, but then I thought that I could pay other people to get them for me. I accepted the offer and went ahead and paid another kid to cut the willows for me. When the other kid had all of them cut, I told Dungmonkey38. He said to give him the willows, so I did. In the end I got my armor, and he got his willows. If u wanna play runescape u can get on. Go to runescape.com. Then b my minion and do my dirty work. Muahahhaha-hahahahahahahhahahah.

Nathan Kapp is an avid *Runescape* fan and a Gamer 4.0 who surfs the Internet daily, makes online purchases, uses instant messaging with wild abandon, and owns a cell phone and a laptop computer. He is looking forward to turning thirteen and entering the seventh grade.

Source: Printed with the permission of Nathan Kapp.

The degree of realism in these games is striking. Moms and dads walk by their kids playing *Madden Football 2007* and ask, "Who's winning?" It looks

so real they think it is an actual game. A Gamer 4.0 controls the look, uni-
form, build, talent, and "coolness" of his or her own football player. The
player can go through a draft after passing an "IQ test" and can then demand
to be traded to another team if he or she doesn't like the drafting team. Not
only is the realism striking, but the interactivity is as well.

As Satoru Iwata, president of Nintendo, stated in a keynote address at a
games conference, "Books, movies, and TV shows are exactly the same for
every user. But our games let players help write their own screenplays and
their own endings."[40] Gamers 4.0 are writing their own stories and endings
over an over again.

For Gamers 4.0, growing up creating their own endings and screenplays
in video games has changed all the rules. They have had to process new, realistic worlds and learn strategies and basic business concepts while running
theme parks or zoos or exploring new online worlds. They have received
instant feedback and hundreds of chances to try something until they get it
right. They collaborate online with friends and strangers from all over the
world to achieve desired goals. Gamers 4.0 are competitive, techno-savvy,
confident, and ready to prove what they know.

Not only have they grown up on games, they have grown up with the
Internet. In fact, 84 percent of people under the age of twenty-nine access
the Internet on a regular basis.[41] The numbers get larger the younger you go.
The U.S. Commerce Department found that 90 percent of children between
the ages of five and seventeen use the Internet: 90 percent of 47 million children.[42] Many use the Internet for e-mail, chats, and games. In fact, over a
third of all Internet users report using the Web to engage in games.[43]

Kids eight to ten years old play video games for about one hour every day.
Male teenagers currently play about thirteen hours of console video games a
week.[44] Their female counterparts play fewer console games (five hours a
week) but make up the majority of PC gamers, at 63 percent.[45] According to
the MediaWise Video Game Report card, 87 percent of eight- to seventeen-
year-old children play video games at home. More than nine out of ten boys
(92 percent) play video games at home, and 80 percent of girls say they play.[46]
By the time a student graduates from college, he or she will have played over
ten thousand hours of computerized games.[47]

You Go Girl. It is not just males who are Gamers 1.0–4.0, females are as well. Although their involvement tends to go unnoticed—even among themselves. As Kirsten Kearney, a video game industry journalist, puts it, "I started off playing *Pong* twenty-five years ago, then I had a GameBoy and played *Super Mario.* There are plenty of girls who did this, but when you ask if they are gamers they say no." Nikki Douglas, founder of www.grrlgamer.com, a site dedicated to girl gamers, adds, "We know that women do play games . . . we have played hundreds upon hundreds of [video] games."[48]

While not as visible as their male counterparts, females are no strangers to the video game world. Seventy percent of the players of the social interaction game *The Sims* are women under twenty-five.[49] The computer game that held the number one position in the Children's PC chart from May 2004 until July 2006 was designed specifically for girls ages six to eleven.[50] In that popular game, *Princess Fashion Boutique,* a player chooses her favorite fairytale princess and dresses the princess in a variety of outfits mixing and matching colors and textures until everything is just right.

A game that has been a hit with older females is Nintendo's *Nintendogs.* This game allows players to "pick out a puppy, name it, and then watch it interact with other dogs." Forty-two percent of *Nintendogs* purchasers are women, with over seven hundred thousand copies of the game sold over the first two months in Japan.[51] When the game hit the United States, it sold two hundred fifty thousand copies the first week and sold out of two major computer game store chains within a month.[52]

Increasingly, females are playing first person shooter games as well. In fact, there are several female-only game tournaments started by women for women. Web sites such as www.womengamers.com, www.ladygamers.com, www.grrl gamer.com, and www.gamegirlz.com have sprung up to eliminate the stereotype of girls not playing video games.

Females are active participants in video games; they are learning the same traits, concepts, and behaviors as their male counterparts when it comes to the influence of video games. While females tend to gravitate toward different types of games, the lessons learned—problem-solving, the benefits of exploration, and the advantages of multiple attempts—are all the same.

Gamer traits are cross-gender traits, because young girls play video games and are growing up in a culture influenced by those games.

The Allure and Power of Games

It is obvious that games are immensely popular. What is less obvious is that they are also powerful teachers that have been schooling a generation of gamers for the past thirty years.

Learning is most effective when the learner has an achievable, well-defined goal. With a goal, you are "willing to be corrected for your mistakes and accept 'try this, do that' advice in order to achieve your success."[53] Games are filled with goals: reach the final level, raise the puppy into a dog, defeat this creature, find the treasure, save the princess, dress appropriately for the royal ball, beat your previous time, defeat the computer opponent, defeat your human opponent. Games induce players to create their own worlds, participate in social activities, form effective teams, reason, and save lives.[54]

Gaming puts the player in control, gives clear, immediate feedback on progress, and offers progressively more challenging levels of achievement that a player reaches at his or her own pace. There are few other environments that offer that level of feedback or critique. Games require observation, rapid and continual choices, thoughtful strategic planning, good eye-hand coordination, and fast physical reflexes.

Contrast that gaming environment with the typical classroom environment that dominated the education of the boomers. In the classroom, the instructor was in control, gave sketchy, infrequent feedback, and expected the entire group of learners to progress at the same rate.[55] There is no contest: gaming wins.

Daphne Bavelier, a researcher who conducted studies with funding from the National Institutes of Health and the James S. McDonnell-Pew Foundation in the area of video games, made the following statement about her research: "Our findings are surprising because they show that the learning induced by video game playing occurs quite fast and generalizes outside the gaming experience." [56] She goes on to say that whatever it is that gamers learn transfers to other situations.[57]

Bavelier is not alone in her research or findings. There is a growing body of research concentrating on the ability of the brain to change in response to stimuli and behaviors that require intense stimulation, such as video game playing. It seems that teenage brains are open to lasting physical changes: "In the late 1990s, neuroscientists discovered that the adolescent brain . . . undergoes a wave of exuberant growth that produces more branches of and connections between neurons in the frontal cortex, in a process that peaks at about age 11 in girls and 12 in boys."[58] As Craig Anderson of Iowa State University states, "Overall, the research is solid. Video games are powerful teachers of all kinds of things."[59]

Emotional Impact. The video game industry has successfully produced games that engender strong emotions like awe, fear, power, and happiness in the players by creating a virtual reality that allows collaboration, social interaction, victory, and defeat.[60] How many times have you been emotionally involved in a classroom experience? Probably not that often. How many times have you screamed or heard your children scream and yell at the screen while playing a game?

Late one night, I was playing the first-person puzzle-adventure game *Riven*. I was alone in the spare bedroom exploring this eerie world. My wife was sound asleep in the other room as I lost track of time engrossed in the game. I was moving from island to island across dirt paths and rope bridges, carefully noting the strange creatures, vegetation, and sounds that were clues to solve a puzzle. I didn't know how they all fit together. Occasionally I came across signs of civilization, but the inhabitants rarely showed themselves. The sounds of the islands were all around me: water splashing against the docks, birds singing in the air, and crickets chirping. As I made a turn down a dimly lit path, a little girl coming out of nowhere darted in front of me, stopped, looked right at me, and ran away. I screamed.

My wife ran into the room to see if I was all right. I was startled and a little shaken (and by this time embarrassed). That virtual girl had given me a fright—not a virtual fright, a real one. I had trouble sleeping that night and didn't play the game for several days after that incident. That's the power of a game. Classroom or training events rarely touch students as emotionally as gaming experiences.

While playing a game like *Riven,* the gamer gets into a state that has been named the *flow state.*[61] The player forgets normal cares and the passage of time in the intense satisfaction from the sheer pleasure of performing the activity required by the game. The gamer is so enthralled that the game becomes a sort of reality, and he or she reacts just as he or she would in an actual situation, like screaming when startled.

"A successful game sucks the player in and doesn't let him go."[62] It immerses the player in the environment of the game. Gamers can get into "a sort of 'groove'" where they become one with the machine and are "no longer aware of the user interface at all." They enter into the "the infamous *Tetris Trance.*"[63]

Motivation to Play. A key prerequisite for entering the flow state is intrinsic motivation. The player must want to be engaged in the game, not because someone tells him or her to be engaged but because of a desire to be engaged. This is also a crucial element in real-life learning.

Under the right conditions, a game player sees each frustration, each failure, as an opportunity to get it right on the next try. Finally getting it right automatically establishes a new level of skill that encourages the player to attempt a more difficult move, and that achievement enables reaching a still higher skill level. The act of obtaining that new skill and the promise of learning a subsequent skill are highly motivating. This is part of the reason gamers can spend all day playing a game. They are slowly but surely learning a new skill at each level and making steady, visible progress toward their goal of defeating the game, bettering their time, or finding the hidden treasure.

The constant visual and verbal feedback is a basic principle of good game design: there must be a reaction to the player's every action to sustain the player's entertainment.[64] If the player hits keys on the controller or clicks the mouse and the game does not respond, the player becomes frustrated or bored and may stop playing. However, the player will quickly recognize a simple beep or tone as a signal that there is no play-relevant response and try another option.

Another key design element is the use of nonlinear stories and nonlinear sequencing. The nonlinear aspect of a game environment enables each player to live the world of the game in his or her own way and enables the player to find different ways to replay the same game, thereby expanding the opportunities for interest and enjoyment.[65]

As a consequence of these interface elements and the immersive nature of the game environment, the gamer generation has picked up tendencies, traits, and behaviors that are very different from those of the boomer generation or even Generation X (people born between 1965 and 1979). Generation X, while having some differences with the boomer generation, did not grow up with the dual technologies of the Internet and video games. Gen Xers are digital immigrants just like the boomers. The first generation to be fully immersed in video games and the Internet is the gamer generation.

Economic Power of Games. The alluring power of video games has created huge financial opportunities for companies that create, market, and distribute electronic games and game consoles. As the video game industry becomes bigger and generates more revenues, it is exerting more and more pressure on popular culture worldwide. Movies now star video game characters like the fictional star of *Tomb Raider,* Laura Croft, who has appeared in two movies. There is even a debate about whether the video game industry is generating more revenue than Hollywood.[66] No matter which side of the debate you come down on, the fact is that video games are generating a lot of money and influence over an entire generation across the globe.

In Europe, video game playing is more popular than ever. In fact, Ireland has the highest per capita ownership of the Sony PlayStation game platform outside of Japan.[67] In Germany, one in ten households owns some type of video game platform.[68]

The French government is using a Web-based game to help its citizens understand the complex issues involved with balancing the budget. The French Budget Minister, Jean-Francois Cope, has supported the creation of *Cyberbudget,* an online game focused on the trade-offs required to balance a national government's budget.[69] The game allows players to manage 300 billion virtual euros as they attempt to balance spending in the areas of education, the military, and social programs.

France also has named three video game creators to its prestigious Order of Arts and Letters. This is the first time electronic games artists have achieved

France's highest award for culture. The honorees are Nintendo's Shigeru Miyamoto, Ubisoft's Michel Ancel, and Frédérick Raynal, director of the original *Alone in the Dark* game.[70]

In Asia, Japan dominates the worldwide console market with Sony and Nintendo games and game consoles. The South Korean game market is expected to reach $2 billion by the end of 2007—an 18 percent increase from its 2006 size of $1.7 billion.[71] In China, increased broadband access has created an online gaming boom. The market for online games in China is about $683 million with twenty-seven million gamers.[72] The Chinese's market is expected to grow at a compound annual growth rate of 24 percent during 2005–2010 until it hits $2.1 billion.[73]

Overall the combined video game market in Europe, the Middle East, and Africa is projected to grow at a compound annual rate of 13 percent through 2010 to reach a $13 billion market size.[74]

This worldwide demand for video games has created huge financial opportunities for companies like Electronic Arts, a Redwood, California, interactive game developer. In fiscal year 2006, the company posted revenues of over $2.95 billion and has over twenty-seven titles that have sold more than 1 million copies.[75] Atari's blockbuster *Enter the Matrix* sold 4 million copies and brought in $250 million worldwide.[76] Electronic games are debuting everywhere, from exercise machines to cell phones.

The gaming juggernaut is not slowing down. It's not even breaking stride. Experts estimate that non-PC devices supporting electronic games will rise from $415 million in 2004 to at least $2.6 billion by 2010. The online Internet game market is forecast to increase to $1.7 billion by 2007.[77] And the worldwide market for video games is expected to grow at an average 11.4 percent compound annual growth rate to $46.5 billion by 2010.[78]

Traits of Gamers

We know that gamers are learning from games. The question is, What are they learning? John Beck and Mitchell Wade discovered some interesting and possibly counterintuitive traits as they conducted research for their book *Got*

Game: How the Gamer Generation Is Reshaping Business Forever. Here are some of the traits they discovered within the gaming generation:[79]

- Analytical/problem solvers

- Multitasking

- Competitive

- Resilient

- Confident

- Sociable

Analytical/Problem Solvers

Gamers are confronted with a problem every time they pick up a controller or a mouse. They spend much of their time analyzing and solving puzzles, working through mazes, searching for objects, keeping characters happy, finding clues, and figuring out the location of the next round of ammunition. They have learned to break down the game environment into its basic elements and then determine how each element fits together:

- Should I take the path on the left or the right?

- What do the clues I have gathered so far tell me?

- Where can I find a locked door now that I have located a key?

- Where do I hit my opponent for the maximum impact?

- What are some other ways I could solve this problem?

- What am I not seeing?

- What other information do I need to find a solution?

- How is this situation similar to others I have faced?

All of this problem solving and analysis is done on-the-fly. The game continues while the gamer figures out what to do next. Gamers must be able to think quickly, react quickly, and make crucial decisions within seconds. A wrong analysis or conclusion means the gamer forfeits a life, goes back a level, or is defeated at the hands of the enemy.

Gamers have to be detailed. They need to observe the environment in which they are playing and determine if a wall contains a secret passage or an enemy is hiding behind the next door. They have to look for subtle cues and make decisions while misleading cues compete for their attention. Gamers are constantly analyzing their moves and actions to figure out how to get to the next level, defeat the monster at the end of the game, or find the next star. They have developed the ability to quickly assess a situation and determine what to do next. This ability translates to the real world.

One unusually hot Saturday in late September, after I had torn my oldest son away from his latest computer game obsession, *Chip's Challenge,* my wife, two boys, and I went to a local corn maze. A corn maze is a lot of fun: it is literally a life-sized maze cut into a corn field that you walk through collecting clues and completing activities found throughout the maze.

After about two hours in the five-acre maze, my wife and I were ready to go home, but we couldn't find the exit. Finally, we came across a rest station that had a huge map of the maze nailed onto a post. My wife and I stared at the map but couldn't figure out how to get to the exit from our location. We were tired, hot, and hungry. Also, my wife was getting a little snippy. I, of course, was calm, cool, and collected. The activity had ceased to be fun. We studied the map but could not discern a good path for our exit.

My oldest son (Gamer 4.0) looked at the maze map for a few moments and then said, "Follow me." We did and were out within five minutes. I asked him how he could read the maze so well. He said, *"Chip's Challenge."*

Chip's Challenge is a game from Microsoft where a small guy named Chip runs around mazes collecting computer chips. You guide Chip as he runs round collecting these prized items. At every level, the player encounters a progressively more difficult maze, and there are about one hundred levels (Figure 1.3). Unbeknown to my son and luckily for me and my wife, he had been studying how to get out of corn mazes for several weeks.

Think how helpful a similar game might be for guiding new employees through the cubicle mazes that are the hallmark of large companies. No matter how many times I visit a mammoth organization, I am always a little confused when trying to find a particular cubical.

Figure 1.3. The First Maze in *Chip's Challenge.*

Source: Microsoft's *Chip's Challenge* product screen shot,
reprinted with permission from Microsoft Corporation.

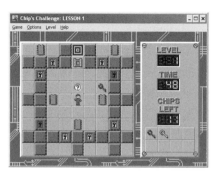

Gamers are not intimidated by mazes or puzzles or problems. They face these challenges and solve them on a regular basis. Gamers are forced to think strategically. They play war and strategy games that previously were reserved for military or industrial strategists. They act as social psychologists when they make sure their *Sims* character has enough human contact, exercise, and food to be healthy. The gamers don't look at pictures of animals in a zoo; they become the zoo keeper, the architect, and the businessperson running the zoo in Microsoft's *Zoo Tycoon.* Gamers are forced to operate at a high level of thinking. Otherwise they would never get past level one.

Game developers understand this analytical and problem-solving allure and even develop games within games to draw in gamers. The developers place extra scenes, help codes, and other enticements in games for the gamer to find. These are fondly referred to as "Easter eggs."[80] An Easter egg is a message, graphic, sound effect, or unusual change in program behavior that occurs in response to some undocumented set of commands, mouse clicks, keystrokes, button presses, or other stimuli intended as a joke, an amusing entertainment piece, or to display program credits. The first known video game to feature an Easter egg was the Atari game *Adventure.* In the game, the designer's name would be displayed if the player moved a hidden item to a certain location.[81]

Gamers like to apply their skills and analytical abilities to solve problems. They tend to have "intuitive technical skills, problem-solving strategies, and attitudes that just couldn't have evolved outside their digital world."[82] They have learned to be keen analysts and problem solvers.

Multitasking

Here is a scene that drives boomers crazy: a gamer sits at the computer working on a project that is due tomorrow. Dozens of open windows are displayed on the screen: the MS Excel spreadsheet for crunching numbers, an Instant Messenger window, a weather ticker, and a search engine page, to name just a few. All the while, the gamer is jamming to the tunes playing on the multicolored MP3 player and watching the cell phone to see if there are any calls. How can anyone work with all those distractions? For boomers, this is information overload. For a gamer, it is standard operating procedure (Figure 1.4). They have never experienced information underload; they've always had too much information.

Figure 1.4. Gamer Working with Distractions.

Source: Reprinted with permission of the artist, Kristin Longenecker.

Information has always been available at the fingertips of gamers. Gamers with a question search the Internet for an answer and instantly look up what they need to know. The television provides twenty-four-hour networks of news, information, and trivia, all with a ticker at the bottom providing—what else?—additional information. You can watch cooking shows all night or cartoons until your side hurts from laughing. Boomers grew up with three channels to choose from, and most of those signed off at midnight.

Gamers have adapted to information overload by embracing the technologies that allow them to be constantly informed and updated. They surf the Web, text-message friends, subscribe to podcasts, and stay connected to information and each other through the dizzying assault of information.

Video games contribute to the information overload of the gamers. To achieve mastery in a video game, you need to know what activities you can ignore or disregard and which activities require your attention.[83] Switching from focusing on one task to quickly focusing on another is an important skill set gamers have learned. "Games might have trained a whole generation to multitask a little more easily, or to routinize tasks the rest of us have to actually think about."[84]

Gamers need to have multiple channels of input. They can easily become bored with just one stimulus. It seems that they want to quickly move back and forth from one activity to another as they are completing tasks and processing information.

Competitive

This is obvious: gamers like to win. Why? Games are about winning. Gamers are motivated to rise to the challenge of a game. "To put it mildly, gamers believe that winning matters."[85] Gamers believe that competition is the law of nature and that they must always compete. This gives them an incredible competitive drive.

While it would seem to make them hypercompetitive and have a win-at-all-costs attitude, this is not the case. Gamers compete against themselves and the game first. They compete against each other second. They admire the skills and abilities that make someone an excellent game player. They reward and exalt fellow gamers who share gaming tips, cheat codes, and Easter egg locations. The competitive spirit of the gamers is mostly a healthy competition, where the gamer wants to be a hero and wants to win but not always at the expense of others.

Gamers are willing to take calculated risks to be successful and win. They have learned through game play that if they take the right risk, they will be richly rewarded, at least virtually. This risk-reward trade-off has preconditioned them to think through situations and determine which risk is worth taking. They don't want to win at all costs; they want to make the right decision that will provide the highest reward for the lowest amount of effort.

Resilient

It is not that other generations haven't been resilient; they have. Everyone has had a coach or teacher who wouldn't let them quit, spurred them on to greatness, or stayed with them until something was finally learned. The difference is that those episodes were sporadic and intermittent; video games allow everyone who plays them to have that experience over and over again.

How can you not learn to be resilient when you have multiple lives or multiple chances to try the same thing over and over again until you get it right? Games teach that if you work hard enough at something, you will eventually master the skill or technique you are seeking (or at least move up to the next level). "Gamers know from countless attempts to maneuver through fictional mazes and dungeons that trial and error is the preferred way to tackle a problem."[86]

It is not like a real-life soccer game where if you touch the ball with your hand in the penalty box the other team gets a free kick and your team risks losing the game because of your mistake. If you mess up in a video game, you just start over. If you do really poorly, don't save the results. Press the Reset button and start over. If you try hard enough, you'll eventually beat the level. This resilience means that gamers are willing to take a chance to see what happens. They don't have to get everything right the first time.

Internet surfing is the same: if you don't find what you are looking for with the keyword search combination you tried the first time, you try another combination and see if it works. Eventually you find what you are looking for. A generation that has grown up searching for information on the Web and playing games over and over again is familiar and comfortable with trial and error. They are willing to fail and then are able, even eager, to bounce back and try the same thing again but in a different way. This is in total contrast to, say, that well-known boomer Wile E. Coyote from *The Road Runner* cartoon. In almost every episode, Wile E. would use some type of Acme device, like the Acme Steel Wall or Acme Tiger Trap, in an attempt to catch the Road Runner. He always failed. However, instead of trying to tweak the product or make minor adjustments and try again, he would simply purchase a new item. He was definitely a boomer.[87] Had he been a gamer, he would have made minor adjustments, tried over and over again, and caught the Road Runner. Beep-beep.

Confident

Progressing from one game level to another, defeating countless villains, and conquering worlds gives gamers a strong sense of confidence. They can handle whatever is thrown at them. After all, they've beaten the final level. "Gamers believe in themselves and in their own ability to create exceptional value."[88] They have been "trained" to be confident by the games they have grown up playing.

In their research, Beck and Wade found that gamers label themselves as experts even at their relatively young ages. They are confident in their technical skills. They believe that because they are talented and smart, they don't need to work as hard as other people to get the job done. They think of themselves as working smart, not hard.

This self-confidence is one reason that gamers believe in a pay-for-performance system. They would much rather be paid for results than, in their minds, unproductive face time. Gamers believe in results and not necessarily in the process. Whatever it takes to get the desired results is what drives a gamer. They are confident they can accomplish whatever needs to be done; they don't want someone looking over their shoulder.

Gamers are also confident because they are digital natives.[89] They see the boomers and even some Generation X coworkers struggling with technology and wonder why. The gamers grew up with technology and are perfectly comfortable sitting in front of a program or game they've never seen before and diving right in. This comfort level with technology has given them confidence in their abilities with computers and related gadgets. No other generation has this confidence level.

Sociable

This trait seems to fly in the face of what everyone intuitively knows about gamers. How can spending all that time alone with a video game make a gamer sociable? Watch a group of kids playing a video game, and you'll find out.

My older son constantly has friends over to play video and computer games. He invites two or three friends over, and they begin to play a game. If it is a single-player game, they negotiate with each other who is going to play first and for how long: "Until you get killed and then it's my turn" or "Until you get to the next level." They provide constant advice and counsel to each other to help their fellow game players beat the level or avoid getting killed. "If you go through the building you avoid running into three bad guys." "No, no, go left at the barrel." "Press square, triangle, circle while pressing R2. It's an awesome combo move."

Inevitably my younger son wanders in and wants to be part of the game play. On a good day, the group will let him play and give him the controller at certain points in the game where they know he can be successful: "Okay, you get this guy through the window and onto the roof and then give me back the controller." Once he is successful, he hands back the controller. The entire exchange, negotiation, turn taking, and playing of the video game is worked out among the kids.

Now, sometimes it gets out of control, but most of the time, they are good for several hours until someone calls in the parents. During the game-playing process, the players learn to delegate, take turns, rely on others for help, and work together to achieve a common goal. They are a self-directed team. There is no authority figure; they determine who does what and how to solve the problem facing them.

Research empirically validates the anecdotal evidence: "Our survey made it very clear: Gamers are not isolated, introverted, or unsociable. In general, they care about people exactly as much as the rest of us do."[90] Gamers are also the IM-e-mail-cell phone generation who are in constant contact with each other. They invented the concept of an instant social event and coined the term *flash mob*. A flash mob is a gathering organized using technology, primarily e-mail and cell phone text messages. A group of people assemble suddenly in a public place, do something unusual or notable, and then disperse.[91] After the event, the participants continue with their other activities.

Flash mobs and other social events indicate that gamers are sociable, but not in the traditional sense of socialization. Gamers don't make phone calls; they text-message. They don't write letters; they send e-mail. Gamers will sit in their home and text-message a friend who lives right next door. They do not require face time to be sociable; they use technology to socialize.

The Chasm

The differences between the gamers and the boomers are not superficial. In fact, some would rename the "knowledge gap" the "knowledge chasm." *Gap* or *chasm,* organizations are faced with a daunting task: transferring the hard-earned knowledge of the boomers to the techno-savvy gamers. The problem is that these two groups have different beliefs, attitudes, and expectations for the workplace. As a boomer writer for *USA Today* comments, "My generation didn't grow up with video games. We don't care much about them."[92] While boomers might not care about them, they have certainly influenced an entire generation—a generation that is now entering the workforce, permeating academic classrooms at every level, and butting heads with the boomer managers, bosses, and instructors.

In the next ten years, the biggest issue facing corporations, academic institutions, and government agencies is going to be the transfer of knowledge from the boomers to the gamers. This issue, if not handled correctly, will have an adverse impact on every segment of society. The stakes are high and the issues real.

With their technology training and savvy coming from playing video games and surfing the Internet, gamers can seem intimidating to boomers. The boomers, though, are in control of the workplace and classroom. They set the rules, teach the classes, and control the capital. Gamers who have grown up with interactive experiences, self-directed work teams, and informal communication channels are not going to want to sit in a classroom or confront online learning modules that have no interaction and no game elements. Gamers are impatient and anxious to get to the next level.

Boomers will find it difficult to articulate and make tangible the knowledge they have in their heads about customers, procedures, operations, and academic subjects. Even the basic everyday tasks of boomers will be difficult for them to explain: "I just see the issue and resolve it. If you put in enough hours, you'll figure it out."

Teachers cannot continue to lecture to rows and rows of gamers sitting in colleges and universities, high schools, or even elementary schools. As Bill Gates said in an address to the National Governors Association, "America's high schools are obsolete. By obsolete, I don't just mean that our high schools are broken, flawed, and under-funded—though a case could be made for every one of those points. By obsolete, I mean that our high schools—even when they're working exactly as designed—cannot teach our kids what they need to know today. Training the workforce of tomorrow with the high schools of today is like trying to teach kids about today's computers on a 50-year-old mainframe. It's the wrong tool for the times."[93]

This chasm between what is taught in high school and what is needed in the workforce is clearly illustrated in Table 1.2. Boomers and gamers have different perceptions of information, work structures, software applications, and communication channels. Each generation has had its ideas and perceptions shaped by its environments and pastimes. The trick is to find a way for the boomers to transfer their knowledge, experience, and know-how to the gamers in a manner that is efficient, practical, and effective for gamers.

Table 1.2. Gamers' and Boomers' Differing Perceptions.

Source: Some material from Prensky, M. (2001). *Digital game-based learning.*
New York: McGraw-Hill, pp. 46–47.

Perception of . . .	Boomer	Gamer
Knowledge	Structured (books, memos, standard operating procedures)	Unstructured (instant messaging, blog, e-mail)
Organizational structure	Hierarchical team-based structure	Level playing field, equality
Communication channels	Formal (face-to-face, telephone calls)	Informal (instant messaging, e-mail, text messages)
Software applications	Interface and information are separate	Information is the interface
Career advancement	Patient ascent	Impatient rapid ascent
Learning environment	Classroom	E-learning
Gadgets	Fun to have	Essential
Video games	Distraction, entertainment, waste of time	Way of life
Information processing	Linear	Multitasking
Technology comfort level	Digital immigrant	Digital native

To make matters worse, gamers are not used to learning in the same fashion as the boomers. Gamers are self-educating. They seek out and learn from the information that is available to them. They do not rely on formal educational settings for their learning. The gamers' learning style:

- Ignores any hint of formal instruction. They are self-directed learners.

- Includes trial and error and approaching a problem from different angles.

- Relies heavily on learning from peers, with a distrust of information from authorities.

- Focuses on small, focused bits of information.

- Demands just-in-time information. They don't want to learn about what they might need.

- Is not focused on books and reading.[94]

In spite of differences in learning style, attitudes, and beliefs, this chasm must be crossed. There is too much at stake in terms of productivity, profitability, and public safety. The differences between the two groups must be overcome with a focused and targeted approach. It's too bad we can't take a page from the baby boomer classic *Star Trek* and do a Vulcan mind-meld between the boomers and the gamers. Barring any mind-melds, the alternative is to find a way to build a bridge over the chasm.

Building the Bridge

Schools are failing gamers, as are corporate training programs. The traditional methods of passing knowledge from one person to another are inadequate for this age and these learners. Our current learning paradigms, institutions, and techniques are a hindrance to learning for gamers. For example, if a company has forty-five hundred employees to train on a new product initiative and it can train only 250 employees a month using traditional stand-up training, it will take eighteen months to train all its employees. If the life of that product knowledge is eighteen months, then by the time the last group is trained, the product information is obsolete. Organizations must find methods for faster deployment of instruction.

Fortunately, many tools already exist to bridge the gap from boomers to gamers. Unfortunately, many of these tools exist in noncorporate and nonacademic settings. The tools that are needed come from the game and electronics industries. Adaptation of these tools will provide an effective method of knowledge transfer. Boomers must understand that the toys of today—the gadgets, games, and gizmos—are the business and academic tools of the future.

Time is not a luxury in this situation; the boomer exodus is happening as you read this page, and the time for action is now. Rules need to be broken, new paradigms established, university structures rethought, and old training techniques replaced with new methods as existing training department structures are torn apart and rebuilt. Schools and academic institutions must redefine learning and redeploy resources. Executives, training managers, employee supervisors, and others must rethink how they educate new employees.

The current boomer-controlled, team-based command-and-control structure must morph into a self-directed virtual learning environment. Organizations need to tap into the existing inclinations of the gamers and provide educational experiences in harmony with the way they learn and seek new information.

What's Coming in This Book

How to accomplish this goal of knowledge transfer is the topic of this book. So far, we have discussed the differences between the boomers and the gamers, as well as examined the tremendous challenge and opportunities that lie ahead in terms of transferring knowledge from one group to the other. Next, we discuss how to accomplish this goal.

Outline of Chapters

The next few chapters introduce tools, ideas, and practical tips for bridging this gap. Stories, anecdotes, statistics, and expert insight provide a foundation for action and practical tips to turn the toys and trinkets of the gamer generation into the business tools of the future.

In Chapter Two, the focus is on using games to teach basic but essential knowledge: facts, concepts, and rules. Chapter Three discusses the use of simulations to teach advanced knowledge like procedures, principles, and problem solving. In Chapter Four, the use of handheld gadgets by the gamers is discussed, and methods of using those gadgets for transferring knowledge are explored. Chapter Five provides a look at how gamers use cheat codes and exploit rules of video games to their advantage and describes methods of incorporating some of that thinking into business and academic settings. Chapter Six describes how institutions must move information and knowledge out of rigid course structures to create small, easily searched bite-sized nuggets. Gamers are used to Googling information, not reading manuals. In Chapter Seven, the concept of replacing education with automation is discussed, and examples are provided to explain why automating a process is often better than trying to develop and maintain a training program. Chapter Eight offers a look at the gamer's expectations of a boss and a teacher. These expectations are far different from those of other generations. In Chapter Nine, issues of recruitment and retention are explored. Gamers will be attracted to certain types of organizational cultures and turned off by others. Chapter Ten provides practical methods of selling the concept of introducing gadgets and games into a corporate or academic environment. Introducing innovative technologies can be difficult, and when those technologies are associated with games or electronic toys, the level of difficulty is magnified. In Chapter Eleven, the concept of knowledge requirements planning is introduced. This is a systematic process for creating an enterprisewide approach to the boomer-gamer knowledge transfer issue. The book concludes in Chapter Twelve with a discussion of personal actions that gamers and boomers can take to better understand one another and provides a glimpse into the future.

In each chapter, I point out workplace implications. This section describes how the concepts discussed in the chapter can be applied in both academic and corporate settings to be successful and what the ideas introduced in the chapter mean when they are applied in a practical setting.

The Best Way to Read This Book

The ideal approach to reading this book is as a team or group consisting of boomers, gamers, and Generation Xers. Divide your team, department, or faculty into reading clubs, and read a chapter each week. Once a week, the group should get together and discuss the salient and thought-provoking points. How is our organization dealing with this issue? Have we seen these traits in new employees or incoming freshmen? Can we sell simple games to our leadership? How do we implement these ideas?

This group approach will spark discussion, provide insightful solutions, and guide you to develop your own methods of transferring knowledge and dealing with the boomer-gamer knowledge gap. It will also lead to discussions between the boomers and the gamers of the organization that would not occur otherwise. These conversations, even when off-topic, will be valuable in strengthening your organization and are one of the first tangible steps you can take to bridge the boomer-gamer knowledge gap.

Continuing the Discussion

A topic like this does not remain static; it is constantly moving. In an effort to continue the dialogue in real time and make progress in bridging the boomer-gamer knowledge gap, I have created a Web site, www.gadgetsgamesandgizmos.com, that contains a space for you to respond to a blog on the subject, a wiki for you to update terms and definitions, and a podcast on the topic. You will find lists of resources and white papers to help you manage the boomer-gamer knowledge transfer. Most important, you will find room to contribute your own knowledge, thoughts, and wisdom on the subject. Visit it and use the tools discussed in this book to further your knowledge and experiment to see how they can help you and your organization.

This book provides a list of recommendations and techniques for recasting our existing training, academic, and computer systems into tools for bridging the knowledge gap. These new tools will push the knowledge and innovation envelope. Academic, corporate, and nonprofit organizations that adopt these tools and techniques will not only survive the transition; they will profit from it as well.

2

It's in the Game

O N THE SURFACE, the easiest place to start bridging the knowledge gap between boomers and gamers is the development of training programs in the same style and quality as video games. Provide gamers with a rich, interactive experience where they can assume a role and guide the company to greatness or learn leaderships skills in a virtual world. Program a corporate version of *Halo 2* or *Star Wars Battlefront II*, and you are set.[1] Instantly gamers have access to the boomer's knowledge in a familiar video game format.

There are only two problems with this approach: time and money. Developing *Halo 2* with its fully interactive game play effects, high-quality graphics, and professional soundtrack took a team of over 190 people three years of development at a cost of about $40 million.[2] Estimates for the development of games for the Xbox 360 and PlayStation 3 are around $20 million a game.[3]

Even if you go for a slightly lower production value, it is hard to develop a video game for less than $8 to $10 million,[4] a price and time frame out of reach for most training departments, corporations, and academic institutions. Of course, that type of investment is worth it when *Halo 2* grosses over $100 million in sales the day it is released. In the training and education market, those returns are not realistic, that level of development not feasible.

Unfortunately, these obstacles tend to halt game development or, more important, even the idea of game development dead in its tracks. There is an attitude in training and academic circles that you need to "go big or go home" when it comes to game development. In fact, you don't need to go home or go big. Beneficial educational games can and are being developed inexpensively. Intertwining learning and electronic games does not require a cinema-like production value. Many advertisers have learned the lesson of short, quick, fun games. Educators, trainers, and corporate managers need to learn the same lesson. Absolut, the company that makes premium vodka, has created a search game that takes only two minutes: you try to find all the Absolut bottles you can in a stylized cityscape (there are eighty-two).[5] The game is fun, draws you in, takes only two minutes to play, and the cost to develop it is a lot less than $10 million.

In the gaming world, simple, easy-to-play, short games are called "casual games" or "coffee-break" games. One well-known casual game is *Bejeweled,* where you make horizontal or vertical lines out of three or more identical gems.

Casual games are designed to be played again and again, are simple to learn, have a short playing time, and are relatively inexpensive to build. The "average casual game is built in months, often by a team of three to five people at a cost of about $100,000."[6] Causal games are perfect for teaching basic knowledge.

Basic Types of Knowledge

There are literally thousands of pieces of information that need to be learned for any position in any field. According to Robert Gagné, a well-known researcher in the area of learning, there is a knowledge hierarchy for learning.[7] The hierarchy progresses from learning basic facts all the way to complex problem solving. Gamers need to climb that hierarchy to reach the knowledge level of the departing boomers. The first three levels of the hierarchy are:

- Declarative knowledge
- Concepts knowledge
- Rules knowledge

The three higher-level knowledge types—procedures, principles, and problem solving—need to be learned as well and are discussed in the next chapter. They do require more sophisticated games for knowledge transfer.

The lower levels of knowledge need to be acquired before higher levels can be obtained. A learner needs declarative knowledge (facts, jargon) before he or she can understand concepts. Likewise, a learner needs to understand basic concepts before he or she can apply them to a rule. The flow of knowledge acquisition from one level to another is essential for the overall learning process. Table 2.1 includes a short definition of the three types of basic knowledge and provides an example of each.

No employee successfully rises through the ranks without moving up the knowledge hierarchy. Savvy realtors don't just know what the letters MLS represent; they know the rules that govern how the Multiple Listing Service works. Good retail bankers don't just know that ARM represents the term *adjustable rate mortgage;* they can state when an ARM is appropriate for a customer and when it is not. A college chemistry student can't conduct an experiment without knowing the chemical symbols for the required elements. Inventory managers can't effectively trouble-shoot high levels of inventory if they don't know the difference between work-in-process and finished goods inventories. Students in a high school math class need to know what the term *variable* means before tackling algebra problems.

One type of knowledge ripples into another, and each encompasses the previous, as shown in Figure 2.1. An employee, no matter how talented or skilled, cannot jump ahead. Either he or she learns the knowledge needed at each level while on the job or is hired with the prerequisite knowledge. There are no shortcuts.

Table 2.1. Knowledge Types.

Type of Knowledge	Definition	Example
Declarative	An association between two or more objects—typically facts, jargon, and acronyms.	*DPW* represents the phrase *Department of Public Welfare. SOW* represents the phrase *statement of work. GPS* represents the phrase *global positioning system.*
Concept	Categories used for grouping similar or related ideas, events, or objects.	Quality means the following: not handing off the customer from one representative to another when the customer has a problem, addressing the customer need in a timely fashion, and providing the customer with alternatives.
Rules	Relationship between two or more concepts.	Typically expressed as an if-then statement: If the customer has exceeded the specified credit limit, then inform the customer of the two options: (1) fax a signed letter of credit, (2) accept shipment Cash on Delivery (COD). If the customer is angry, then contact the manager.

Figure 2.1. The Interrelated Nature of the Different Types of Knowledge.

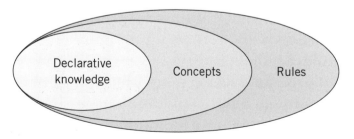

However, as Mark Oehlert, an associate at the consulting firm Booz Allen Hamilton and the former director of learning innovations at the online learning think tank the MASIE Center, points out, "Learning hierarchies can be problematic for gamers. Their experience with non-linear games means that they tend to have a different understanding of how complete their knowledge set needs to be before moving to the next level. Gamers are comfortable with ambiguity, so they sometimes attempt to move forward without all of the information they need."[8] The challenge is to provide gamers with basic knowledge quickly and effectively.

This nonlinear approach for learning content means that creating a game to help employees work up to the proper level of knowledge becomes more complicated than creating a cute user interface and setting the learner loose. Effective knowledge transfer requires careful game design to ensure that the prerequisite knowledge levels are learned. Game types must be aligned with the content being taught.

If you design, develop, or commission a game for teaching gamers, you need to be sure the right type of design is being used; otherwise, resources will be spent designing and developing the wrong game for the wrong content. Let's look at the games designs for declarative, conceptual, and rules-based knowledge.

Declarative Knowledge

Declarative knowledge deals with memorization of information. Every organization and academic discipline has names, jargon, facts, and acronyms that members must memorize to communicate effectively. New employees have no choice but to memorize the fact that the letters *S-O-P* represent the phrase *standard operating procedure*. Otherwise they will not be able to converse with their boss or coworkers. New students have no choice but to memorize the names of the Great Lakes. Some types of information can be learned only through memorization. Information to be memorized can be divided into four categories:

- Names and labels
- Jargon

- Facts

- Acronyms

Memorizing basic information is essential. You need to identify the parts of the machine you are operating or correctly recognize the form that needs to be completed by the customer filing a complaint. You need to know the acronym for your company's hottest-selling product; you need to understand what the technical support person is telling you about the customer relationship management (CRM) application. You must be able to discuss job performance with your manager using acronyms as language shortcuts (Figure 2.2 gives a typical example). Declarative knowledge is essential for basic survival in any organization regardless of size or industry.

Figure 2.2. Knowledge of Acronyms Is Essential for Survival in Any Organization.
Note: The assistant vice president (AVP) from the Department of Public Works (DPW) left a voice mail (VM). She needs the statement of work (SOW) as soon as possible (ASAP) for the General Accounting Office (GAO) before the end of day (EOD).
Source: Reprinted with permission of the artist, Kristin Longenecker.

In school, students spend a tremendous amount of time memorizing facts. They learn the names of countries, key historical dates, and fundamental language terms and structure. Without memorization, higher-level learning cannot occur. Although this type of information is critical for organizational and individual survival, it is not always exciting to learn. To make matters worse, the learning techniques can be, well, painful. Think back to when you were preparing for spelling tests or memorizing important historical dates: you drilled and practiced until your brain hurt.

The goal of the drill-and-practice technique is repetition. You repeat a piece of information over and over again until it is burned into your memory. Think about multiplication tables. In elementary school, your teacher had you complete pages and pages of multiplication problems or review flash cards until you were ready to scream. That is drill and practice. The result is that to this day, you know $9 \times 7 = 63$ without using a calculator. You know the times tables, but the process of learning that information was not pleasant. Let's face it: drill and practice works, but it is boring or even painful at times.

Corporate training programs aren't any better. Most traditional classroom training sessions present information to memorize on overhead slides that are heavy with text. The attendees furiously take notes, and on occasion, the trainer asks a couple of questions to keep learners interested (or awake).

If the content is online, the format becomes page-of-text, page-of-text, page-of-text, multiple-choice question, repeat. The entire process is a little insulting. The technical term for this type of online training is *page turner.* All the learner does is click the Next button to move to the next screen or page. This method is absolutely ineffective for gamers who "control-alt-delete" out of these types of e-learning modules as quickly as their fingers can move. Traditional corporate methods of teaching declarative knowledge offer little enjoyment, excitement, or motivation.

While boomers might have tolerated this type of instruction (and even that is questionable), gamers quickly become bored and listless, and they opt out of the learning. This is one of the reasons that e-learning dropout rates are so high. There is a better method of teaching declarative knowledge: casual games.

Declarative Knowledge Games

Games can quickly teach basic declarative knowledge to anyone who takes the time to enjoy the game. Information to memorize will naturally be repeated as the player engages in the game over and over again to obtain a high score or beat an opponent. The games do not need to be complex or have elaborate graphics to be educational. They simply need to follow a proven format honed over decades.

The technology of television enabled boomers to transform the games their parents played around the kitchen table—charades, card games, trivia, and basic word games—into television shows like *Card Sharks, Wheel of Fortune,* and *Jeopardy.* Now the technology of the Internet is enabling those games to be played online, and organizations are taking advantage of these games to help their employees learn new information.

Johnson & Johnson, a broad-based manufacturer of health care products and related services, is using simple games to convey basic legal concepts to employees. This is no small introduction of games; Johnson & Johnson has over two hundred operating companies employing approximately 115,600 men and women in fifty-seven countries.[9]

When the corporate legal department wanted to create learning around the concept of effective communication, it developed a Web site with a number of simple but fun games for learners to play while they learned about the elements of clear and effective communication. The site features a variety of games:

- Crossword puzzles
- Hangman
- Word searches
- Cryptograms
- E-mail games
- Interoffice memo games

The goal was to attract learners to the content through games, tricking them into drill and practice. The legal education team created a game room and invited learners to come and play. The game room is shown in Figure 2.3.

Figure 2.3. Johnson & Johnson Legal Education Page.

Source: Used with permission.

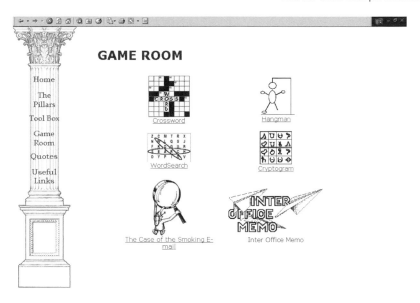

Johnson & Johnson took advantage of simple game designs to teach declarative knowledge. A review of various game designs from hangman to racing games reveals how games passed down through generations and altered each time by technology, can be used to teach gamers new knowledge.

Hangman. Hangman is a popular game. It is a simple concept but fun to play because the elements of surprise and competition are built in. Kids played it on paper or a chalkboard in the past, and boomers created the television show *Wheel of Fortune* based on its elements.

Hangman can be made into an educational game to teach acronyms or memorized information by adding a definition to the game. Instead of simply

guessing a word by providing a bunch of letters, the learner is given a definition and must guess the letters that represent the term related to the definition. The player thinks about the definition and associates it with the term
while playing the game. The player competes against the clock, seeing how
quickly she or he can guess the right term. This simple game can greatly speed
the time it takes for employees to learn new terms and definitions.

The hangman concept can be modified to be played in several different
ways. For example, the traditional game has a decidedly negative connotation
(a person hanging by the neck until dead), so one solution is to change the
theme but keep the basic elements. It is possible to change the "hang-the-
man-until-dead" theme to one of "freeing a road runner," as shown in Figure
2.4. The road runner wants the learner to guess the right word before a cage
completely traps him. The concept is the same: guess the correct letters when
given a definition within a certain number of tries; only the graphics are
changed to be less offensive.

Figure 2.4. Game Based on the Concept of Hangman to Teach Facts.

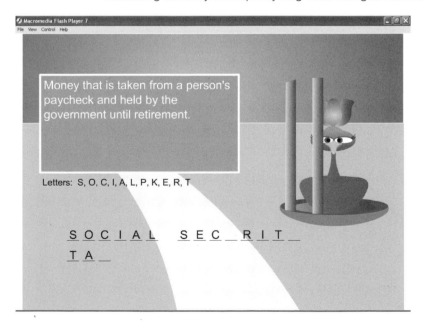

The game elements in this case are time and number of incorrect answers. Posting the top ten scores on a Web site visible to the group playing the game increases the sense of competition and encourages players to play again and again. If posting actual names creates a problem within the organization, allow the players to use pseudonyms for both personalization and to hide real identities. Using real names or pseudonyms, players will volunteer their time for drill and practice in an effort to better their times and post the highest score. The players conduct the drill-and-practice elements of learning on their own without external encouragement or boredom.

Word Search. Another effective game for teaching declarative knowledge is a computerized version of a traditional word search, as shown in Figure 2.5. This online version helps students recognize terms and jargon, as well as learn definitions. The gamers like the online challenge of the puzzle, and the boomers are familiar and comfortable with the format of word searches. Words are circled with the mouse

---

Figure 2.5. Johnson & Johnson Word Search Game.

Source: Used with permission.

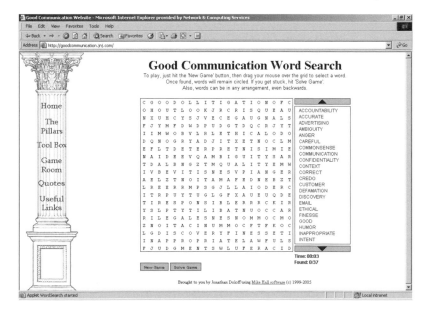

instead of a pencil. The searches can be timed to add a little competition and motivation. These are used in a variety of industries, from banking to consulting to sales organizations. The example here is to teach terms related to clear and effective communication used by Johnson & Johnson.

Drag-and-Drop Exercises. Naming the parts of a machine or steps in a particular process or elements of a computer network are important pieces of declarative knowledge workers need to know. Proper identification of the parts of machinery helps with maintenance, operation, and safety. Knowing the proper sequence of steps for creating a product or completing paperwork is essential for the effective flow of information.

In a drag-and-drop game, the learner recognizes the location of various parts of a piece of equipment and properly labels each part by dragging a name from one part of the screen to its proper location on a diagram.

A timer and an indicator of the number of attempts are added to create competition. It is also possible to add, for correctly completing a drag and drop, rewards such as a small, entertaining video clip related to the content being taught or several tokens that can be collected. In the latter case, the learner with the most tokens may win some type of group competition. Again, this is consistent with the gamers' philosophy of game playing, where success is rewarded by receiving a prize or moving to the next level.

Figure 2.6 shows a drag-and-drop game developed to teach people statistics related to Japanese and American beliefs about certain business principles. In the game, the learner plays a samurai who must avoid various men dressed in suits. The samurai grabs a number and drags it to either the American or Japanese flag. If the answer is correct, the number stays in position; otherwise, the number returns to its original position, and the samurai must retrieve another number. This game, created by GameTrain, includes a sophisticated scoring system that tracks how many attempts the learner has taken, how much time he or she took during the game, the number of correct answers, the pace of learning, and the percentile rank as compared to others.[10]

Figure 2.6. Drag-and-Drop Game for Teaching Statistics Related to Japanese
and American Beliefs About Certain Business Principles.

Matching. This is a variation of the classic card game where players flip over all fifty-two
cards face down and then turn them over two at a time to find a match. In
this version of the game, the learner matches a term listed on one card to a
definition listed on another. The learner turns over the cards by clicking on
them two at a time. This game provides a good method of linking terms with
definitions. The learner must understand the definition of the term, read each
definition, think of its meaning, and then find the match. The example shown
in Figure 2.7 is of a matching game teaching the various parts of a memo to
employees who will be responsible for creating memos at a law firm.

Figure 2.7. Matching Game.

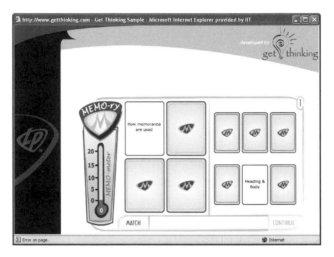

Duck Shoot. This game is based on the old carnival game where the person attempts to shoot the duck worth the highest number of points. The person with the highest number of points gets a prize. This version of duck shoot requires the learner to click on the duck when the correct definition appears, as shown in Figure 2.8. This game is used by a pharmaceutical company to help production employees become familiar with dangerous chemicals they may encounter in the manufacturing process.

Acrophobia. Not only can traditional games played by baby boomers around the kitchen table be turned into educational online games, but early Internet games can be modified to provide an educational experience as well. One such game is *Acrophobia.* With a little modification, this game is a great way to teach acronyms to new employees. This Internet game was created by Anthony Shubert in the mid- to late 1990s and incorporates a chatroom, voting on other players' answers, and the element of speed.

The game play involves entering a chatroom and being presented with a series of randomly generated letters that players see, for example, ELO or MLAN. The players then type an acronym as quickly as possible matching those letters—perhaps Electric Light Orchestra or Enterprising Ladies Organization. After all the players submit their acronym and time has expired, the acronyms are displayed, and the players vote for the best one. The winner is the acronym-definition combination with the most votes. During the game play, a chat box is available for the players to discuss the various acronyms and what they liked or didn't like.

Now imagine this game with a few modifications for use as a training tool. Instead of randomly generated letters, the letters represent actual acronyms commonly used in the organization. The players are new employees who compete with one another to see who recognizes the acronym the quickest. Instead of voting, the system determines the winner based on speed. The chatroom is monitored by a veteran employee (a boomer), who comments on the meaning of the acronym and how it is used within the organization. The gamers enjoy the game while learning acronyms used within the organization. Simultaneously, they are mentored by a seasoned boomer who is monitoring the chat. Players don't even have to be in the same building or state; they don't even need to leave their desk.

Concept Knowledge

A concept is a series of traits that classifies an object or event. For example, you can classify e-mail as junk mail or business related. You can classify a production process as value-added or non-value-added. Employees must learn hundreds of concepts to perform their job. Policies, procedures, and protocols all contain concepts requiring employees to classify information.

A call center employee needs to classify the type of customer request to handle it properly. A worker on the manufacturing floor needs to classify different defects when conducting a quality inspection. A hospital worker must correctly classify symptoms to diagnose a patient. A bank employee must classify the needs of a customer to offer the right product.

Teaching concepts involves two general strategies. The first is to present examples and nonexamples of the concept to the learner and ask him or her to deduce or, discover, the concept. The learner, in other words, is presented with an example and must indicate if it illustrates that concept. After each response, the learner is given feedback indicating if he or she was right or wrong. Through the feedback process, the learner eventually determines the characteristics of the concept.

Using this technique, an instructor might present a series of images of defective and quality parts and ask learners to classify the parts based on the visible characteristics. The learners would then be asked to list the characteristics of a good part and the characteristics of a defective part, learning in the process the concepts of quality and defective parts.

A second method of teaching concepts is to provide a best example of the concept and then highlight the attributes and characteristics of that concept. Learners would then be asked to identify other instances of that concept. An illustration of this method would be an educational experience that discusses the concept of value-added by providing an excellent example of a value-added process and then asking learners to identify what makes that process value-added. The learners would be presented with a series of processes and asked to determine if those processes were value-added or non-value-added. They might be asked as well to generate their own examples of non-value-added and value-added processes.

There are two types of concepts: abstract and concrete. An abstract concept is one that cannot be seen, for example, the concept of value-added. You cannot see the value being added, but you can tell when that is the case. Abstract concepts—safety, honesty, customer service, innovation, quality, and literally hundreds of others—are essential to the effective running of almost any organization.

A concrete concept is something you can see, such as a defective part or a laptop computer. You can look at several examples of a computer and identify which is a laptop and which is a desktop by identifying the physical characteristics of a laptop, such as an integrated screen and keyboard.

Although these methods of teaching concepts are effective, the instructional sequence leads to boredom and disinterest if it is not presented correctly. Games can be used to help learners work on classifying and identifying the traits of various concepts and add a little fun to the experience.

Concept Knowledge Games

The goal of a concept game is to allow the learner an opportunity to identify the traits of the concept or encourage the learner to generate ideas about the traits of the concept on their own. These types of games can be presented as multiple-choice exercises or identification games.

Sorting Games. In a sorting game, the learner is required to distinguish between examples and nonexamples of a concept. For example, in Figure 2.9, the learner

Figure 2.9. Sorting Game.

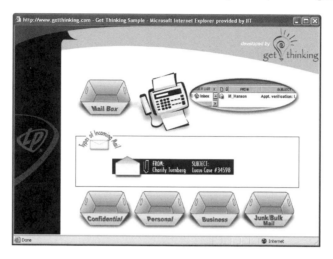

must properly identify the type of mail he or she is receiving by category. The learner must understand the meaning of each type of mail—confidential, personal, business, junk, or bulk mail—and properly categorize an incoming piece of mail. This reinforces the concept of each mail type and forces the learner to identify the traits of an incoming piece of mail and match the trait to the appropriate concept. Learners must identify what distinguishes a personal letter from a junk mail letter, for example.

In another version of a sorting game, the learner selects the location of a file based on alphabetical order. The learner is presented with a file and is then required to click on arrows to ensure that the file arrives at its proper location. To be successful, the learner must understand the concept of alphabetical order and be able to identify the proper method of alphabetizing information, as shown in Figure 2.10. The game includes time elements as well as audio and visual feedback.

Another sorting game that can help learners identify the traits of a concept is based on the popular child's game Bop the Fox or Whack a Mole. In

Figure 2.10. Alphabetizing Sorting Game.

the physical world, the player tries to hit as many foxes, moles, or other animals as possible with a rubber mallet as they pop up from the ground within a specified time period. The animal receiving the hit may change, but the concept is the same: score points by bopping the animal on the head.

This game can be modified for teaching concepts by attaching a trait or concept to each animal as it appears. The learner then identifies the correct information by bopping the animal with the mouse. For example, in a Bop the Fox game used to teach the attributes of acids and bases for lab technicians, foxes are labeled as "acid" or "base," and the learner clicks on one of the choices based on the attribute provided. Figure 2.11 shows an example where the learner must correctly classify an item as an acid or base depending on a particular trait of either the acid or the base.

This game can be used to classify any type of information or list any attributes or characteristics of a concept. The learner determines the proper categorization by clicking on the correctly labeled object. The game can be

Figure 2.11. Teaching the Attributes of Acid and Base Chemicals to Technicians.

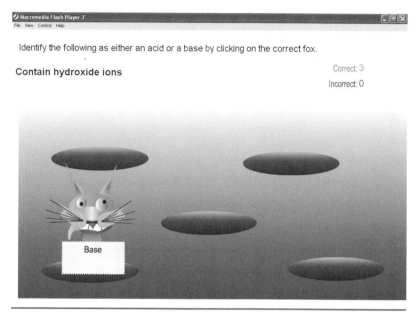

programmed to provide either examples or nonexamples, and the graphics can be changed to be appropriate for the audience playing the game.

Race Games. Most people enjoy some form of racing and are motivated by a competition to the finish line. To teach concepts, two game variations can be used to challenge the learner to get the right answer to win a race. If the learner gets more answers correct than incorrect, he or she wins. Otherwise the race is lost.

One game involves two goats racing to the top of a mountain. The goal is to beat the computer to the top by answering correctly. If the user progresses up the mountain faster than the computer goat, the user wins, as shown in Figure 2.12. A similar version, shown in Figure 2.13, is a road race. Once again, the user races the computer by getting answers correct, except instead of going up a mountain, the race is for a finish line. These games can be given a more professional look by changing the graphics, as shown in Chapter Ten.

Figure 2.12. Learner Races the Computer up the Mountain.

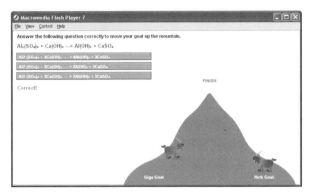

Figure 2.13. Racing Game for Answering Questions Against the Computer.

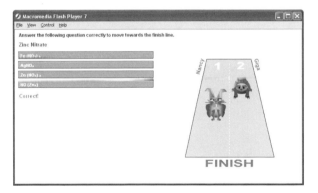

These racing games are really just multiple-choice questions disguised as a game. However, the game elements of racing the computer or racing against time make the interaction more fun and energetic than simply answering a series of multiple-choice questions. Games provide a little extra incentive and motivation.

Drag and Drop, Redux. The drag-and-drop game design mentioned earlier for teaching declarative knowledge can also be used to teach concepts by asking the learner to identify elements of a particular class of items. In Figure 2.14, the learner is asked to drag the family members who are exempt from a certain policy onto the tree. The simple game works effectively and provides reinforcement of the concept of exempt family members to the learners as they drag the correct family member leaves onto the tree.

Figure 2.14. Drag and Drop onto the Tree Matching Game.

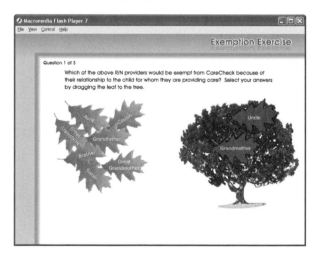

Rules Knowledge

Rules are statements that express the relationships between two or more concepts. Rules provide parameters dictating a preferred behavior with predictable results. For example, "i before e except after c" is a rule that provides predictable results. Most of the time, rules are stated in an if-then format. In a restaurant, if the seafood to be preserved is salmon, place it on indirect ice. If the seafood is a bushel of claims, place it on direct ice. In retail banking, a rule might be that if the customer has more than $25,000 in a savings account with the bank, she is eligible for a higher interest rate in her interest-bearing checking account. If the person has less than $100,000 in an account, it is covered by the Federal Deposit Insurance Company.

Every industry and academic discipline has rules that must be followed. In the retail industry, there are rules that tell the buyer when to place a new order. They are called reordering rules. Rules govern the operation of computer systems and many corporate policies and procedures. In chemistry, there are rules about reactions. In math, there are rules governing the solving of equations. Organizations are simply a set of rules by which members of the organization agree to function and operate.

When teaching a rule, it is necessary to ensure that the learner knows all of the prerequisite concepts required to understand and apply the rule correctly. When a learner is having difficulty learning a rule, often it is because he or she has not fully grasped the prerequisite concepts.

One method of teaching a rule is to allow the learner to apply the rule to a specific situation. You can also provide the learner with the rule and then explain the concepts behind it. These instructional methods can be employed using simple games.

Rules Knowledge Games

Teaching rules can be done in such a manner that the learner has fun applying the rule to a specific situation. These types of games provide a little more challenge than declarative or concept games. The learner must think about the rule and then apply it to the specific situation provided by the game.

Application Games. Application games offer an opportunity for the learner to apply the rule just learned to see if he or she fully understands it and its implications. To teach food service employees how to preserve fresh seafood, a large chain developed a selection game where the learner must recognize the seafood product, determine the type of preservation method needed, and then click on a button to drop the seafood on the proper ice configuration, as shown in Figure 2.15. This game forces the learner to apply the rule to a number of situations. It reinforces the application of the rule by incrementing or decrementing points depending on whether the player correctly applies the rule.

Figure 2.15. Screen Capture from a Selection Game for Teaching Rules.

A variation on this game is used to teach servers at Cold Stone Creamery stores. In the game, the learner is working in an ice cream store. Customers come into the store at various times asking for different-size servings. The server must scoop out the proper size serving for the customer within a certain amount of time. Score is kept by showing how much over or under the server is in the scoop of ice cream. Too much ice cream, and store profitability suffers; too little, and customer satisfaction ratings decline. The player must keep a balance of the two. As the game progresses, more and more customers arrive to be served.

Board Games. An online board game can ask a learner to apply a rule to a situation presented by the game. This is usually done using a multiple-choice question format. Board games are familiar to all types of employees, gamers and boomers, and the basic premise behind them does not need much instruction or explanation. Learners understand they have a "piece" on the board that is moved through the process of rolling a die (or dice). They also understand that they have to answer a question correctly to proceed. These types of online games can be used in a variety of industries and settings.

For example, in a manufacturing organization, a question could be "The Just-in-Time (JIT) method for reordering product requires what prerequisites?" The learner responding to the question has to understand the concept of "JIT" and of "reordering" and know what rule to apply when reordering in a JIT environment.

The rules that need to be learned such as, "Don't keep a customer on hold for more than two minutes," can be incorporated into the rules of the game or can be taught as the learner moves around the board. The designer of the game can use chance or other factors through different cards or through game conventions like having the player land on a "go back" spot on the board.

The manufacturing game shown in Figure 2.16 teaches inventory control rules by having learners answer questions based on several categories: work-in-process inventory, maintenance inventory, and raw materials inventory. The types of questions are based on the color of square on which the

---

Figure 2.16. Board Game Screen Capture.

Source: Courtesy of the Institute for Interactive Technologies, Bloomsburg University. Created by Frank Brophy and Adrienne Marquette. All rights reserved.

learner lands. Common inventory rules are provided to learners in the form of questions. The learner must answer the questions correctly in moving around the board. The learner takes turns "rolling" the die by clicking on the button in the right-hand corner.

Board games teach many different types of rules and provide learners with a simple method of applying rules to different situations. The universal convention of the board game means that the learners are not caught up in the rules of the game; rather, they are able to focus on the rules that are presented in the content of the game.

If the underlying logic and functionality of the game are developed effectively, they can serve as a game engine, with the cosmetic elements around the game changing while the underlying functionality remains the same. A game engine is the code and software that run the "behind the scenes" activities of a game, such as the process of turn taking or the mechanism for keeping score. It controls the game play and rules of the online game. The use of a game engine reduces development time for future versions of the game and allows the game to be refreshed with new questions and a new look without reprogramming the underlying code every time. Figure 2.17 shows the basic board game concept used in the manufacturing game with a new look for use in a retail bank setting. The idea is to keep the basic game play elements and functionality while adding new questions and graphics. Intelligently designing and deploying games helps to reduce costs while allowing for fun game play.

Versatility of Multiple-Choice Questions

One of the fundamental elements in many of the games described in this chapter is the use of multiple-choice questions. Effective use of multiple-choice questions can test a learner at various levels of the learning hierarchy, from declarative knowledge to the application of rules. Effective transfer of knowledge from boomers to gamers requires that the multiple-choice questions be well written. Games can seem simplistic and boring with poor question writing.

Figure 2.17. Same Board Game as in Figure 2.16 But with Different Graphics and Questions.

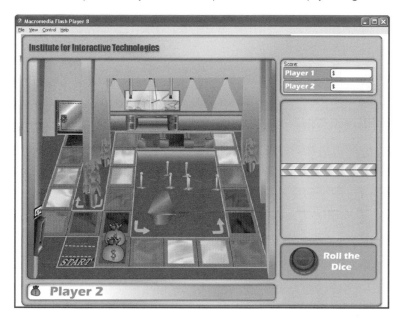

Well-written multiple-choice questions teach and assess knowledge within the context of a game. Poor questions simply allow the gamer to play a game without learning. Work to develop effective questions to force learning and require learners to think as they play the game.

Keep in mind that when developing games using multiple-choice questions, you can move the learner up the learning hierarchy by structuring more and more difficult questions. This provides the learner with an initial sense of accomplishment but challenges the learner to move up to more difficult levels because the types of questions become increasingly challenging. Gamers like a good challenge and expect the games they play to become progressively more difficult as they master basic knowledge. Table 2.2 shows the different levels of knowledge that can be addressed with multiple-choice questions.

Table 2.2. Types of Multiple-Choice Questions.

Declarative knowledge/memorization

In terms of computer hardware, what does the term *CPU* represent?

    a. Central processing unit

    b. Core processing unit

    c. Central planning unit

    d. Core planning unit

Concepts and comprehension

If a customer needs to create budgets, sort financial information, and create a cash flow statement for her small business, what type of software application would you recommend?

    a. Fully integrated accounting software suite

    b. Basic spreadsheet program

    c. Word processing program

    d. Basic database program

Application of rules

If your client received the following error message, "Inventory Item Not Found," when searching on the item number field in the Enterprise Resource Planning system for an item he swears is in the database, what should you do?

    a. Ask the client to enter the item again.

    b. Ask the client for the item number and check it yourself.

    c. Ask the client to conduct a search for the item using the text field.

    d. Check to see if the server is still communicating with the inventory database.

Workplace Implications

You can almost hear the boomers screaming in the background: "Wait! We don't want employees playing games on company time!" Why not? Games are engaging, interactive, and an effective method of learning. The gamer generation doesn't want to learn in the traditional manner; in fact, some experts would argue that they can't learn in the traditional manner. They have been changed by technology.

Whether that is indeed the case, there are plenty of examples of how playing games can be advantageous to an organization. Here is a classic example. In the late 1980s and early 1990s, when MS Windows started to gain widespread popularity, the first thing that the information technology department did in every organization when they installed the new operating system and the newfangled thing called a "mouse" was to remove the *Solitaire* game from the desktop. Let's not tempt employees with frivolous, time-wasting games. It might cut down on productivity.

Next, training departments invested thousands of dollars and hundreds of hours teaching employees how to double-click, drag and drop, and right-click mouse buttons, the very skills that can be learned in fifteen minutes of playing *Solitaire*. And as a bonus, *Solitaire* was fun as opposed to being lectured on the functionality of a mouse. In the case of learning to use a computer mouse, games would have saved organizations a ton of time and money.

The intelligent application of games for teaching declarative, concept, and rules-based knowledge is an important aspect of transferring knowledge from the boomer generation to the gamer generation. Organizations that want to be successful are going to find methods of teaching gamers using the language and tools of gamers.

When an organization takes the time to design effective games using the information shown in Table 2.3, it will be able to create workplace games that

Table 2.3. Types of Games and Appropriate Content.

Game	Definition	Example	Type of Knowledge Taught
Declarative knowledge and labeling games	Game that provides matching, labeling, or question answering based primarily on knowing facts	Word search, free the road runner, drag-and-drop exercises	Declarative
Concept games	Game that requires learner to understand concepts and apply those concepts in limited situations	Bop the fox, race games	Declarative and concepts
Board/trivia games	Game that requires learner to move a piece around a board or answer questions when provided some type of stimulus	*Jeopardy, Who Wants to Be a Millionaire, Wheel of Fortune, Hollywood Squares, Monopoly, Risk*	Declarative, concepts, and rules

provide gamers with the entertainment of a game while teaching them the fundamentals required for workplace success.

While boomers may find the games in this chapter simplistic and a waste of time, they provide an excellent instructional design for a generation that grew up on games. Gamers quickly learn declarative, conceptual, and rule-based knowledge. An aversion to casual games can cost corporations hundreds of thousands of dollars in training and lost productivity.

■   ■   ■   ■

SUMMARY

When thinking about adding games to an academic or training department curriculum, consider casual games. These types of games can be powerful tools for transferring basic knowledge. They can be played quickly and over and over again, making the repetitive process of learning basic knowledge fun and exciting. Casual games engage employees and students by providing essential gaming elements while transferring basic knowledge.

Although simple games are a good start in any learning effort, they do have limitations. Preparing gamers to be good technicians, research scientists, sales-people, CEOs, and production managers requires more than basic knowledge. Incoming gamers need to be taught procedures, principles, and problem-solving skills to gain the knowledge level of the exiting boomers. The next chapter discusses how that can be achieved through the development of edu-cational simulations.

3

The Virtual Apprentice

WHEN YOU PLAY THE JAMES BOND 007 *NightFire* game on the PlayStation 2, you don't tell James Bond what to shoot, you don't direct him where to go, and you don't give him commands to follow. No, you don't control James Bond because you *are* James Bond.

The first-person viewpoint puts you neatly into Bond's tuxedo. It is as if you were in a Bond movie drinking the martini yourself. You learn as James Bond how to approach a potential enemy, which gun has the most firepower, and which button activates the car's missile defense system. (Trust me, that comes in handy when you are being chased by heavily armed jeeps.)

You learn more than you would if you were merely controlling some external character's movements. You wince when you are shot; your stomach drops when you fall off a cliff. You understand the implicit rules of the world in which you are operating as Bond. Parameters are revealed to you as you play. Some are obvious and predictable, like gravity. Some are not so obvious, like detecting enemies by using the "Bond Focus" power.

Figure 3.1. Gamers Can Easily Imagine They Are Superspies When Playing
First-Person Video Games.

Source: Reprinted with permission of the artist, Kristin Longenecker.

You are actually serving as an apprentice to the game environment. The game patiently teaches you lessons about how Bond would behave. You have an initial tutorial where you learn how to fight, how to aim a gun, and how to rappel up walls—skills that you need later as you encounter increasingly difficult levels of your mission. Each mission builds on skills and behaviors learned in the previous level, and the game corrects your actions by giving you continuous feedback.

You can look at your health meter to determine if you did something correctly. Full health means you made it through the mission with no mistakes. A health meter that is less than full indicates you took some damage; you made some mistakes. If you do really poorly, you are reprimanded by the game in the form of death. You receive the message "Mission Failed," and you must start over, just as a watchful master tells an apprentice to "try again" when not pleased with the apprentice's action or, worse, tells the apprentice, "You're fired." The game kicks you out and makes you do it over again until you get it right. These types of games are a great lesson in perseverance and have taught gamers that "of course you got only 50 percent through; now try again and get 52 percent of the way through."

For an even more realistic first-person perspective, play Microsoft's *Flight Simulator 2004* (Figure 3.2). In this game, you don't read pages and pages of text instructing you how to fly an airplane. Instead, you are placed in the cockpit with an instrument panel in front of you. You then need to begin to fly your plane or end up on the ground in a pile of twisted metal. The simulator becomes the master instructor, and you become the apprentice pilot.

Figure 3.2. Plane Cockpit in Microsoft's *Flight Simulator 2004.*

Source: Used with permission. Screen shot reprinted by permission from Microsoft Corporation.

You are immersed within the environment of the cockpit and must act as if you were flying the plane. You use the same instruments, observe the same feedback, and make the same adjustments as an actual pilot. The simulator teaches what you need to learn by trial and error: "Okay, so last time I ignored the altimeter and I crashed. This time I will pay attention to my altitude."

In both cases, the game acts as a master, patiently teaching procedures, principles, and problem-solving skills needed for success. In fact, in these cases, the game is more of a simulation than an actual game.

Games typically do not attempt to mimic real-life situations. While playing hangman, for example, you do not play from the perspective of the person being hanged or the executioner. Playing Whack a Mole does not cast you as a hunter. There is a clear division between the environment in which the learning will be used and the environment in which it is being taught. You might learn about the parts of a memo by flipping virtual memory cards, but you will never encounter those cards when actually typing a memo.

There are times when games are appropriate, mostly for teaching the first three levels of the learning hierarchy. Other times, the learner needs an environment that is closer to the actual work situation.

Simulations are meant to blur the line between playing a game and being involved in the actual situation. Yes, you know that you are not James Bond or that you are not flying an actual airplane, but the immersive and engaging nature of the simulation means that you react in a similar manner, with similar emotions and feelings, as you would when placed in the actual environment. Your palms sweat, you jump when a character pops out of the dark at you, and you feel threatened when a heavily armed jeep pulls up behind you.

Our minds can easily place us in a faraway village or on a distant planet by simply reading text on a white page. If you have ever been emotionally moved by a book or cried while reading a sad story, you understand that we can easily be placed into a desired environment with little external stimulation. Now add high-quality graphics, animation, and realistic sounds, and suddenly you can be transported into the world of James Bond or the cockpit of an airplane.

Gamers are used to all kinds of simulations, from console games to PC games to simulated online cell phones. They are comfortable with virtual objects and operating in virtual worlds. They have run kingdoms with *Age of the Empires* and have been railroad tycoons, city planners, and owners of theme parks. Gamers have created simulated families with *The Sims* and raised virtual dogs with *Nintendogs*. They have joined entire online worlds simulating a different way of life in such online role-play simulations as *Runescape, Everquest,* and *World of Warcraft.* As the introduction to *World of Warcraft* explains,

World of Warcraft enables thousands of players to come together online and battle against the world and each other. Players from across the globe can leave the real world behind and undertake grand quests and heroic exploits in a land of fantastic adventure. At long last, the world of Azeroth . . . is realized in glorious detail and ready for the arrival of millions of prospective players. So step upon the hallowed shores of this embattled world, and see what journeys await for those who would plumb this ancient realm's many secrets.[1]

It turns out that these simulations are effective teachers. Boomers might not always agree with the content being taught, but these simulations do teach. Simulations provide training and education with a high level of clarity and detail. More important, they connect learning to the affective domain, the emotions of the gamer. This type of connection rarely occurs in an instructor-led training program. Simulations are necessary tools for teaching gamers how to be good technicians, scientists, managers, and salespeople.

Simulations are patient and understanding teachers: they don't get bored, tired, or frustrated, no matter how many times you make the same mistake. A simulation simply repeats the sequence over and over again until you determine what actions are needed to land the plane, create armor out of the materials lying around the countryside, move to the next level, or defeat the relentless jeeps.

Games Versus Simulations

"We cannot define anything precisely! If we attempt to, we get into that paralysis of thought that comes to philosophers, who sit opposite each other, one saying to the other, 'You don't know what you are talking about!' The second one says 'What do you mean by know? What do you mean by talking? What do you mean by you?' and so on."*

What can I say about a debate that routinely chews up chapters in books, occupies entire blogs, and can cause heated discussions between normally well-mannered thinkers from both camps? You can definitely say that we aren't going to solve the problem here, but at least we wanted to make sure people were aware of some of the high points.

One of the most important points on the entire issue is the realization that there is a difference. You run this risk, once you get known as the "game guy," of getting called on all the time to speak or write about the topic. That's fine, but usually it's a call to talk about "games and simulations," as if they were the same thing. They're not; they never have been and never will be. So what is the short answer? The most compelling distinction for me is that games construct their own reality, but simulations seek to recreate a certain slice of an existing or past reality.

Let's also be clear that neither games nor simulations require technology to exist and that both have enjoyed long lives prior to the computer. Think about a nontechnology-enabled game like soccer. Soccer has a unique set of rules. The penalty kick, the rule disallowing the use of hands (except for the goalie), the indirect kick; none of these rules has any meaning outside the magic circle, that is, the context of the game. Those rules are bedrock foundations of the reality inside the game, but they do not seek to replicate any particular law or rule found in the nonsoccer world.

What about simulations? Let's look at one of the most popular simulations available (which does happen to be technologically mediated): Microsoft's *Flight Simulator*. The rules that govern someone's experience within *Flight Sim* are primarily the same ones pilots face in the physical world: Newton's laws of motion and Bernoulli's principle, for example. The creators of the simulation sought to model these certain physical laws as closely as possible in order to most closely approximate the experience of flying a plane. They did not seek, however, to recreate all physical world laws such as those governing economics or quantum mechanics, since simulations seek only to recreate manageable, relevant slices of reality.

The savvy reader will almost immediately realize that this bifurcation is not impermeable and in fact has considerable bleed. There are any number of games with rules that in some way seek to represent some portion of reality; in many games, resource constraints are placed on the player (for example, you have only so many players or only so much time). These mirror constraints are also found in reality but do not seek to accurately and directly model the behaviors and characteristics of exact conditions.

There are also simulations with pieces or elements that do not seek to march in lockstep with reality. Scores, time limits, the ability to pause the simulation, the ability for a teenager to fly a military jet; these are not typically elements found in the reality of our daily lives. But for the most part, these elements do not form the core of the simulation experience.

So how do we come to a conclusion or a decision here, and who are some of the folks thinking about this and writing about it? While the description of games having their own rules and simulations seeking to model reality's own rules is useful for telling the two apart, we should ask why it matters.

The two big forces, aside from intellectual curiosity, that power the drive to make a distinction between games and simulations are design and purchasing.

Design is an important force. If you are looking to design a game or a simulation, you need to understand both the common and distinct elements of each. You need to understand what elements of games and simulations can be mixed and matched and which should be left to their own respective areas.

Purchasing in this instance refers to going out and looking to buy a game or a simulation for you or your company. If you are talking about a technologically mediated situation (a PC-based game or simulation), there will probably be both a price and a development time frame differential between the two products. This will depend greatly on the scope of the effort, but in general, given similar scope or subject matter, a well-done simulation will cost more and take longer to develop than a well-done game. The reason is simple: in reaching for that near-reality level of fidelity, the simulation will require greater subject matter expert input, greater resolution of images, and other components.

Mark Oehlert is an associate at Booz Allen Hamilton, a global technology consulting firm. He works on the learning team as a learning strategy architect and provides leadership and enterprise-level insight on a number of issues, including game-based learning, mobile learning, emerging technologies, and strategic planning. Before returning to Booz Allen, he served as the director of learning innovations for the MASIE Center.

Source: Printed with the permission of Mark Oehlert.

*Feynman, R. (1994). The Feynman lecture on physics. In *The character of physical law.* New York: Modern Library.

Higher-Level Types of Knowledge

While the casual games discussed in Chapter Two are adept at teaching declarative knowledge, concepts, rules, and even abstract thinking, simulations are more appropriate for direct, one-to-one transfer and application of higher levels of learning, such as procedures, principles, and problem solving, directly to the situation in which you need to exhibit those skills.

The real danger of losing boomer knowledge is not the loss of basic declarative knowledge, concepts, or rules. It is the loss of problem-solving knowledge, business acumen, and knowing when to apply the right steps in a procedure.

Basic knowledge is relatively easy to transfer; transferring higher-level knowledge is more difficult. Higher levels of knowledge can be divided into three types. Table 3.1 lists these three types (procedures, principles, and problem solving) with a short definition and an example of each.

Unlike the lower levels of knowledge, these three types of knowledge are not necessarily hierarchical. The lower levels of knowledge are required as pre-

Table 3.1. Higher-Level Knowledge Types.

Type of Knowledge	Definition	Example
Procedures	Ordered sequence of rules or steps a learner must complete to perform a task.	First type the customer name; then click Next; then type customer address; click Save.
Principles	Guidelines for behavior or actions that are not sequential.	There are five leadership principles to follow. Different situations call for emphasis or deemphasis of one or more of the principles (for example, crisis leadership may be different than day-to-day leadership).
Problem solving	Learner is confronted with novel situation and must use previous knowledge to solve the problem.	Determine the best way to confront an employee who seems to be having personal problems.

requisites, but knowledge of a particular procedure may not be required for solving certain problems. Knowledge of the principles of good communication is not necessarily a prerequisite for solving a problem related to a piece of heavy machinery. The skills of good communication will facilitate the process and may provide needed information, but typically, the problem can be solved without having learned the principles of good communication. However, in some cases, procedures are a prerequisite for problem solving. For example, you cannot solve the problem of having too much inventory if you do not know what procedures should be in place for reducing inventory. In that case, prerequisite knowledge of how inventory is affected by shipping and production is key to solving the excess inventory problem.

Since sometimes prerequisite knowledge is required and sometimes it is not, the teaching of the higher-level skills to gamers by the boomers is somewhat problematic. The gamers may have enough knowledge and skills to apply their problem-solving abilities to a specific set of defined problems but may be completely devoid of the prerequisite skills necessary to solve other types of problems or problems outside their comfort zone. It is important for gamers to receive as much training as possible in applying their sharp problem-solving skills to a variety of real-life situations. Practice in applying these skills to different contexts will help them to transfer their learning from simulations to actual situations.

Successful boomers are adept at quickly analyzing and solving problems. Research shows that the difference between experts and novices in problem solving has to do with the expert's ability to internally organize a domain of knowledge and then quickly search that knowledge to develop a plan of action. "The problem-solving difficulties of novices can be attributed largely to the nature of their [internal] knowledge bases, and much less to the limitations of their process capabilities, such as their inability to use general problem solving heuristics or strategies."[2]

The ability of experienced boomers to quickly solve a problem is possible because they have seen dozens, if not hundreds, of instances of the same or similar problem, not because they have better problem-solving techniques. Experts can distinguish between the sound of a piece of machinery running properly and the sound of that same machine not functioning properly. When experts "look at an apparently complicated situation, they are able to represent it in terms of a small number of patterns or chunks." They perceive the problem in a way that restricts the problem space.[3] These are difficult skills to teach in a classroom, but this is the knowledge boomers need to pass on to gamers, and this is where multiple experiences are needed.

Fortunately, the experiences can be real or simulated. "If a simulation is done well, it seems real and becomes a labeled memory that's triggered by a similar experience."[4] Therefore, providing gamers with simulated experiences will help them when they encounter actual experiences involving the same issues. Virtual experiences can make up for a lack of real experiences.

We took my gamer son to New York City for the first time recently, and he swore he had been there before. He hadn't. Yet he did seem to have an uncanny knowledge of some landmarks and streets. He even correctly recognized and pointed out specific parts of Times Square. When we asked him how this was possible, he said that he had raced in New York before. Raced in New York? He can't even drive. He was talking about the time he spent playing *Gran Turismo 4,* a driving game that bills itself as a "The Real Driving Simulator." You can choose from real cars, real race tracks, and real cities in which to race. New York is one of those cities. In this case, the racing simulation created memory points in my son's mind that he keyed on when he was in the actual city. To him, the line between memories and reality was blurred by the high-quality simulation. Similar reactions occur when discussing dog ownership with someone who has never owned a dog but has played *Nintendogs,* where you are required to raise a virtual dog from a puppy.

Tapping into the power of simulations to transfer knowledge from the boomers to the gamers makes sense for a number of reasons:

- Gamers are familiar with the genre of simulations and are comfortable working within the conventions of simulations.
- Well-developed simulations can provide a wealth of virtual experience and help learners build an experiential knowledge base in a safe environment.

- Simulations can be developed by boomers to contain the rules, parameters, and guidelines that gamers need to learn in a manner conducive to how gamers prefer to learn.

- Simulations can teach subtleties and nuances not possible with text-based e-learning modules.

- Simulations are appropriate for teaching higher learning, such as procedures, principles, and problem solving.

- Simulations can tap into the emotions of the learner and provide a realistic version of a situation or piece of equipment. The high level of realism helps reinforce the learning.

Because of their ability to transfer higher levels of knowledge, simulations have to be carefully constructed. "A good simulation cannot be slapped together," maintains Rich Mesch, a developer of simulations for over twenty years.[5] Mesch, now the director of simulation and special projects at a Philadelphia-based performance improvement company, Performance Development Group, reminds us that "simulations need to have certain elements to be effective. Simulations need to replicate a slice of reality. They should be something that the learner cares about, and they should be engaging. A good back story helps. In effective simulations, like good games, people need to care about the story. If they don't care, they will not be engaged." He goes on to point out that effective simulations also "need to contain specific and accurate job-related elements. Things that are difficult on the job should be difficult in the simulation. The answers in the simulation need to be the answers to the real-world problem."

Now that we understand the strengths of simulations and some of the caveats, let's look at how simulations can transfer the three types of high-level knowledge from boomers to gamers in the form of different types of simulations.

Procedural Knowledge

A procedure is a set of steps that must be completed to achieve a desired result; procedures string together rules and concepts to achieve a particular outcome. They are a vital element in the daily operation of any organization.

There are procedures for opening a store, developing a new product, logging on to an intranet, and handling customer complaints. Without procedures, organizations would not function. No one would know what to do.

In fact, many common business procedures become codified into software. Software applications are simply a list of steps that need to be followed in a certain order to achieve a desired result. A software application walks employees through the proper steps time and time again.

The manufacturing process, tracking customers, human resources, logistics, and countless other common business processes have been turned into software sold across industries and companies because of the commonality of many business processes. One of the most common examples is accounting software. Almost every organization has accounting software to assist with the process of collecting financial data and creating monthly and year-end reports. If the employee follows the screen sequence and enters the requested information, the proper reports are created.

Some people spend all day working through the procedures of a software application. A claims adjuster at an insurance agency inputs information in the proper sequence into a software application to determine the proper disposition of a claim. Welfare caseworkers complete screen after screen of information in the proper sequence as they input information about their welfare clients. There are even jobs designed to ensure that others are following correct procedures. Auditors monitor, maintain, and enforce organizational and governmental procedures.

Boomers have focused on procedures within the corporate environment for years in an attempt to improve quality and increase productivity. They have led the workplace in seeking a variety of methods for improving procedures through Six Sigma, just-in-time initiatives, and statistical process control. They have spent a lot of time thinking about process and procedure improvement.

Through the years, it has been discovered that the best procedure for teaching procedures seems to be this sequence:

1. Present an overview of the procedure from start to finish and its desired outcomes.

2. Break the procedure into discrete steps.

3. Teach each step individually.

4. Combine multiple steps.

5. Focus on putting the entire procedure back together.

6. Allow learners to practice the entire procedure.

7. Introduce variations to the standard procedure.

8. Allow learners to practice the variations and the standard procedure.

While it is initially difficult to learn step-by-step procedures, over time most people internalize procedural knowledge. The routine procedure becomes automatic through practice or repetition. The learner no longer has to concentrate on the skill to accomplish the task. It becomes internalized. The academic term for this is *automaticity*.[6]

Once the procedure is internalized, employees are able to perform a procedure fluidly without thinking of the discrete steps. A good example is logging on to an organization's intranet. After several weeks of logging on to the system, most people no longer think about individual steps; they simply log on and go about their business.

In fact, once a procedure hits the level of automaticity, the individual can often perform additional procedures at the same time because the procedure that has reached automaticity no longer requires thought. A common example is driving a car. Many people are able to eat, drink, and listen to the radio while driving because the procedures for looking in the rear-view mirror, staying in the proper lane, and appropriately accelerating and decelerating have been internalized. The process becomes so automatic the person doesn't even think about the steps.

Procedural knowledge can become so internalized that a person is no longer able to break the procedure into discrete steps. The steps are too automatic. This often happens with boomers who have been doing the same procedure for years and years. This inability to distinguish the discrete steps can make the transfer of procedural knowledge difficult. It is not that the boomer doesn't want to provide the detailed step-by-step information; it is that he or she can't. Automaticity has set in.

Procedural Knowledge Simulations

Because of automaticity, often an experienced master performer is not the most appropriate teacher. A master performer may be unable to recall how he or she got to such a high level of performance. Simulations can be developed by observing several master performers, recording their efforts, and evaluating what they do. This level of analysis can be used to create a simulation providing instruction on each discrete step and on the overall combined procedure.

Creating a procedural simulation codifies the steps of the procedure and allows the learner to review them over and over again until they are learned. A well-built procedural simulation acts as a patient master, teaching each new apprentice the proper steps, with no chance of forgetting a step and no automaticity. There are basically three types of procedural simulations:

- Physical

- Software

- Operational

Physical Procedural Simulation. The proper operation of physical objects requires the following of specific procedures. This is especially true when working with expensive or dangerous machinery or equipment. Unfortunately, written standard operating procedures (SOPs), developed and used by many companies, do not convey specific tasks or steps as accurately as they should. Employees often have difficulty translating written instructions into tangible actions when they are using the equipment.

In addition, problems arise when trying to give new employees enough time to learn how equipment functions. Some specialized machinery can cost as much as $1 million. It is understandable why companies are reluctant to interrupt the production process to conduct training. They are too busy recouping the cost of the equipment, and there is a risk that the new employee may make a mistake and damage the equipment. The high price tag for the equipment also means that there isn't any possibility of having a spare available for training purposes.

The alternative is also unacceptable. Companies do not want a new, untrained employee operating a million-dollar piece of equipment. As a remedy, new employees are supervised by a more experienced employee for months until the new employee is skilled enough to operate the machinery alone. With operators retiring and new employees under increasing pressure to produce more quickly, the learning curve required to make this type of training feasible is too long. Learning times need to be reduced safely and effectively.

One method of shortening this learning curve is to develop physical procedural simulations: simulations of equipment that function like the physical object they represent but are available using a computer. They are virtual renderings of the physical machinery or equipment that the operator must use. These are sometimes called *emulations, virtual labs,* or *virtual products.*[1] These simulations range from mimicking a simple item like a cell phone all the way to functioning like a million-dollar plastic extruder.

These simulations do not replace the need for hands-on training with the actual equipment or machinery. Instead, they make the limited time available on the machinery or equipment more productive. A simulation of a machine or piece of equipment allows the learner to determine what the equipment is capable of doing, how it operates, and its limitations in a safe and risk-free environment. Many objects that are too costly or dangerous for training on the real thing are ideal candidates for physical simulations. The simulation allows trial and error while presenting feedback and advice to the person operating the simulated machinery.

Simulated Blown Film Extruder. One example of a simulated piece of large equipment was developed by Kirk Cantor, a faculty member at the Pennsylvania College of Technology. The project, funded by the National Science Foundation, involved the creation of simulations of several pieces of equipment used in the plastics manufacturing process. One of the simulations was of a blown film extruder.

The simulation was created in part to train workers within the plastics industry how to operate a blown film extruder safely and effectively. Employees use the simulation, shown in Figure 3.3, to practice running the virtual machine before using a real one on the shop floor.

Figure 3.3. Simulation of a Blown Film Extruder.

Source: Created by Kirk Cantor. Used with permission.

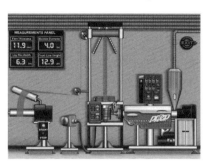

Properly running the extruder is important. If an employee doesn't run the extruder at the right temperature, speed, or pressure, the screw may break. Each screw costs thousands of dollars, not to mention the cost of time and effort to extract and replace the broken screw, on top of any lost productivity or possible injury—an expensive lesson. Learning that same lesson virtually is practically free after the initial cost of developing the simulation.

Employees can practice the proper procedure for starting the machine, operating the machine, and shutting it down over and over again without the risk of damaging it or taking it out of production. Employees can even practice troubleshooting and reacting to different scenarios involving the functioning of the machine.

Multiple learners can be working with the simulation at the same time, as opposed to each new employee trying to obtain time on the actual machine. Safety concerns (other than carpal tunnel) are eliminated. Workers can practice what they need to learn virtually, so they spend much less learning time on the actual blown film extruder. This is effective when a new employee needs to get up to speed on a piece of equipment within a manufacturing process, and it frees the time of the more experienced boomer operators, who need to be operating the machinery for the company to remain profitable.

The knowledge of the master operators is incorporated into the simulation, so it functions and operates as the actual equipment and, through feedback and programmed parameters, can instruct a new employee on proper procedures and functions. The operator of the simulation must start, operate, and stop the simulated blown film extruder using the same procedure as the physical blown film extruder.

Simulated ATC-600A Test Box. Small pieces of machinery can be simulated as well. In this example, a piece of equipment called the ATC-600A is recreated virtually. The ATC-600A is specialized hardware designed to test an aircraft's transponder while the aircraft is on the ground (see Figure 3.4). It is a delicate piece of equipment and easily damaged if not properly set up before testing.

Figure 3.4. Simulated Test Box Screen Capture.

Source: Courtesy of the Institute for Interactive Technologies, Bloomsburg University. Created by Frank Brophy, Adrienne Marquette, Nick Pastore, Ula Konczewska, and Norm Verbeck. All rights reserved.

To help teach the proper procedure for operating the ATC-600A test box, three modes of operation were programmed into the simulated ATC-600A. In the first mode, the learner watches a demonstration of the proper procedure. An overview of the entire procedure is presented, and then the learner observes the placement of the ATC-600A in relationship to the airplane's antenna. The learner observes the cord being plugged into the box and watches as the system is configured, tested, and made operational by following the proper procedure. This is called the Demonstration mode.

The next mode is the Practice mode, which allows the learner to interact with the ATC-600A under the watchful guidance of the simulation. The simulation provides arrows, hints, instructions, highlights, and advice to the learner as he or she follows the procedure for setting up and operating the test box. It is almost impossible for the learner to get lost using the simulation. Once the learner performs a step in the procedure, the simulation checks the step and provides immediate feedback. This mode provides the learner with a chance to learn each step individually.

The final mode is the Test mode. In this mode of the simulation, the learner receives no guidance, help, or assistance from the simulation. The learner must know what to do. Each step in the procedure is evaluated by the simulation, and at the end of the procedure, the learner is evaluated. If the learner "fries" the test box before reaching the end, he or she is made aware of that situation and must start the test over. He or she failed the procedure.

These three levels are not unlike the levels in a video game. In many games, the gamer is able to choose an easy, medium, or hard level. In the James Bond video game, the three levels are named Operative, Agent, and 00 Agent. Multiple levels of difficulty provide variety of game play and allow players with different levels of knowledge to enjoy the game. The use of three levels in this simulation and others accomplishes the same goal. Different learners with different knowledge levels can all use the same simulation. They simply pick the mode most appropriate for them. This allows for an effective and timely transfer of know-how. Time is not wasted going through the parts of the simulated procedure already known.

The advice and guidance provided in the first two modes of the simulation is information and knowledge from experts familiar with the ATC-600A.

These experts have worked with the test box in the past and have, in some cases, broken the test box by not following the proper procedure. Their knowledge and experiences are passed on every time a learner goes through the simulation. They are masters and mentors to apprentices they will never meet.

Software Emulation. One of the most obvious areas for simulating a procedure is software applications. Since these are codified procedures, it makes sense that a software simulation is an effective tool for teaching the functionality of software, not to mention that companies have literally dozens of software applications that new employees need to learn.

Software emulations or simulations are programs that look like and function in a manner similar to the live software but are more controlled and limited than the live system. They are typically created by taking screen shots or small videos of the software and then adding in functionality. A number of software programs exist that make it possible to create software simulations without needing to know programming. The user simply "records" events on the screen, adds text boxes or voice-overs, and creates a simulation of the actual software. In many cases, the developer can even add input fields and provide feedback to the learner as he or she progresses through the simulation.

Software simulations eliminate a number of traditional problems with classroom-based software training. In many cases, as with the machinery example above, it is not possible to train employees on the production version of the software. This can be due to the sensitivity of the data (client information) or the fact that managers in the organization do not want garbage data in the live system (input from the trainees may have an impact on real data as they are aggregated for reports).

The difficulty with using a live system for conducting training is that trainers have only one of two choices. The first is to ask the information technology department to create a duplicate version of the live system for training purposes. In this scenario, the department makes an exact duplicate of the live version and places it on another server for use during training classes. This works for some software functionality but has a number of associated problems. One problem is dealing with multiple people logging in to the same record and performing the same task using the same information at exactly the same time, as happens in a class when they all work in unison. Another problem is that the instructor ends up spending a lot of time establishing test cases and configuring data so the right results occur when the learners are guided through the scenario by the instructor. In addition, students in class can inadvertently hit a wrong key and go off to some foreign screen and not know how to return to the screen the instructor is describing. The instructor must stop the class, help the learner return to the correct screen, and then continue. Everyone waits while the instructor guides the learner back or the instructor leaves the lost learner and proceeds with the instruction and attempts to help that person catch up later.

If the purpose of the class is to teach a process that ages, such as accounts receivable or a customer follow-up three months later, the instructor has to hope an aged receivable is in the database to teach the correct lesson. If the instructor is teaching the learner what to do with aged information, he or she cannot speed up time on a duplicated live system. With a copy of the live system, one hour equals one hour.

The second choice instructors have is to use screen captures in paper-based manuals to discuss the process. This means that the learners read about the proper functioning of the software and fill in fields on paper as they would when using the software. This type of training is not effective since the learners aren't actually using the software.

A software simulation solves both problems with classroom software application training:

- It allows aging. In a simulation, five minutes can equal one hour or longer.
- There is no danger of corrupting real data.
- There is no danger of revealing sensitive data from an actual system.
- The trainer doesn't have to spend hours setting up scenarios ahead of time.
- Multiple trainees can log in to the same account with the same data at the same time.

- Software simulations generally require less memory for storage than an exact copy of an actual system.

- Learners stay on a prescribed screen path. A simulation is not as wide open as an exact copy of the actual system, so it is harder for learners to get lost on the wrong screen.

- It provides the physical simulation of using the mouse and pressing the right keys, something that doesn't happen with paper-based screen captures.

- Software simulations provide gamers with a chance to practice computer procedures in a computerized environment, one with which they are familiar.

Figure 3.5 displays an example screen shot from a training program designed to teach the learner how to create online surveys and quizzes. The

Figure 3.5. Software Emulation Screen.
Source: Courtesy of Helmut Doll. Used with permission. All rights reserved.

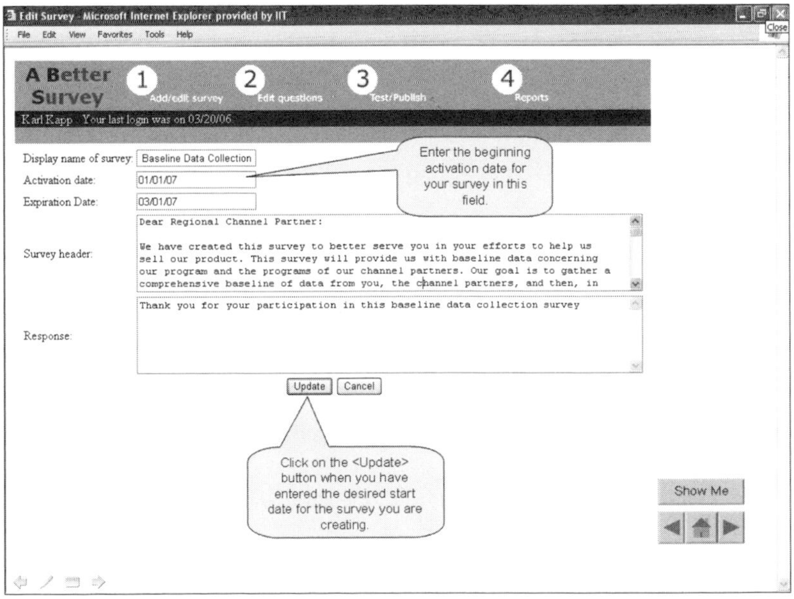

simulation allows the learner to move through the simulated software learning the definitions of each field. As a final exercise, the program walks the learner through the process of creating a survey.

Operational Procedural Simulation. This type of simulation covers common procedures used within an organization that are not software or object based or that contain elements of both. These are simulations of a meeting to determine contingency plans for potential disasters, using job aids to assist in a sale, conducting an employment interview, or running a football play.

An example of this type of procedure is opening a retail store in the morning. The procedure involves unlocking the door, turning on the lights, opening the cash register, counting the money in the drawer, arranging displays, and possibly logging on to the corporate intranet. The procedure is a mix of online activities and physical activities.

Another is the running of football plays. Joe Paterno has been coaching the Penn State football team for over forty years. One new trick he has adopted is providing his quarterbacks and receivers with copies of the Penn State playbook on a PlayStation 2 memory card. The players plug in to the game *Madden 2006* and practice running the plays to learn the routes and moves.[8] The playbook combined with the simulated game provides the players with an opportunity to practice plays and run routes virtually. This allows them to be better prepared to run routes and make moves during practices and on game day.

These types of simulations provide a broad range of opportunities to simulate organizational procedures, including knowing what steps need to be taken to document an employee absence or the process for documenting a hostile incident in the workplace. These training situations can consist of a diagram showing the flow of paperwork, schematics, videos, or photographs of people and even software screen shots. The goal of the simulation is to walk the learner through the procedure in as realistic a manner as possible.

Hazardous and Operability Study Simulation. A chemical manufacturing plant needed to train its workers on the proper procedures for conducting a hazard and operability study, or what is commonly referred to in the chemical industry as a HAZOP. A HAZOP is a systematic, rigorous methodology used to identify potential hazards and operability concerns when implementing new processes or equipment.

The procedure for conducting a HAZOP consists of meetings of a multidisciplinary team of individuals knowledgeable and technically qualified in the process or with the equipment. Most often these are the senior-level people within the organization, that is, boomers. During these sessions, the team systematically follows procedures for questioning each part of the process or equipment to determine how deviations may occur. The outcome of these meetings is a list of potential hazards and brief recommendations explaining how to mitigate identified hazards.

This simulation places the learner on a HAZOP team consisting of virtual teammates with whom he or she needs to interact. The learner can click on each teammate to hear his or her viewpoint on the implementation of a new piece of equipment and then has the opportunity to ask questions from a multiple-choice menu. Each question chosen elicits a different response from the virtual team. If wrong questions are asked or if the proper procedure is not followed, wrong decisions are made and lead to a HAZOP failure.

The technique employed for the functionality of the simulation is known as the branching story technique. Based on the learner's responses, the simulation branches in one direction or another. It is an appropriate branch if the learner is following the correct procedure. If it is an inappropriate branch, the learner is not following the correct HAZOP procedures. In this case, the simulation branches down an inappropriate path where the learner can observe the consequences of not following the right procedure.

The simulation provides learners with tips and prompts, helping them to follow and learn the proper procedure for conducting a HAZOP. The content for the simulation was provided by experienced workers who have conducted one or more HAZOPs.

Tips and hints are placed into the simulation so some of the nuances of human interaction that cannot be captured in written procedures can be conveyed. The goal is to transfer the knowledge of conducting a HAZOP, as well as the lessons learned from previous HAZOP studies, to those who participate

Figure 3.6. Simulation of Team Meeting.

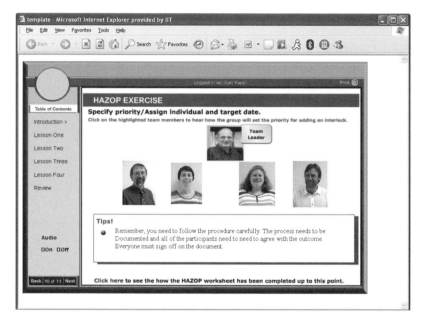

in the simulation. On successful completion of the HAZOP simulation, the learner knows the proper procedure for conducting a HAZOP and gains knowledge and expertise from experts who have participated in actual HAZOPs.

Teaching Sales Reps to Use the Proper Tools. In an ongoing effort to increase sales productivity, a pharmaceutical company performed an analysis to see what issues the sales representatives were encountering. It discovered that one critical issue was that sales representatives didn't feel they had all of the selling tools they needed to be effective.

The training department was puzzled by this finding because they provided extensive training and had issued a number of job aids and other performance support tools to the sales representatives to use to manage an effective physician call. The tools were comprehensive and explained in detail the techniques used in planning and executing a successful sales call. The sales representatives, however, were not using them. The problem was that the representatives did not understand what was contained in the performance support tools or when it was appropriate to use them.

A simulation was created by the instructional systems design and development firm Performance Development Group located in Wayne, Pennsylvania, to give pharmaceutical sales representatives a place to practice and to discover which tool was appropriate at what time. Using the simulation, the sales representatives practiced their selling and relationship skills in an environment that was safe but realistic. To make the simulation feel real, the storyline was based on war stories from experienced representatives in the field; in order to make it immersive, realistic three-dimensional environments were created and extensive video was used.

Since the reps had already received training in the skill sets, the simulation used a discovery learning format. After a brief call planning exercise, the representatives were placed in the doctor's office and required to initiate the call. They had the opportunity to interact with the doctor, along with members of the doctor's staff, such as the receptionist and a nurse. The sales representatives made several decisions, some of which led to a successful call, some to a less successful call, and some that could actually get the representative kicked out of the office.

Figure 3.7. Pharmaceutical Selling Simulation.

Source: Created by Performance Development Group
and used with permission. All rights reserved.

Representatives who made a mistake or weren't sure how to handle a decision had the opportunity to link to different selling tools that helped them understand how these tools were used in the context of a call. In addition, they received extensive performance feedback on each of their decisions.

Principles Knowledge

A principle is a nonsequential guideline for behavior or action. Principles deal primarily with the development of communication, leadership, ethics, team building, negotiating, and other social skills—what some call soft skills, social skills, or far-transfer learning.[9] The need for employees to know when and how to apply certain principles is critical for an organization's long-term success. The interrelationship between people is what makes an organization effective. Fortunately, gamers have more social skills than most boomers think they do, but gamers can still benefit from learning how to apply those skills in the workplace. They need to learn the right context in which to apply the principles they have learned through their social interactions with other gamers.

Principles should be thought of as nonsequential guidelines as opposed to step-by-step procedures. Guidelines can be applied differently at different times. Sometimes the team-building guideline of "include everyone in the discussion" is needed, and sometimes the guideline of "cut off someone who tries to monopolize the discussion" is required. Different situations require a different application of the guidelines. This becomes especially important when boomers are retiring and gamers need to be groomed for leadership roles within the organization.

Simply memorizing guidelines for a particular principle does not mean the learner has learned anything. To teach principles, the learner must be placed in the context in which the principles are to be applied. The learner then needs to apply what he or she thinks is the right principle and observe the results. This can be summarized by the term "learning as interaction."[10] You learn leadership, for example, by leading, not by reading about it. Unfortunately, it is not possible to place every employee in multiple real-life leadership positions and hope they turn out to be a leader. An alternative is needed.

Principle Simulations

While it is not possible to place every employee in an actual leadership situation to develop his or her leadership potential, it is possible to place each one in a leadership simulation. No person can become a leader just through simulated experiences; nevertheless, virtual experiences can dramatically cut the learning curve and make the few opportunities employees do have to practice leadership within the organization more effective.

Teaching principles requires learners to have an opportunity to practice the principles in an environment that provides feedback on their behavior and actions. To transfer the necessary knowledge, skills, and abilities and foster social skills, an interactive learning environment is needed.[11] This can be done electronically by immersing the learner in a simulation where he or she must apply leadership skills to navigate through the environment successfully.

Interactive learning environments designed to teach principles or social skills are often referred to as social simulators. They teach principles in the same way that procedural simulators teach the functionality of software or the physical operation of equipment. The key feature of a physical simulator, like a machine simulation, is that the operator is allowed to practice a skill in an environment that mimics the real world as closely as possible, except that in the simulated environment, it is okay to make a mistake.

Similarly, a social simulator permits discovery-based learning through open-ended experimentation. A social simulator can play a valuable role in teaching principles. It offers a work environment in which the employee can interact with simulated characters through conversations. As learners move around in the simulated world from the shop floor to the customer's place of business, images of the scenes and characters provide visual realism. Social simulators are "perfect learning environments for the training of social skills, the (re)construction and sustainable development of social systems, and dealing with the complexities of modern corporate life."[12]

The real benefit of social simulators is their ability to help learners discover and test hypotheses. There is hardly ever one correct way to implement principles. Not only are there countless ways principles may be applied, but there are even more ways that principles are received by the recipient. For example, gamers may react differently to a leader who steps up and takes absolute control than boomers do. A social simulator is an excellent way to account for the variability of human perceptions and to bridge the gap between boomer and gamer expectations.

Implementing a New System. In this principle-based simulation, the learner must form a team that will be responsible for implementing a piece of software into the organization. The simulation challenges the learner to visit with potential team members throughout the organization and recruit them for participation on the team.

During the process, the learner must negotiate the number of team members with upper management; he or she must then recruit members by exhibiting leadership skills and properly selling the implementation to potential team members. The learner must choose the appropriate team members and then negotiate with either the team member or his or her boss for a certain number of hours that the team member can devote to the project each week. The simulation requires the learner to communicate effectively with management, peers, and subordinates to build the ideal team.

While the learner can visit offices and even tour the plant floor in the simulation, the main parts of the simulation take place at the employee's desk. The employee can receive e-mail, voice mail, and even in-person visits within his or her office. He or she can also choose other locations to visit and take notes. The employee will ultimately use the information gathered to help form the team.

If the team leader is too pushy or demanding, no one will join the team or will join reluctantly. If the team member is too passive, no one will join the team, and the learner will not have successfully completed the task.

This principle-based simulation requires a careful balance of activities and actions. The team that built the simulation consisted of a number of project managers who have established teams in various situations for different types of projects. The goal was to use their insights and ideas to form the foundation for the social simulator. The insights help to guide new learners as they attempt to form the team. A "coach" appears from time to time if the learner has traveled too far down an inappropriate path.

Problem-Solving Knowledge

In educational terms, problem solving is the application of previously learned rules, procedures, declarative knowledge, and concepts to remedy a previously unencountered situation. It is different from rule or procedural learning because it involves the simultaneous consideration of multiple rules and procedures, the selection of the appropriate rules and procedures, and finally the proper sequencing of the rules and procedures to achieve a satisfactory answer.

Teaching problem solving requires three elements: teach the underlying rules and concepts that can be generally used to identify and solve problems, teach learners how to look at the interrelated nature of problems, and provide practice for learners to rehearse problem solving in a nonthreatening environment.

The first element of problem solving is teaching names, jargon, facts, acronyms, concepts, rules, and procedures. A learner must have prerequisite knowledge in order to be able to solve problems. Most effective problem solving involves identifying a potential problem and decomposing the problem into subelements. A common problem among novice problem solvers is their inability to identify the problem correctly. Without fundamental knowledge of the environment in which the problem is occurring, identifying and eventually solving it becomes extremely difficult.

The second element of problem solving is to understand the interrelatedness of the problem elements. Most problems are difficult to solve because of the quantity and interaction among variables. When one variable decreases, the other increases; when one process is in balance, another is out of balance; when one element is favorable, another is unfavorable. The trick is to understand how variables react with one another and consider multiple interactions and consequences prior to presenting a solution.

The third element in teaching problem solving can be summed up in three words: *practice, practice, practice.* Errors in problem solving by novices frequently result from their unfamiliarity with the type of problem they are attempting to solve. Experts have less trouble solving a variety of problems, because they most likely have encountered that type of problem before.

An expert problem solver in a particular area first reflects on the new problem and then uses existing knowledge to construct a solution. This means that instruction designed to teach problem solving must present a number of situations in which learners have an opportunity to practice solving problems they are likely to encounter. It also means that novice learners must be taught the skills necessary to learn how to link new problems with previously encountered problems.

As Mark Oehlert points out, "Gamers are used to learning about problem solving by learning the prerequisite knowledge through trial and error. First, the gamer jumps into a game (no need for the stupid manual), then they practice what they think are the right skills (concepts, rules, procedures). When they fail, as expected, the gamers start to look for the prerequisite knowledge and the interconnected pieces needed for success. After they have learned the requisite elements, they finally master the techniques and begin to understand the underlying rules and concepts involved with the problem they are solving."[13]

Problem-Solving Simulations

One method of providing practice opportunities is to immerse the gamer in a problem-based simulator. It is possible to design simulations in a way that presents learners with a variety of problems to solve. Those problems can be with machinery, managing team members across the world, or even learning to find a bar in a foreign land.

Speaking Spanish. One innovative application of simulation technology is *3D Language: Spain.* The simulation is a language-learning tool that combines aspects of video games, speech recognition technology, and proprietary language management process to place the learner into a town in Spain. The developer, David Dunlap, is a former airline pilot who wanted to create a "flight simulator" for learning a language.

The simulation is a virtual world that the learner inhabits. The learner can wander around, interact with the townspeople, and simulate activities that he or she would participate in if actually in Spain. The idea is to immerse learners in the language and culture of a country to allow them to learn about the country and the vocabulary in the proper context and to solve common problems like ordering a drink, checking into a hotel, and asking for directions.

Before developing the simulation, the developer conducted a study to identify the major impediments for learning a new language. The first impediment found was that the majority of language learners have a real fear of making mistakes in front of native speakers. This fear restricts the chances they are willing to take and arrests their progress with the new language.

Second is having a realistic place to practice the language and the communication of that language. At the end of the day, learning a language is all about communication and the ability of one person to convey to another what he or she desires. The simulation provides that type of environment.

To start the simulation, the learner arrives in a town somewhere in Spain. The learner is then free to move around the town and visit the town square, go to a hotel to check in, visit a local bar, or converse with people in the street. There are eight characters with whom the learner can interact. Each character supplies different information and helps the language learner work through the different problems most people encounter when in a foreign land, such as speaking more slowly, asking the proper questions, and using the correct pronunciation. Figure 3.8 shows an image of a restaurateur in the town and allows the learner to ask him when the restaurant opens for dinner.

Upon meeting a person on the street, the learner can begin an interactive conversation (Figure 3.9). The learner speaks into a microphone attached to the computer and interacts with the virtual Spaniard. The simulation evaluates the learner's Spanish and either continues the conversation or tells the learner "Más despacio, por favor?" ("Could you say that more slowly?"). The learner has the opportunity to speak into the microphone again, this time correcting his or her pronunciation. The simulated townspeople patiently wait until the learner gets it right.

In addition to the option of listening to the townsperson, the learner can view only the Spanish version of what is being said, the English translation, the phonetic spelling of the words being spoken, or any of these. There are hot spots throughout the town that the learner can click on to learn simple vocabulary words or information about Spanish culture.

Managing Team Members Across the World. SAP, an inter-enterprise software development and implementation company, needed to provide project managers with a learning experience to address a specific challenge: managing teams whose members were scattered across the globe. With team members in Germany, Japan, the United States, and India, a SAP project manager must contend

Figure 3.9. Image of a Citizen of a Virtual Spanish City.

with cultural differences, time zones, disparate expectations, communication styles, and other issues a local team may not encounter.

SAP partnered with the e-learning design company Enspire Learning, located in Austin, Texas, to craft six hour-long modules tackling six major difficulties with distributed, or virtual, teams. The training included a twenty-minute capstone simulation for each of the six modules.

The capstone simulation allows the learners to experience virtual team management as a team leader (as shown in Figure 3.10). The learner makes key strategic decisions about a simulated project and assigns work packets to three distributed segments of the team, based on their skills, cultural differences, and the work in question. Then the project is executed, and the learner experiences the effects of his or her actions, mitigating any issues that arise.

Figure 3.10. Assessment of the Virtual Team's Skills.

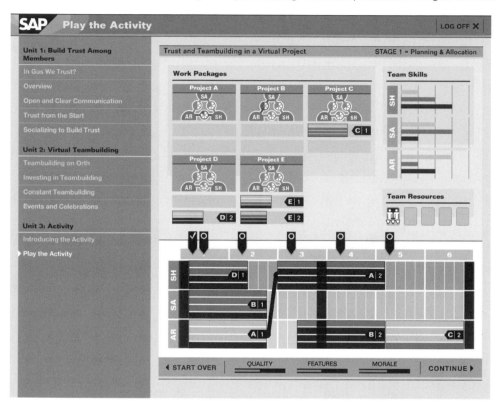

Enspire and SAP recognized the significant design challenge of meaning-
fully discussing cultural differences while remaining sensitive to the cultures
of learners worldwide. This challenge was addressed by using a trick from the
gamer's massively multiplayer online role-playing games. The team created a
fictional world called Orth with its own fictional cultures. The team from the
Orthian region of Sampo considered timeliness as paramount, while the culture from Shananees viewed time very loosely. Understanding and decipher-
ing these differences influence how the learner makes decisions.

So how does the learner measure progress? To coincide with SAP's standard
processes, the simulation fixes the time line and resources, leaving three measures

of a successful project: quality, feature set, and team morale—the QFM score. Choices the learner makes directly or indirectly affect her ability to deliver a finished project of high quality, with a maximal feature set, and high team morale.

As with many other problems that actual executives and managers face in a business setting, there is no one way to win the virtual team management simulation. You simply develop the most appropriate balance. Each course of action comes with different costs and benefits in terms of QFM scores and the time available. If you choose to hold an in-person meeting for all three teams, you may increase team morale, but you lose one week of production time. Canceling in-person meetings provides more production time, but may result in miscommunications between the teams later in the project.

The simulation also tackles the common problem of resource allocation. The learner must allocate work packages that make up the project. However, just as in real life, there are restrictions. Certain work packages require certain skills to complete; others must be addressed sequentially. Experiencing the difficulty of complex work allocation puts pressure on a learner's other decision points, such as whether to give a team time off to celebrate a local holiday, and helps drive home the points of the simulation.

The simulation provides the feedback to the learner throughout the execution stage. A team leader may complain of being assigned work his team finds boring, or he may thank you for providing them with new communication technologies. At the close of the module, the learner's virtual mentor, Linda, provides the final QFM score, general feedback on performance, and feedback on specific learner decisions that had significant impact on the learner's scores (Figure 3.11).

Although the learners operate in a fictional world with fictional teams, the issues they face are the same ones they face with actual teams and actual work flow processes. The use of a fictional world, to avoid offending any specific culture, may seem abstract, but the carefully crafted fictional world is based on patterns of the real world, so the learning transfers. The simulation in this case has more in common with how our brain visualizes patterns and relationships than it does with the details of reality, such as having a real project or using real cultures. But the rules learned in the simulation—the

Figure 3.11. A Virtual Mentor Providing Feedback.

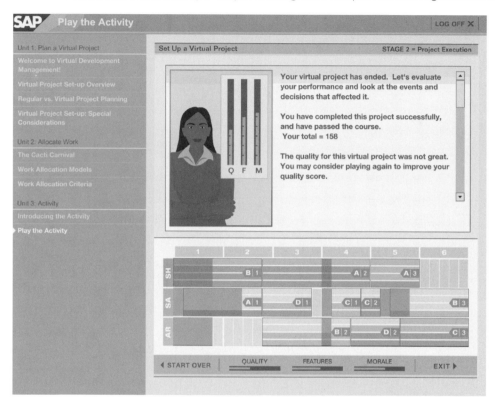

underlying relationships and patterns—get processed exactly the same way as we process real things like "working on a holiday causes low morale" and "allocating resources requires trade-offs."[14] The lessons of the simulation are learned even though the events take place in a fictionalized world.

Workplace Implications

Video games act as mentors and instructors all the time. Organizations need to take advantage of the power of simulations to teach and affect behavior. Simulations and emulations are useful methods for transferring knowledge from boomers to gamers. Immortalizing key boomer knowledge in a simulation provides an effective method for helping gamers reduce the natural learning curve. Different simulation types are appropriate for transferring different types of knowledge. Focusing on the type of knowledge needed to be transferred will help organizations create the most effective simulations, as shown in Table 3.2.

Table 3.2. Simulation Types and the Knowledge They Teach.

Simulation Type	Definition	Example	Type of Knowledge Taught
Physical procedures simulator	A simulated object, piece of equipment, or machine. It works and functions like the actual physical device.	Simulated ATC-600. Simulated piece of machinery or even a cockpit of an airplane.	Procedural: operation of equipment or machinery
Software emulation	Simulated software that works and functions in a fashion similar to the software that it is teaching or emulating.	Tutorial on how to use MS Word or Excel. Simulated SAP software.	Procedural: software features and functionality
Operational simulator	Simulates common procedures used within an organization that are software or object based or contain some elements of both.	Using Madden 2007 to teach plays to quarterbacks and wide receivers.	Procedural: proper steps for completing a desired task
Principle-based simulator (social simulator)	Situation in which the learner is placed in an environment in which he or she must interact. Environment changes based on learner's actions.	Simulated team meeting or simulated negotiation with certain steps needed to achieve the desired outcome.	Principles: soft skills, skills used when interacting with people
Problem-solving simulator	Learner is presented with a new problem to solve. There is not a single method or process for solving the problem; multiple avenues are available for solving the problem.	Roller Coaster Tycoon, where the learner is given an environment with rules and told to accomplish a broad task like building and maintaining a profitable amusement park.	Problem solving: confronted with a new problem to solve

Perhaps the best use of simulations is in a blended approach, where the learner spends time working through the simulation alone—learning the subtlety and the nuances of the information. After a period of time, the learner teams with an experienced employee and reviews lessons learned and insights gained. Finally, the employee should be given opportunities to apply the new skills under the watchful eye of a skilled mentor. This combination provides the best advantage to the employee and employer as the gamers learn to apply newly gained skills in a manner that provides direct payback to the organization.

SUMMARY

Simulations can be a powerful tool, providing gamers with experiences specifically designed to shortcut lengthy learning curves. Well-designed simulations compact years of experience into the parameters of a well-crafted environment that can be explored in a manner of hours or days. Carefully constructed simulations are an asset to any organization that needs to transfer higher-level knowledge to gamers as quickly as possible.

Games and simulations are not the only tools that can be used to transfer knowledge—gadgets can be used as well. Next we discuss gamers' fondness for gadgets. They love gadgets, grew up with gadgets, and communicate with gadgets even when they are sitting next to one another. Innovative organizations take advantage of the gamers' love of gadgets by capitalizing on the portability, size, and power of these handheld devices.

4

Go, Go Gadget

IT HIT ME ONE DECEMBER when I asked my eight-year-old son, "What do you want Santa Claus to bring you for Christmas this year?"

"I only want three things."

I thought to myself, *Great, only three things! I am getting off easy this year. Maybe he wants an action figure or a race track or something.* "What are the three things, son?"

"Okay, I want a big-screen TV for my room, a laptop computer, and a cell phone."

"What?" I was stunned.

"I want a big-screen TV for my room, a laptop, and a cell phone."

I was almost speechless, "You're eight years old. Wouldn't you rather have an action figure or an electronic handheld game or something?"

"Dad, that is soooo 1990s."

Gamers don't play with toys; they play with gadgets and gizmos (Figure 4.1).

Figure 4.1. What Gamers Want for Christmas.

Source: Reprinted with permission of the artist, Kristin Longenecker.

Gamers love gadgets. They grew up with gadgets, work with gadgets, and communicate using gadgets. It's all about the gadgets. It's no wonder two of the largest toy retailers filed for bankruptcy within the past eight years and a third is struggling to stay relevant.[1] Interest in gadgets has pushed toy manufacturers into creating more tech-focused toys as they work to win back gamers who have abandoned toy stores in favor of electronic boutiques.[2]

Perhaps gamers like gadgets as opposed to toys because a toy represents someone else's fully realized idea of fun, while a gadget allows the gamer to modify and change the outcome according to his or her own wishes. Or perhaps the gamers' affinity for gadgets started in the early days of handheld games, when the portability of the game allowed them to play wherever and whenever they wanted. In those early days, a single LED dot represented a football player running down the field. Those handhelds, like the one shown in Figure 4.2, were purely for pleasure. They allowed players to pass time with an interesting activity, no matter where they were: in the car, waiting in line, waiting for a bus.

Figure 4.2. Early Handheld Football Game.

Source: Author.

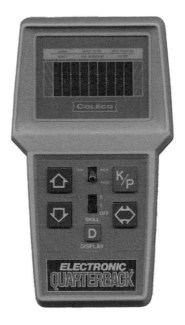

Since that time, handheld games have morphed into Nintendo Game Boy, Game Boy Advanced, Nintendo DS, and the PlayStation Portable better known by its acronym, PSP. The PSP is no mere handheld game console. It comes complete with Internet access and the ability to store photos, music, and videos, and, by the way, it plays games. It is estimated that non-PC devices that support paid-for electronic games will number over 2.6 billion by 2010.[3]

These non-PC game platforms are enabling multiplayer games with wireless connectivity. Nintendo has entered into an agreement with McDonald's to create wireless zones in its restaurants. Gamers can now bring a Nintendo DS unit and a wireless-enabled game into McDonald's and launch a multiplayer online game while munching on a Big Mac.[4] No setup is required. As many as eight players can play Nintendo's *Mario Kart* simultaneously.[5]

Other fast-food restaurants are getting into the gadget frenzy. The chicken-based restaurant chain KFC doesn't sell kid meals; it sells "laptop" meals. Even cereal companies are appealing to gadget-oriented kids. You don't send away cereal box tops for secret decoder rings anymore; you send away for a Toucan Sam computer microphone delivered in four to six weeks for you to hook up to your laptop or workstation.

Gamers aren't just purchasing game-based gadgets; they are purchasing cell phones, personal digital assistants (PDAs), handheld computers, MP3 players, BlackBerry devices, digital cameras, video iPods, and even Swiss Army knives with built-in jump drives. A majority of all teenagers, 84 percent, report owning at least one personal media device: a desktop computer, a laptop computer, a cell phone, or a PDA. As many as 44 percent say they have two or more devices, 12 percent have three, and 2 percent have all four. Only 16 percent of teens report not having any of these devices.[6] The most targeted markets for consumer electronics are teenagers between ages fourteen and eighteen and "tweens" between ages ten and thirteen. More than half of American teenagers will spend over one hundred dollars on their next consumer electronic purchase and one-quarter more than two hundred dollars.[7]

The proliferation of gadgets shows no sign of slowing. Increasingly, gadgets are communicating with corporate intranets, the Internet, and each other. Gadgets are a big part of the gamer ethos.

This love of gadgets can be converted into new and exciting ways to transfer knowledge from the boomers to the gamers. The gamers' affinity for gadgets enables continuous contact with their company, coworkers, and clients. A strategic use of gadgets provides employees with access to information, data, and knowledge from experts wherever and whenever it is needed.

Gadgets Allow Access

The convergence of three elements is making the use of gadgets feasible in the quest to transmit knowledge from the boomers to the gamers:

- Broadband wireless
- Automated cataloguing of digital assets
- Increasing power of gadgets

Broadband Wireless

Wires are a major headache. They are expensive to put into place, eventually require upgrading, and limit the range a gadget can travel. Game developers understand this and have created a number of wireless game platforms. The PSP is wireless, as is the Nintendo DS.

The advent of wireless has enabled all types of gadgets to work in all kinds of locations. Factories can install data collection equipment in places previously too cost prohibitive. DHL, UPS, and FedEx drivers can scan packages and relay information back to a database that can be accessed by a client tracking the progress of a package from point A to point B. And lawyers can transfer notes and information about a case to paralegals for research.

Initially, wireless networks were limited in both distance and download speed. These wireless local area networks (WLANs) began showing up at coffee shops, schools, home offices, and businesses. Often referred to as Wi-Fi, these inexpensive, easy-to-set-up networks and devices give desktop and PDA users untethered access to their data and the Internet whenever they are in reach of a network. Unfortunately, Wi-Fi access has a limit of about 330 feet and includes restricted bandwidth.

The Wi-Fi standard limits the amount of information that can be quickly downloaded to a gadget and the mobility of the person who wants to stay connected. Leave the coffee shop or home office, and you are out of range. Slow download speeds and restricted access also mean that gadgets had limited usefulness. They were not ubiquitous. No one wants to wait too long for a critical document or key piece of video-based instruction to download.

Fortunately, the limitations of distance and speed are being rapidly overcome. One initial solution was the creation of wide area networks (WAN), which have a range of about a mile but provide a large area of coverage when strung together. The future, however, lies in broadband wireless networks that are as efficient and far reaching as wired networks. New broadband wireless networks are being referred to as worldwide interoperability for microwave access (WiMax), which is a type of wireless metropolitan access network (WMAN). WMAN is a wireless communications network that covers a geographical area such as a city or suburb, with a range of about thirty miles.

WiMax networks, as opposed to less powerful Wi-Fi networks, are geared toward higher download and upload speeds for data, voice, and video—known in the industry as the triple play. WiMax networks are based on the IEEE 802.16e standards, which describe greater interoperability between broadband wireless access equipment than the fading Wi-Fi standard.

As a result, the WiMax market is predicted to grow to over $1.9 billion in 2008 from a mere $125 million in 2005.[8] The attraction of WiMax networks is obvious: "Sales and field forces can connect to the Internet and corporate applications from virtually anywhere, network speeds are reasonable, and deploying the technology requires only minimal IT investment."[9]

On a personal level, the advent of wireless personal area networks (WPAN), using Bluetooth (802.15) technology, ultra wide band (UWB), and wireless USB, allow gamers and others to remove the cables from their keyboards and cell phone headsets, enabling an unwired personal work space and wireless connectivity between devices such as a personal digital assistant and a laptop.[10] The various wireless networks, their ranges, and their primary uses are shown in Figure 4.3.

The proliferation of wireless broadband allows gadgets to go anywhere and download any size data, from entire manuals to lengthy video clips. On-demand video and other triple-play bandwidth-intensive media will soon be an option in even the most remote locations. Cities like Philadelphia and San Francisco think wireless Internet access is so important that they are undertaking initiatives to make their cities wireless havens for gadget-carrying gamers.

A group called Wireless Philadelphia aims to strengthen the city's economy by providing wireless Internet access throughout the downtown area.[11] Wireless Philadelphia is trying to create a digital infrastructure for wireless Internet access. The goal is to help citizens, businesses, schools, and community organizations use wireless technology to achieve their goals, as well as provide a better experience for visitors to the city. This initiative will enable gamers' gadgets to work anywhere at any time within the city. Once this type of initiative takes hold, other cities will follow suit.

Figure 4.3. Range and Applications for Various Wireless Standards.

Devices: PDAs, cell phones, smart phones, laptops/tablets via PCMCIA card

Speed: 384 kB per second (and reaching 2 to 3 Mbits per second in the future)

Range: About 1 mile

Primary uses: Voice, data

Devices: Desktops, laptops, tablet PCs, PDAs, cell phones

Speed: 70 MB per second, maximum

Range: About 30 miles max (unobstructed)

Primary uses: Data, voice via VoIP

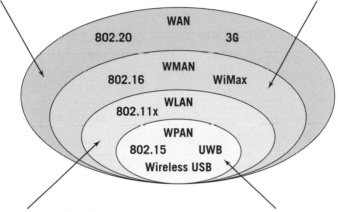

Devices: Laptops, tablet PCs, PDAs, smart phones

Speed: 11 to 108 MB per second

Range: About 330 feet

Primary uses: Data, voice via VoIP

Devices: Laptops, tablet PCs, PDAs, smart phones, cell phones, headsets, keyboards, mice

Speed: 2 MB per second, maximum

Range: About 30 feet

Primary uses: Replace propriety cables

Automated Cataloguing of Digital Assets

An organization's data, information, and knowledge taken in their entirety resemble the scene in the movie *Raiders of the Lost Ark* where the Nazis open the ark: text, audio, video, and graphics in all shapes and sizes dangerously flying around in erratic patterns with no organization or structure.[12] You have to close your eyes or be turned to dust (actually, the analogy ends right before the "be turned to dust" part).

Getting a handle on all of that information, data, and knowledge is a daunting task. Organizations have islands of knowledge everywhere: in databases, PowerPoint slides, computer code, standard operating procedures, corporate manuals, and, increasingly, the heads of retiring baby boomers.

In an attempt to capture and catalogue some of these data, companies are recording exit interviews with retiring boomers. They are turning on video or audio recorders and asking retiring employees a series of questions to find out everything about a particular job or subject. This knowledge transfer process is appealing because it is so cost-effective. All you need to do is sit the boomer in front of an inexpensive video camera, ask questions, and start taping. When you are done, simply place the recording in a DVD player and let the new recruit learn the lessons from the expert. In theory, it seems like a good idea. In practice, it is not.

What gamer wants to sit down for ten hours and watch an interview with an R&D scientist who is trying to tell the camera everything he or she knows about a job or topic?[13] Even if the interview is watched, remembering ten hours of rambling is a challenge for even the brightest gamer. It might be critical and important information, but anything over twenty minutes is rambling (Figures 4.4 and 4.5). Unfortunately, organizations "don't anticipate the difficulty of converting raw interview data into knowledge that is accessible and useful."[14] The value in recording the knowledge of the boomers is not in capturing the knowledge; the value is in applying or accessing the knowledge at just the right time.

To be effective, the video must be catalogued and available in small, well-marked chunks—the YouTube approach. YouTube, a Web site that displays videos posted by visitors, provides short video clips that are ranked by viewers. The short clips are easy to download and watch and few are longer than ten minutes.

For the exit interview, the ideal situation is for the key parts of the interview to be accessed exactly when the gamer needs the expert's insight. This can be accomplished through the process of editing the tapes into smaller snippets of information and adding meta-data, which allow a search through

Figure 4.4. What Happens in a Knowledge Dump Interview from the
Boomer's (Instructor's) Perspective.

Source: Reprinted with permission of the artist, Kristin Longenecker.

Figure 4.5. What Happens in a Knowledge Dump Interview from the
Gamer's (Learner's) Perspective.

Source: Reprinted with permission of the artist, Kristin Longenecker.

the clips to find what is needed. A meta-tag is data about data. A meta-tag for a video describes what the video is about, notes the length of the video, and provides key words for retrieving the clip when needed. This tagging process makes it easy for anyone to find what they are looking for: just type in search criteria, and the system will retrieve all video that is tagged accordingly. Once tagged, the videos could be placed on a corporate Web site and accessed when needed. Employees could rank the usefulness of each clip, giving other employees insight into how useful the information is for a particular situation.

It takes a long time to watch a video and decide how to dissect and meta-tag all of the information. Someone has to watch the video, transcribe the information, break the clips into reasonably-sized chunks, and then decide if any of the information should be codified into policies, procedures, or protocols for the organization. Then the person has to add the correct meta-tag information so the material can be searched. This can be an expensive and time-intensive process.

The technology is not quite ready to catalogue video or audio tracks automatically, but it is getting closer and closer to commercial availability. A number of projects are focused specifically on cataloguing video and audio information automatically so that it can be retrieved using a key search term or phrase. Automatic retrieval will greatly increase the usefulness of recording a boomer's departing exit interview.

One possible solution, among many, is MARVEL (Multimedia Analysis and RetrieVEL), a project conducted by IBM. This system automatically annotates multimedia, making it possible to search and retrieve content of interest. "The objective of MARVEL is to help the media industry, including stock photo/video and broadcast companies, as well as libraries, organize large and growing amounts of multimedia content much more efficiently and automatically."[15] The project uses both video and audio to do searches and has already developed a list of over a thousand terms for classifying clips. Some are relatively generic descriptors ("landscape"), while many are more specific ("tennis," "basketball").

Video assets are not the only information that organizations need to collect, catalogue, and search. Audio, text-based, and other information needs quick retrieval. A class of software emerging in this area is known as digital asset management (DAM) software. This software is related to video cataloguing, document management, content management, and search engines.[16]

Another organization working in DAM software is Virage, with offices in San Francisco and the United Kingdom. The company has technology that automatically catalogues and understands video-based content and allows users to search video assets with a high degree of accuracy. The company's software can conduct searches by audio, scene, speaker, location, key frame, image, on-screen text, face, and even concept. The goal is to be able to search video and other assets at a granular level to find precisely the right media element.[17]

As DAM software matures, it will allow more and more gadgets to quickly and easily search for all types of corporate information, from audio and video files to text contained in an online brochure or even a statement made in a corporate blog.

Needle in a Haystack. Once all of the video, audio, and textual information is stored and given tags, how does one decide what tag was used to name what information? Automated tagging systems provide their own labels for all of these digital assets, and they might not be the same labels you would use to describe an asset. For example, you could have an image of a doctor, and the tag might read "doctor" or "physician" or "woman in white coat" or "health care professional" or even something else. Multiply that one image by the thousands of images, pages of text, and animations housed on a typical company's intranet, and it is like trying to find a needle in a haystack.

One solution is to allow the system and the employees to tag items. Gamers have become comfortable tagging items and content any way they see fit when they store their digital assets online. They do this all the time at YouTube when they tag their videos and the videos of others. This same concept should be extended to items within an organization.

Allowing people to tag content in an unstructured manner even has its own name, *folksonomy,* a play on the concept of a *taxonomy*—a set of controlled vocabulary terms, usually hierarchical, used to classify information and data. Stewart Butterfield, a cofounder of the photo self-storage site Flickr, stated that the job of tags isn't to "organize all the world's information into tidy categories. It's to add value to the giant piles of data that are already out there."[18] Many Web sites that rely on user-created content encourage those same users to create their own tags. The same concept can be used in a corporation. If the company had tagging software, employees could tag the data and retrieve them based on their own tags.

Thomas Vander Wal, the information architect credited with coining the term *folksonomy,* describes the concept as people "tagging information so that they can come back to it themselves or so that others with the same vocabulary can find it."[19] This means that organizations should not worry about setting up an elaborate tagging system to help employees find data; instead, they should allow the people who use the data to do the tagging themselves.

Since many systems allow multiple tags for data, both boomers and gamers will be able to tag and subsequently search the data according to their own folksonomy. This will allow for multiple paths or channels back to the desired information. Each group can search for the proverbial needle any way it wants.

Increasing Power of Gadgets

Gadgets are becoming increasingly powerful and small. Handheld devices can now bring tremendous amounts of computing power to the fingertips of any user, as predicted by Moore's law.[20] Today most portable, handheld gadgets have more computing power than the *Apollo 13* spaceship, which had two computers, referred to as the Block II Apollo Guidance Computer. One was in the command module and one in the lunar module. Each ran the guidance, navigation, and control systems. These computers had 36,864 words of read-only memory (ROM), 2,048 words of random-access memory (RAM), and a clock speed of 2.048 MHz.[21]

Today, game platforms work not with thousands of words of memory but with millions. The PSP game platform has a main memory of 32 megabytes and 4 megabytes of dynamic random access memory (DRAM). Each megabyte holds about 1 million bytes or characters of information. The PSP's clock speed is 333 MHz. You could literally travel to the moon with the power contained in the PSP (command module not included), as shown in Table 4.1.

Table 4.1. Comparison of *Apollo* Computer and PSP Game Platform.

Capability	Block II Apollo Guidance Computer AGC	PlayStation Portable PSP
Memory	36,864 words of ROM	32 MB
Storage	2,048 words of RAM	4 MB DRAM
Clock speed	2.048 MHz	333 MHz

The trend in the gadget industry is lower cost, smaller size, reduced power consumption, and integrated features. As gadgets become smaller and more powerful, they contain more and more features. It used to be that cell phones were just telephones; now they are cameras, date planners, jukeboxes, and Web-enabled devices. Some even still make calls. Many telephones have built-in global positioning satellite capabilities. A driver, jogger, or walker can receive turn-by-turn directions beamed right to his or her cell phone.

In digital audio, many devices and technologies are available for recording and playing audio files, with one of the most interesting features being the elimination of tapes. Digital recording devices now have hard drives that record the conversation and download the information directly to a laptop or a server. Digital players using the MP3 format can carry thousands of songs in the space of a deck of cards. Many of these music players also have games, a calendar, and other features. It is now possible to conduct an interview with a digital recorder and store the information in a handheld device for retrieval at any time. MP3 players are so powerful that they can contain an audio recording of an entire book or collection of books.

Graphical images are not being left behind. Digital cameras can double as a video camera if the user needs a few minutes of video. These cameras can even store and catalogue the images. Digital video cameras are coming equipped with the ability to take digital memos or record in total darkness, as with Sony's NightShot feature. This feature allows you to shoot about ten feet in front of you in total darkness using infrared light. This type of technology was available only to the military a mere fifteen years ago.

To view digital video, a consumer can use a video iPod or other handheld video player. Many cell phones can download and play videos. Handheld pocket PCs can show videos as well as run spreadsheets and word processing programs, send e-mail, and run any other applications the user wants to access away from his or her desk or laptop.

Personal Digital Assistants

PDAs, or handheld computers, are quickly emerging as an important educational tool as they gain more features, more acceptability in the marketplace, and more applications in many areas of daily life. Schools are using them to automate routine, time-consuming (and often excruciatingly boring) tasks like taking roll and handing out daily assignments. Using PDAs, students come into the classroom and access the day's to-do list, which appears on their screens. The teacher presses a button and sends the attendance report to the administration office. During the day, students use their PDAs to access the Internet, communicate by e-mail, take notes, and collaborate on projects and homework.

A cursory investigation of a half-dozen professional journals—*T.H.E. (Technological Horizons in Education) Journal; Social Education; Communication Quarterly; Journal of Physical Education, Recreation and Dance; Journal of Accountancy; and Annual Review of Psychology*—shows PDAs being applied to widely diverse endeavors. In elementary schools, they are used to teach basic language skills through instructional games. In social studies classes, they are used instead of and in conjunction with full-sized computers to surf the Internet and complete class projects. Researchers in communication have found them a convenient means of gathering data to evaluate the effects of computer-animated figures. Physical education personnel use them to assess skill acquisition. Accountants use them to retrieve, store, manipulate, and send data from practically anyplace. In psychology research and therapy, they are used to record accurate, immediate diary-like data for research. As these highly portable and increasingly powerful devices evolve, their scope of use will continue to broaden and deepen.

Celina Byers has extensive experience in public service, industry, and higher education. She has worked in various companies as a psychologist, programmer, systems analyst, manager, and computer-based training developer. She is currently teaching in the instructional technology department at Bloomsburg University.

Source: Printed with the permission of Celina Byers.

How Gadgets Will Be Used to Transfer Knowledge

Handheld devices enable boomers and gamers to access information, clients, learning tools, competitors' Web sites, and even each other. Gadgets allow boomers to remain at the home office while transferring information and knowledge to numerous gamers in the field. It will be an ideal working relationship because boomers need to be in the office to feel connected and coordinate activities face-to-face, while gamers connect through technology and are comfortable working virtually. This will allow the boomers not to have to deal with the wear and tear of being on the road and traveling all the time. Gadgets allow the gamers to have access to the experience and knowledge of the boomers, who are valuable but less inclined to travel than the gamers.

Properly deploying gadgets provides a competitive advantage for organizations of all sizes and design. However, it is not enough just to hand out gadgets to the workforce, cross your fingers, and hope for the best. Gadgets need to be used properly, or the efforts will be wasted. Perhaps the best way to illustrate effective deployment of gadgets is to look at a series of scenarios. Each scenario uses technology that is available today and can be adapted to any industry.

Flash Teams

A flash mob is a group of people who assemble suddenly in a public place, do something unusual or notable, and then disperse.[22] It is possible to envision the flash mob scenario applied to more profitable and productive situations than showing up at McDonald's and clapping for five minutes. With a little adjustment, the flash mob concept can be changed into a productive flash team.

Building on the technology-enabled networking skills of gamers, organizations can create flash teams. An ad hoc flash team is a group of employees focused on solving a problem in a short period of time. Flash teams of engineers spread out on a massive corporate campus can be summoned through a text message on their cell phones and instantly swarm a service problem. The team converges in a designated conference room and addresses the problem.

In a retail scenario, a flash team quickly helps a customer shopping for her senior prom. A text message is sent to various sales clerks within different departments when the customer explains her needs to the lead saleswoman. The saleswoman sends a text message and a photograph of the senior to other sales clerks. Instantly someone from the makeup department arrives with a shade of makeup that matches the young woman's complexion. A clerk from the dress department arrives a few minutes later with several dresses, all color coordinated with the makeup. At the same time, a person from the floral department arrives with sample flower arrangement suggestions designed to complement the dress. The goal of this flash team is to quickly deliver the required items to the shopper in the shortest period of time. The team communicates using text messages and digital photographs.

Flash teams do not need to be physical. A corporation can summon a flash team to a specific virtual location regardless of their physical location or proximity to each other. The team, once assembled, uses collaboration software to work together solving an internal or external problem. All that is needed are the gadgets and collaborative software that allow connectivity among team members.

Virtual Mentors

Gadgets enable the concept of a virtual mentor to be employed in a variety of settings. A virtual mentor is a live person who provides assistance to one or more gamers at a customer site working on a problem. The mentor remains at a central location so he or she can assist several teams of individuals.

Perhaps the most dramatic example of a virtual mentor comes from the animated cartoon series titled *Batman Beyond*. The series takes place in the future when the original Batman, Bruce Wayne, is in his late eighties. He is too old to fight in hand-to-hand battles with the forces of evil, but he still has the knowledge, experience, and wisdom necessary to keep Gotham streets safe.

Eventually a seventeen year old named Terry McGinnis becomes the new Batman. Bruce outfits his new apprentice with all the latest gadgets and sends him into Gotham to fight crime. Although he is physically strong, the boy is at a serious disadvantage: he doesn't have the years of experience or the necessary training to fight crime expertly. He is full of attitude and believes he is a hero but has a lot to learn. The boy needs coaching and additional training, but the criminal elements in the city won't wait around until the new Batman is fully trained and operational. Terry has to fight as Batman immediately.

To remedy this situation, Bruce Wayne coaches Terry using a headset from an operational command center in the BatCave. Terry relies on Bruce's experience and knowledge to guide him in his crime-fighting activities. Bruce is in constant contact with Terry, providing advice, insight, and directions.[23]

In the virtual mentor scenario, the mentor knows what needs to be done but is more valuable coordinating activity from a distant location than actually doing the work at the customer's site. The mentor provides guidance and direction so the tasks are successfully accomplished by each team he or she coaches. Gadgets allow the virtual mentor to keep in constant contact with the members of the team. The gadgets send back visual images or even plug into devices at the customer site. The boomer transfers knowledge and information as he or she helps the gamers develop the skills and competencies they need to be proficient on their own.

On-Demand Text

One of the most obvious methods of recording the knowledge of boomers is documenting that knowledge in writing. This is done when organizations document processes and procedures and use those documents as a road map for how to do business. Evidence of these efforts can be found in employee manuals, policy documents, and corporate procedures for handling everything from customer complaints to shipping product.

Although this is helpful, few gamers will read any type of manual or procedures cover to cover unless they are under duress. The gamers' hierarchy of searching for information seems to be as follows: search engine first, then Instant Messenger (to see if anyone in their network knows the answer), and then, as the last resort, the manual. This makes sense since the first thing that goes in the trash after a game is purchased is the user guide. Gamers don't read even those tiny little booklets. They want to get into the game and start exploring as soon as possible.

Enter the handheld gadget: pocket PCs, PDAs, notebook computers, and other small devices that can be networked using a wireless network to access thousands of searchable documents. These devices can use text search applications to find just the right information at just the right time. This immediate access to information means that the gamer doesn't have to memorize information; he or she can just look up what is needed. Forgotten steps are retrieved through a gadget.

Information is continually updated in a central location by experts and then made available to anyone needing it. The information can be in the form of frequently asked questions, online databases, manuals, job aids, and any other type of text-based documentation.

Picture a scenario in which a gamer prepares to consult with a client on ways to improve the order entry process. While waiting in the client's lobby, the gamer accesses text documents about the client's history, looks up techniques for improving order entry process from his company's database, and reviews information about what data should be collected on the first consulting visit.

Podcasting: Audio on Demand

Often a short audio narration provides the information and coaching needed to help an employee solve a problem or deal with a customer issue. The widespread adoption of Apple's iPod products has led to an entire ecosystem of tools, accessories, and content providers. You can subscribe to a podcast on any topic through iTunes or other subscription services. A podcast (for the boomers) is a Web-based audio file distributed over the Web. The file can be downloaded onto a handheld device that plays audio files, the most popular of which is Apple's iPod family.

The concept is just getting started and has room to move in exciting directions. One appealing concept in this area is the creation of a type of corporate Napster-type software for the exchange of audio files among experts and members of an organization. Originally Napster allowed the free exchange of audio files among a virtually limitless group of Internet users. Imagine a corporate Napster where you upload audio files of information about competitors, new product launches, corporate directions, and other valuable information, all easily searchable and downloadable by members of your organization. Once loaded onto a portable MP3 device, the information can be listened to anywhere at the exact time of need. Creating files could be easily done with a handheld digital recorder.

Imagine a pharmaceutical sales representative waiting in a doctor's office who accesses a corporate audio server, downloads the necessary information, and listens to the drug detail recording just prior to meeting with the doctor. Or imagine a doctor downloading an audio file of a patient's medical history. The doctor listens to the file while preparing for the patient to arrive or fast-forwards through the audio file to learn key patient information.

A strong advantage of audio is that it provides the proper tone of voice, inflection, and other information necessary to assist sales representatives, doctors, and others. Audio can provide information with relatively little bandwidth requirements as opposed to video.

Drexel's University's LeBow College of Business has 150 online students all over the world enrolled in its M.B.A. program. LeBow is using podcasting for both lectures and distribution of administrative information. Students can view a slide presentation of an economics lesson along with the audio, download just the slides, or download just the audio. This gives the learners the flexibility of how they prefer to receive the information. The podcasting allows the students to learn at lunch, after work, or when they are exercising. It provides an opportunity for them to multitask.

LeBow College officials like the podcasting of administrative information. It helps to ensure that the students get the right information and are able to navigate requirements, scheduling, and other tasks critical to successful completion of the program. At least every two weeks, the college issues a podcast explaining everything from course schedules to scholarship rules and regulations to upcoming events.

The students can subscribe to the podcast through iTunes or listen to the information online using a Flash player interface. Erik Poole, associate director of Online M.B.A. Programs, explains: "The students are receiving the administrative information they need. They are responding to the podcasts and are incorporating both the administrative podcast information and the lectures into their M.B.A. experience here at Drexel."[24] One student summed it up:

Usually prospective students who are interested in pursuing an online degree are the ones whose everyday schedule would conflict or interfere with standard classroom studies. During my first semester as a Drexel M.B.A. Anywhere student, I have found an incredibly useful tool that is being used by professors and program managers: podcasts. Professors and administrators record an audio lecture and then upload the file to the server. In the evening, when I turn on my PC, I launch my iTunes application and click on Update: all of the new podcast files are automatically downloaded into my PC. When that is done, I can either listen to the lecture from the comfort of my house or, in my case, burn the MP3 audio files onto a CD and listen to the lectures while I sit in traffic on the way to work. I find this tool extremely useful for my busy schedule. It really makes a big difference.

Not only is sound important for lectures or giving administrative instruction; sometimes sound itself contains important knowledge. A boomer production employee may be able to hear when a machine is running out of spec. He can hear the abnormal vibrations of the equipment or the sound the die makes when it is hitting the raw material. A newer employee hearing the same sound or change may not know what it means or even be aware of a sound change. If the various sounds of the machinery can be recorded and placed on an iPod or other MP3 player, a newer employee could learn, through repetition, the different sounds of the machinery and what each sound means.

A similar process is being used to teach young doctors how to distinguish heart sounds. After hearing a recording of different heart sounds about five hundred times, young doctors reliably discriminate among different sounds made by various heart problems. Before listening to the recordings, the young doctors correctly identified only 50 percent of the heart sounds; after the test, they could identify 80 percent of the sounds correctly.[25]

Nike, the athletic footwear, equipment, and accessory company, has even created an iPod-enabled shoe. The shoe has a built-in sensor that communicates with the runner through an iPod receiver. The runner can receive real-time audio feedback about his or her time, distance traveled, calories burned, and pace. Steve Jobs, Apple's CEO, states that "the result is like having a personal coach or training partner motivating you every step of your workout."[26] It even has a feature that plays your favorite running tune when you are near the end of your workout, so download the Rolling Stones' "Start Me Up" or Survivor's "Eye of the Tiger" and run off those boomer pounds.

Vodcasting: Video on Demand

Handheld video devices such as the video iPod provide access to a variety of recorded video archives as well as real-time video feeds. Archived video information can be an efficient method of transferring boomer knowledge to gamers. Recording the knowledge of boomers, archiving that knowledge, and allowing gamers' searchable access to exact sections of recorded knowledge is extremely valuable.

Archived and live video feeds enabled by the Web technology of RSS (really simple syndication) have led to the coining of the terms *vodcasting* and *vidcasting:* the delivery of video clips over the Web for display on handheld devices.

With a handheld device equipped with access to a video archive of information, a new employee can walk up to a piece of equipment, pull out the video-enabled gadget, type in the necessary search criteria, and, through a broadband wireless network, access a video of a boomer describing the proper steps for changing a timing belt or replacing a critical piece of tooling. This can be valuable to engineers trouble-shooting machinery in the field, auditors at a client location, salespeople preparing to present to a client, and in a variety of other settings where a video of the action conveys meaningful and valuable information.

If an employee needs to view a process or gain access to recorded boomer knowledge, access is only a few clicks away. The same technology and concepts that are available today from a commercial standpoint can be used for transferring knowledge. Today, technology allows telecommunication network operators to offer such services as home shopping, games, and movies on demand. The consumer simply clicks through a series of menu screens and navigates to the information required. This same concept can be used to provide instant access to manuals, videos, and even experts. An employee who requires help enters the appropriate search criteria, navigates to the appropriate topic, and accesses the information, all using a handheld video player.

One company delivering training and sales-related content specifically designed for the video iPod is AXIOM Professional Health Learning, a division of AXIS Healthcare Communications, a global medical communications agency that provides educational services to pharmaceutical companies. AXIOM is creating two types of content for the video iPod. One type is designed to train pharmaceutical sales representatives in the areas of product knowledge and information. The goal of this type of vodcast is to optimize the sales representative's time. Representatives are always on the road and spend a good deal of time in their cars or waiting to see a doctor. This time can be nonproductive unless training intervention is available. For audio or video content, sales representatives sometimes receive CD-ROMs or DVDs but the expense of sending a single mailing to over ten thousand people can be as high as sixty thousand dollars.

Andrew Howe, the client service director at AXIOM, explains, "With the video iPod, they can simply attach the iPod to their computer at night, initiate the download, and in the morning, updated content can be on their iPod ready to go. With a car adapter, they can play the audio-based information as they drive to their first appointment. As they wait to see the doctor, they can view 3D animations with voice-over explanations or 'eavesdrop' on a model sales call, and learn the latest information in the medical specialty into which they are selling."[27]

The value of the video iPod and similar devices is that they can store and play video files, animations, still photos, and even audio files. Multiple channels of learning are contained on a single portable device that fits in the sales rep's pocket, ready to use at a moment's notice.

The second use of the video iPod that AXIOM is creating for pharmaceutical firms is to assist sales reps in making a sale. These devices can help sales reps make better presentations to doctors. On a sales call, the rep shows visual information and animations to the doctor through the iPod. The rep can show an interview with a key option leader or an animated sequence of a drug interacting with human cells, or the rep can allow the doctor to watch a patient describing the benefits of a certain pharmaceutical product. The video iPod gains the attention of the busy doctor and makes information available instantly through the use of already downloaded video clips. There is no need to lug around a DVD player; the on-demand video fits in the palm of the hand.

Another application of handheld video devices is the use of a real-time vodcast to monitor and track information. One use of this technology is in agriculture, where wireless video cameras are set up to monitor livestock movement and births. This allows for quick interventions or remediation if the person monitoring the livestock views a problem or issue with the livestock. This concept can be used in almost any production environment to monitor lines of automated equipment or help troubleshoot on the production floor.

The video can be combined with the virtual mentor. For example, a person performing work who needs assistance aims a wireless camera or video cell phone at an electrical problem. Then a boomer views the feed in real time and offers assistance. This can be done for assembly work, repair work, or any other type of job requiring visual cues during the troubleshooting process. The combination of the real-time video feed and a competent guide watching the video can be a powerful method of transferring knowledge just when it is needed in just the right amount.

Text: We Don't Need No Stinking Text

Imagine yourself as a new employee in a manufacturing facility, where every machine has detailed and specific procedures that must be followed carefully in order to ensure process quality or a safe work environment. Now imagine a thick binder of standard operating procedures (SOPs) that stores this information or a set of files in a document management system that must be read and applied on the job. How does this critical information become knowledge you can use consistently and reliably?

Add to this challenge the trend of an increasing number of procedures to be learned because of greater work complexity, increased worker mobility, impending retirements, and the sheer competitive drive to work faster, better, and cheaper. In the past, workers needed to know only a handful of procedures. Today, they need to master hundreds of them.

Often, written procedural information is supplemented by the mentoring and on-the-job training of an expert performer. These master performers are known to use best practices that they acquired from reading the documented procedures, their own experience, and sometimes information from other experienced colleagues.

As a means to capture that expert knowledge and then organize it and distribute it for all to use, EduNeering, a provider of engineered knowledge solutions to pharmaceutical, health care, food, and energy industries, has developed a tool called the Visual Job Aid (VJA). The VJA can be used as initial training and as reference material on the job at the point of need. Leveraging expert advice for all to use, the VJA embodies the essence of the written procedures and illustrates them to make it easier to follow for a generation that has grown up with visual images.

In a recent study at a client organization, one hundred workers in a pharmaceutical manufacturing facility needed to learn a new procedure. Fifty of them were given the typical paper version of the SOP, and fifty were given the VJA version. In a written test of SOP knowledge, only 42 percent of those who received the paper SOP passed the test, while 82 percent of those who learned using the VJA passed. And although VJAs, as shown in Figure 4.6, are particularly well suited to regulated SOP-driven industries, they are useful in any work environment where documented procedures need to be followed consistently.

Figure 4.6. Visual Job Aids on a Video iPod.

Source: Screen capture courtesy of EduNeering Holdings, Inc. Used with permission. All rights reserved.

select   navigate   watch

So what makes VJAs so powerful? As the name suggests, they emphasize the visual. Building off the adage that a picture is worth a thousand words, every visual in the VJA is designed to communicate the proper procedural step with few or no words. The visual area takes up virtually the entire screen and is a holding place for any media—for example:

- Photos with call-outs such as "Push this button, not that one"

- Animations to illustrate a proper motion or emphasize a particular spot on the screen

- Sound clips, for example, "This is the sound the machine makes when it's about to overheat" (frequently expert performers use auditory cues to assess the health of a machine or process)

- Embedded video clips, such as an expert performing the task or relaying an important tip

- Words (Because text is used sparingly, the few words that *are* used get noticed and become verbal cues to expert actions.)

VJAs are portable; they are digital files that can be placed on a video iPod or other personal digital devices and accessed when needed.

One manufacturing client is creating a large suite of VJAs that will be delivered using a wall-mounted touch screen on the manufacturing floor. This type of delivery integrates the knowledge into the day-to-day work flow. This method is also integrated with the knowledge learning platform to allow usage tracking and instantaneous update of materials.

VJAs are particularly useful in helping organizations capture and retain the knowledge of retiring boomers and other expert performers who may be changing jobs. They can be generated based on a twenty-minute video interview with an expert who is a master performer. Large quantities of boomer knowledge can be captured, organized, and made available to the organization before it walks out the door. VJAs have a contemporary, visual interface with search and browse capabilities. They are appealing to gamers and effective learning tools.

> Matt Adlai-Gail of EduNeering is involved with research and development of industry-leading knowledge solutions that support business improvement and client success. The group focuses in the areas of high-efficiency knowledge transfer, work flow integration, and compliance solutions.

Source: Printed with the permission of Matt Adlai-Gail.

Smart Equipment

The ability to miniaturize gadgets and place them in almost any environment has led to the creation and deployment of a number of different sensors and identification tags that provide information in a variety for formats. These smart sensors take the guesswork out of many production and paperwork processes.

One emerging technology that has taken off in the retail supply chain space is the use of radio-frequency identification (RFID) tags. An RFID tag is a transponder used to store data and information. The information is then read by a transceiver and fed into larger applications to track movement and location of items.

RFID tags are small and therefore can be placed on just about any object, including animals and humans. The tags contain tiny antennas that enable them to send and receive information. There are passive RFID tags that have no internal power sources and active tags that require a power source to transmit. For example a piece of equipment containing an RFID tag would "speak" to a gadget and describe information essential to understanding the machine's standard operating protocol. This information could include temperature, operating speed, and other critical pieces of data. The person assigned to repairing the machine could use a gadget to read the RFID tag and determine what parameters of operation were running according to specifications and which were out of specification.

RFID tags are starting to be used in hospitals to track patients and provide staff with the ability to access patient information when needed. A company named VeriChip makes a human-implantable RFID tag approved by the Food and Drug Administration. It is implanted in the patient's arm in a process similar to getting a shot. It contains a sixteen-digit identification number that can be used to retrieve data from an external system. The chip is scanned, and the identification number is used to bring up records from a patient tracking system. The advantage of the chip is that patient information is always linked to a specific patient. There are no lost charts or paperwork. This identification leads to a reduction in errors and mistreatments.[28]

Eventually, implantable tags could be developed to contain treatment protocols specific to the patient. These protocols could be developed by expert doctors and then placed into the tags for each individual patient and accessed and followed by less experienced doctors. The treatment recommendations for the patient would travel with the patient, reducing the need for relearning by each subsequent doctor encountered by the patient.

In addition to the use of RFID, the technology associated with sensors has progressed to the point where a series of sensors mounted on machinery can record production rates, temperatures, vibrations, and other critical information. This information can be fed into an enterprise resource planning (ERP) system or even digitized and sent to a person's e-mail or voice mail. This can be a method of informing a manager of a problem or issue. The ERP application could literally call your cell phone and let you know if a production line was falling below a certain rate. Boomers could help program in the operational parameters, and the ERP system could then call a designated person, who could respond to the problem.

This can be used in nonmanufacturing situations as well. Orbitz, the online travel agency, has a feature on its Web site called "Care Alerts."[29] Every time a flight changes, the Care Alerts feature calls your cell phone or sends you an e-mail informing you of the change. The system automatically contacts you, with no human intervention. You can even set up the system to contact up to six different people. Now imagine this system used for alerting a salesperson of a customer purchase, a manager of an employee completing a deliverable ahead of schedule, or a homeowner about what time the repair person will arrive to fix his or her refrigerator.

Imagine an employee receiving a phone call as he or she works on a piece of equipment from that piece of equipment. The self-diagnostic equipment monitors what is being done and what needs to be done. The equipment interfaces with the person doing the repair work for a machine-person dialogue. To enable this exchange, boomer knowledge about the proper operation of the machinery is captured in terms of parameters and limits built into the machine. When problems arise, the machine sends information directly to the gamer's gadget.

Workplace Implications

These scenarios make it clear that information is valuable when it is easily accessible in a variety of formats. Transferring knowledge from boomers to gamers requires parsing information into multiple channels for access by all types of networked gadgets.

Capitalizing on gamers' love of gadgets will provide a strategic advantage to organizations that are able to see past the handheld football games to the multifunctional handheld computers that are capable of allowing constant contact among an entire organization.

If a video recording is made of a boomer exit interview, the information contained in it must be made available using video with sound, sound only, and as a text transcript, or any combination desired by a person seeking the knowledge. Too often, information is tagged for the person encoding the information, not the person retrieving the information.

Companies like Cisco are already providing training, product, and other key information to their employees in a variety of searchable channels.[30] They take a video of a training event and separate the audio track from the video track. Employees can download the complete video track to a laptop or a video iPod, just download the soundtrack to an audio MP3 player, or print out a transcript of the recorded information in the form of a text file.

It is difficult to predict what information format will be most valuable to gamers in the field as they work on a particular problem. Organizations that are able to deploy information and training across all forms of digital communication channels will have an advantage. They will be able to quickly and easily transfer information from experienced, knowledgeable boomers to novice gamers, who will be able to apply the information sent to them over their gadgets to solve the right problem in a just-in-time format.

Gadgets are a link between the boomers and the gamers. Gadgets give boomers a chance to remain in a single location while providing gamers instant access to the information they need to do the job. Organizations that properly deploy gadgets to their workforce will have a networked, highly responsive, highly knowledgeable team connected by gadgets but with the freedom to operate in a variety of situations.

■   ■   ■   ■

SUMMARY

Gadgets can be powerful tools for transferring knowledge, although some changes still need to be made. For example, iPods aren't currently password-protected, so many large organizations are nervous about putting sensitive information on an iPod. Leave an iPod at the airport or in a rental car, and key information could slip into the wrong hands. Gadgets are still thought of by manufacturers and many executives as toys. Once this attitude changes, the use of gadgets as knowledge transfer devices will skyrocket.

Cheat codes, the topic of the next chapter, are a hot topic among gamers and boomers. These codes enable gamers to obtain increased power, lives, and skills in a game without having to earn those privileges. They are a free pass to the head of the line. They shortcut convention and give some players an unfair advantage. But they are not all bad. Learn about the positive aspects of cheat codes in the next chapter.

Cheaters Never Win . . . or Do They?

THE YEAR WAS 1982, the movie, *Star Trek: The Wrath of Khan*:

Kirk: What's on your mind, Lieutenant?

Saavik: The Kobayashi Maru, sir.

Kirk: Are you asking me if we're playing out that scenario now, Lieutenant?

Saavik: On the test, sir. Will you tell me what you did? I would really like to know.

Bones: Lieutenant, you are looking at the only Starfleet cadet who ever beat the no-win scenario.

The dialogue from *Star Trek: The Wrath of Khan* is reprinted courtesy of Paramount Pictures. Copyright: STAR TREK II: THE WRATH OF KHAN © by Paramount Pictures. Rights Reserved.

Saavik: How?

Kirk: I reprogrammed the simulation so it was possible to rescue the ship.

Saavik: WHAT?

David: He cheated!

Kirk: I changed the conditions of the test. I got a commendation for original thinking. I don't like to lose.[1]

To Use a Cheat Code or Not to Use a Cheat Code

When boomers decide to play a video game with gamers (it happens occasionally), one of the biggest points of contention is the use of cheat codes. Boomers forbid them. Gamers love them.

To clarify for nongamers, a *cheat code* is a word or a sequence of controller buttons that, when pressed, gives the player extra abilities or powers during a game. The extra powers can include such things as unlimited life or unlimited ammunition or the ability to hit a home run every time the player is up to bat. Employing a cheat code alters the rules of the game.

In the PlayStation 2 game *Enter the Matrix,* created by Atari and the Wachowski Brothers, typing in the code 0034AFFF gives you maximum firepower. This means you start with the biggest and best guns and do not have to earn them by completing missions. You skip the "earn better weapons by defeating more enemies" rule in the game.

It is widely believed that cheat codes started because game developers needed a way to test a game without getting killed all the time or without having to go back to the previous level. So they invented codes that would prevent their character from being killed, and therefore they could test all aspects of the game. These types of codes later became known as "god mode," because the player was a god who could not be killed, stopped, or injured. Then at some point, early in the evolution of games, a cheat code leaked, and the gamers loved it: they had found a secret method of achieving success.

Another theory is that the gamers wanted to be able to play an entire game whether they defeated every level or not. The gamer paid all that money for the game and wanted to play the entire game, not just the levels he or she could beat, so game developers added cheat codes. With cheat codes, a player can play any part of the game at any time without following the standard rules. Cheat codes also work when a player is having difficulty getting past obstacles on a particular level. They provide unlimited access to all aspects of the game.

Regardless of origin, the use of cheat codes is now widespread and popular. They are not necessarily easy to use; you have to work to use them. If you want full ammunition in EA's *James Bond Nightfire* for the PlayStation 2, press Circle, Circle, Triangle, Square, Square after you have achieved platinum status. If you want invulnerability in *Star Wars Battlefront II,* you have to, while playing in off-line mode, pause the game and then press Up, Up, Up, Left, Down, Down, Down, Left, Up, Up, Up, Left, Right. If you are successful, you will hear a sound similar to the sound the game makes when you press Pause. (Boomers, if you are confused by the previous paragraph, just pretend it never happened.)[2]

The difficulty of the codes adds a little excitement and intrigue. It is not something that is commonly known; you need to work at it. Cheat codes are now part of the development and release process of games, and these codes drive many boomers crazy.

They can also cause game developers problems. When it was determined that a cheat code revealed a rather explicit scene in *Grand Theft Auto: San Andreas,* the Federal Trade Commission opened an official investigation into the marketing practices surrounding the controversial game. The cheat code that was found for the PlayStation 2 version of the game became a rallying call for a recall of the game. The game developer estimated a $50 million shortfall in revenue for the quarter in which the games had to be recalled, an expensive cheat code.[3]

To boomers, cheat codes are, well, cheating. Gamers consider them just part of the game. As my Gamer 4.0 son once told me, "Dad, they wouldn't make cheat codes if they didn't want you to use them."

Cheating in Video Games Isn't Cheating at All; It's Part of the Game

The first must-have game for my Nintendo Entertainment System (NES) was Konami's *Contra*. The graphics were great, and the sound was amazing to a kid coming off the Atari games of the early 1980s. To a thirteen year old, *Contra* had everything I needed in life: elite soldiers, incredible aliens, incredible weapons, and, of course, elite soldiers using those incredible weapons against those incredible aliens. The only part of the game I didn't like was the difficulty of playing it.

Although the game play was difficult, the object of *Contra* was simple enough: start on the first level and work your way through level eight. Along the way, you battled aliens disguised as soldiers, as well as avoided fatal obstacles like cliffs and industrial machines. Your guns could be upgraded by shooting canisters that dropped weapons like machine guns, flame throwers, and lasers.

The levels were either side scrolling (running left to right), climbing, or third-person quasi-three-dimensional. The action took place in the jungle, on mountains, in the snow, and inside alien bases. Each stage had a boss character who was harder to beat than other enemies in the level and required you to figure out when and how to shoot it. You started with three lives and could continue only three times. That gave you only nine chances to beat the game's eight levels, not very good odds when playing against forty to fifty aliens at a time.

Of course, you could play with a friend and have two soldiers on the screen at once, but that still wasn't good enough to beat this game. My friends and I were no match against the relentless attacks by the alien enemies.

I would have given up in frustration had it not been for a small piece of information I learned in *Nintendo Power* magazine. The article told of a code that, if entered, would allow you to start with thirty lives and have three continues. That was ninety chances to beat the game! The code was simple: when you turn the game on, hit Up, Up, Down, Down, Left, Right, Left, Right, B, A, and then the Start button.

My friends and I used the code daily when we played. Of course, we beat the game (eventually), but we kept on playing with the cheat code enabled. It became part of the game. I'm not even sure how far we would have gotten had it not been for the code or even if we would have continued playing.

Was I a bad kid for cheating? To be honest, I don't think I ever thought of it as cheating. To me, cheating was copying answers from another kid's test or cutting in line in the cafeteria or cherry-picking when playing flashlight tag. I did none of those things, but here I was entering codes and extending my play time. I thought the code was a trick that the designers put in there for us—kind of like a password that meant you were in the club. I thought, "Why else would they have a code?"

Years later, I found out that it wasn't really a secret password for membership into gaming's elite, nor was it even intended for my friends and me. In fact, it was meant only for the game programmers and testers. You see, it gets hard testing a game with eight levels if you can make it through only two because you keep dying. The programmers put this code in to enable them to beat each level with ease to check graphics, collisions, sounds, and so forth. The codes were never taken out after the game passed testing and went to production. It turns out thirteen year olds weren't even on their radar.

In reality, thousands of other kids and I were exploiting a flaw in the programming for our own gain. Another popular cheat for the NES was for the game *Super Mario Brothers.* When you ran out of lives, you could press the A button and start at the same time to begin at the beginning of the level you died in. The same game allowed players to set up the right conditions to earn hundreds of lives, a perfect storm of cheating.

But I wouldn't say we were cheating. We were just enhancing a difficult game to make it more fun for us. I think that's the key. Cheating implies that one person has gotten a significant upper hand against another person by not playing by the rules. In my circle of friends, it was agreed that we would play with thirty guys. That was our rule. There was no rule being broken. In fact, if one person entered the code, then both players would get thirty lives. I'm sure if we had entered a competition that stated no enhancement codes could be used, we would have complied.

Were we doing something wrong by playing like this? Were we cheaters? I asked some of my friends to let me know if they ever used cheat codes, and their answers were surprising. My favorite answer was also the most naive one: "There are cheat codes?"

Of the nineteen polled, ten had used cheat codes. Some people used cheat codes to visually enhance the game play, like my friend who had used a code in a football game to make all the players have giant heads. Another friend used codes after he finished a game to go back and unlock hidden features.

One surprising result was that eight people still knew the *Contra* code, and even more surprising, one person claimed she didn't play video games or use cheat codes but she knew the *Contra* code from memory!

In games with finite endings and computer-controlled enemies, cheating is a valid strategy for gamers in the quest to beat the game and get the most out of their game time. When kids play games, they play to have fun. Most of the time, fun happens when you win. No one wants to play a game that is so hard you can't progress. Cheating levels the playing field for younger or novice players by removing barriers that prohibit them from moving forward.

Greg Walsh is an interactive media developer at Black & Decker University and adjunct faculty in the ISD Training Systems Master's program at the University of Maryland, Baltimore County.

Source: Printed with the permission of Greg Walsh.

Rules Were Made to Be Broken

Do cheat codes have any value? The short answer is yes. They allow the gamer to circumvent the rules of the game and search or go places he or she may not have been able to go to without the code. They allow the gamers complete freedom to test and retest various aspects of the game.

Cheating is nothing new. People have been cheating since the beginning of time. Eve cheated by biting the apple. The concept isn't new, but the idea of building cheating directly into the rules of the game is a newer construct, and gamers now look for these codes in single-player and PC-based games.

In an extreme example of searching for cheat codes, one gamer who goes by the screen name of edisoncarter hard-wired a game controller to a parallel port of a computer. He then ran a software application he had developed that mimicked various key combinations until he unlocked a number of undiscovered cheat codes.[4] He then posted the "found" cheats online for the entire world to use. He was hailed in many cheat code communities as a brilliant, mad genius.

Gamers look for cheat codes. They expect a way to work around a difficult situation. This expectation of cheating can be valuable if it is handled correctly. Encouraging the right kind of cheating can lead to productive results.

Cheating Works

One example of how cheating can enhance an organization is explained in a book titled *Ideas Are Free*. The book describes the system by which Boardroom, a publisher of direct-mail newsletters and books, encourages employee ideas. The CEO put in place a policy stating that employees who failed to give an average of at least two improvement ideas each week lost their quarterly bonuses. The authors were shocked that that seemed pretty severe. They asked the CEO how many times bonuses were withheld, and he said, "None." Every employee, for seven years, had produced two ideas per week without fail.[5]

The authors were skeptical. Every employee had come up with two ideas every week for seven years? How could this be true? So they did some investigation and found a black market of ideas had emerged within the company. An employee who was short an idea could barter and trade for an idea to be paid back later with another idea. The authors couldn't believe all the cheating that was occurring. Being good consultants and knowing who was paying the bill, the authors went directly to the CEO with this scandalous information about a black market of ideas. No wonder everyone had two new ideas per week. They were cheating!

When confronted with this startling information, the CEO replied, "Of course, I know about this, but I think it's great." The authors were shocked. The CEO continued, "We have succeeded in creating a culture that values ideas and gets people to share and communicate them. Wasn't that the goal in the first place?"[6]

The CEO had used cheating to his advantage. The employees were sharing and exchanging as many ideas as possible every week. They were focused on the exchange of ideas for the betterment of the company. If a situation can be set up properly, cheating actually becomes a valuable tool in helping to form a corporate culture.

A Community of Cheaters

The idea of cheating behind someone's back (even if that person knows what is going on) is appealing. We all like the idea of getting away with something. Cheating, or "working together" to solve a problem, is frowned on in formal educational settings: "Do your own work." "Keep your eyes on your own paper." These phrases are often the mantra of middle school and high school teachers. However, in business, collaboration and working together is not viewed as cheating; it is how work gets accomplished. No one person can know or do everything. Cheat code use is a form of working together through collaboration.

Cheat codes are typically passed from one gamer to another through word-of-mouth. A gamer will discover a code online or through a special promotion by the game maker and eagerly share the information with a fellow gamer, who in turn shares that information with other gamer friends. This is how cheat codes are spread. Sharing cheat codes builds a kind of camaraderie that is difficult to equal.

This sense of camaraderie has created entire online communities dedicated to the exchange of cheat codes, taking the word-of-mouth concept to a higher level. These online communities support the sharing of cheat codes much like the sharing of ideas explained above. You can go to www.cheatcodes.com and look up cheat codes by platform, game, or "What's New." There is even a section on the Web site honoring members who have contributed the most cheat codes. Or go to cheat code central at www.cheatcc.com and find codes by posting on a message board or opening up an e-mail account. It is easy to join the cheat code community and start participating.

Cheat codes have encouraged, fostered, and taken advantage of the gamers' need and desire to network and be networked. The exchange of cheat codes is a social act that keeps gamers talking to one another and builds a bond. It creates a mentality of, "Hey, it's me and you against the computer."

Cheat codes not only allow the player to have special powers and abilities in the game world; they can also be used to foil an opponent. In the *Madden Football* franchise, there are cheat codes that will force your opponent to fumble more often or drop a higher percentage of passes. This forces gamers to make agreements about when cheat codes are "legal" and when they are not and even how many are allowed in a game. There is an entire negotiation and bargaining process that occurs when gamers get together to play each other.

Organizations can pick up on the cheat code culture by creating ways in which sanctioned cheating can occur, like the example of the CEO encouraging a black market of ideas. Organizations can tap into the sharing aspect of cheat codes by setting up internal Web sites for the posting of shortcuts, cheat sheets, and information about competitors or the marketplace. The sharing of semisecret or even hard-to-find information can be appealing and help to build a corporate culture of sharing.

A form of cheat code already exists in many organizations. It is called expediting. When a product or service is expedited through an organization, the normal processing time is circumvented. The rules are broken, and a product or service is delivered much more quickly than normal. If a product typically takes twelve weeks to go through the manufacturing process in a particular plant, expediting can sometimes cut that time to a few days. When the president or vice president of sales has a rush order for the company's biggest client, cheat codes are enabled, and the time is reduced. The rush order bumps other orders, shortcuts are taken through the production process, and transactional information may be suspended as the items are quickly shipped. The paperwork then catches up later (everyone hopes).

Many businesses would benefit from looking at the cheat codes they use to expedite a product or service and converting some of those practices into standard operating procedures. Observing what happens when rules are broken can help to establish what rules should be eliminated or changed.

I once consulted with an organization with a rule that raw material requisitions needed to be created and approved before material could be purchased. It makes sense to require formal approval before purchasing raw materials. When the company was implementing a new purchasing system, it asked the software vendor if it could modify the system to automatically create a raw material requisition after the raw materials were received at the plant. The software vendor notified me of this out-of-order request and asked me to see why such a request had been made.

It turned out that requisitions were never approved in enough time to purchase the raw materials needed for production, so rather than shut down the production line, the production manager simply purchased what was requested, whether it was approved or not. No one stopped him; after all, he needed the raw materials to do his job. He had implemented his own cheat code for purchasing material: if the purchase is not approved and you need the material, order it anyway. It turns out that no requisitions for raw material were ever turned down. He said to me, "If the answer is always yes, then why do I always have to ask?" The company needed to look at its processes and modify them to be in line with the reality of their production environment.

Cheat Sheets

Another method of taking advantage of the gamers' fondness for cheat codes is to create corporate cheat sheets. When a gamer joins your company, give him or her a book of cheat sheets in the same spirit as the For Dummies series of books (Figure 5.1).

Figure 5.1. Giving Gamers Corporate Cheat Codes.

Source: Reprinted with permission of the artist, Kristin Longenecker.

The first For Dummies book was, not surprisingly, written to help readers understand how a computer works. Back then, computer commands were run from the C prompt in a language called DOS. *DOS for Dummies* was written in November 1991 by Dan Gookin. The book, written in easy-to-understand language with plenty of pictures, is a giant cheat code, actually, a collection of cheat codes. The series has sold over 125 million books on every topic from computers to choosing a dog to bipolar disorder.[7]

Since gamers like to cheat and then discuss their cheating among themselves, a good idea in a corporate environment is to create a number of documents that provide quick and easy-to-understand instructions for being successful within the organization. Then encourage the gamers to discuss these cheat codes with each other and with their boomer coworkers.

No gamer wants to read the lengthy corporate handbook. Instead they want the cheater's version. Have boomers create bulleted lists of what should be done to complete certain tasks or achieve particular goals. Create a cheat sheet for customer interactions, working with raw materials, and getting work done under deadlines. Collect the wisdom of the boomers in small, easily digestible chunks. These cheat sheets can be physical pieces of paper distributed to each new employee. Even better, make them available online in a searchable format so gamers can access the cheat sheets with their Web-enabled gadgets.

Using corporate cheat codes and cheat sheets is not necessarily a bad thing. Cheats are really shortcuts or abbreviations for standard operating procedures. The trick is for management to enact, monitor, and guide the use of these corporate cheats to the ethical benefit of the organization, its employees, and its customers.

Bending the Rules

In addition to cheat codes, gamers like to play at the edge of the rules in the game. The most successful gamers exploit the rules of a game to their advantage. The same can be said of successful businessmen and businesswomen. Successful people learn the unwritten rules of engagement and push those rules, work around those rules, and subvert those rules until they are successful.

As the saying goes, "history books are not filled with people who followed the rules." The remarkable accomplishments of Rosa Parks, Martin Luther King Jr., Susan B. Anthony, and the founders of many companies all point to examples of people who worked at the edge of existing rules and forged a better future, refusing to follow the written and unwritten rules of society.

Working at the Edge

Gamers continually work to find the weaknesses, mistakes, and boundaries in games. Once they locate them, gamers use those weaknesses and mistakes to their advantage.

Being between a boomer and a gamer (I'm an Xer), I have a general rule of no cheat codes, and my son knows this (he's not happy about it, but he knows it). I still think cheat codes are generally on the side of cheating, so we play without the aid of cheat codes.

One day I was playing a computerized hockey game with my son. We were playing against the best team in the virtual league we had established and were winning, seven goals to zero. I started to get suspicious that my son had used a cheat code and that was why we were winning so handedly.

"I said no cheat codes."

"Dad, I didn't use a cheat code."

"Come on, we can't be beating this team seven to zero. They are too good." I was starting to get upset that my son was not being honest with me.

"Dad, really, I didn't use a cheat code." He did his best to keep a straight face.

"Okay, then how can we be winning by this much?"

"Well, ah, before the game, I went into the other team and changed their goalie's power to zero and his ability to see the puck to zero. But I didn't use a cheat code. The game lets me do that."

"Oh."

My son had pulled a Kobayashi Maru; he had reprogrammed the computer to his advantage so he could win. I would have never, in a million years, even considered changing the ability of the other team's goalie to help me win. I would consider boosting the power of my own forwards or making my goalie's power 100 percent, but the manipulation of the other team's players was not something that I would have considered. To a gamer, it's part of the game. It may not be the letter of the law, but it is certainly within the boundaries of the game. The explanation: the game lets me do it.

Don't Take Off

Another time I was playing a military game with my son. The goal of the game was to take off from an aircraft carrier, fly a plane over enemy carriers and islands, and bomb or torpedo the enemy forces. I could not take off from the stupid aircraft carrier. I was able to get a little lift but could never get high enough. I was shot down or crashed into the water every time. I was half paying attention as my son took his turn. When I turned my attention back to the game, he was destroying every enemy in site.

"How are you doing that?"

"Doing what?" he smiled.

"How are you shooting down every enemy in sight when I can't even take off from the aircraft carrier without crashing?"

"Oh, I don't take off," he said matter-of-factly.

"What do you mean, you don't take off?"

"I just drive the plane off the aircraft carrier and onto the water. You don't have to fly."

"Huh?"

He had found a flaw in the game that wasn't even in my realm of consciousness. As a pilot sitting in a plane on an aircraft carrier, you can only do one thing: take off from the carrier. Even if you get shot down again and again, you still try to take off. What else can you do?

My son, not constrained by that little convention of "a plane must fly," simply drove off the carrier. For some reason, this was never considered by the game developer, and my son was driving below the enemy aircraft, at the same level as the ships. No enemy could shoot him. The planes couldn't get low enough, and ship guns were aimed too high. My son had found a way to work the system and play at the very border of the rules and was still doing what the game allowed him to do. He completely exploited a flaw in the game, to the utter defeat of this father.

Improving Customer Satisfaction Ratings

My son is certainly not the only gamer to game the system. We were running a workshop for middle school children one summer, and I learned just how brutal the concept of gaming the system can be.

The workshop was designed to teach business concepts using the game *Roller Coaster Tycoon*. (Don't laugh.) In addition to allowing you to build roller coasters and theme park rides, the game provides players with a budget and a small profit-and-loss statement that you can manipulate to ensure the park is profitable. Players can spend money on marketing, building rides, or hiring personnel to keep the park clean and safe. It is really effective at teaching business basics.

One of the goals we set up early in the workshop was to have the middle school students create a park with a high customer satisfaction rating. This was round one. It was designed to get the kids familiar with the rules of the park and how the game operated, although many of them already knew the game inside and out. To achieve a high customer satisfaction rating, the majority of the guests needed to be happy. To make guests happy, the park had to have plenty of eating and restroom facilities, prices needed to be reasonable, and the rides needed to be the right mix of excitement and relaxation.

While I was walking around the room looking at the achievements of the students, I noticed that one group had an extremely high park rating. I stayed for a while to watch their park and see how they had achieved success so quickly. The more closely I looked, the more puzzled I became. The park was extremely high priced, it had virtually no restaurants or restrooms, and it had several dangerous rides. Yet the customer satisfaction rating was through the roof. I asked the students why they didn't have any unhappy guests.

They replied that they did get unhappy guests but that whenever they located unhappy guests, they eliminated them.

I asked, "What do you mean eliminated them?"

"I'll show you." The student located an unhappy guest, picked him up, moved him over a pond they had built, and dropped him.

I was stunned. "You drown unhappy guests?"

"Yes. You are allowed."

The middle school students had found that unhappy guests could be eliminated quickly by drowning them. If you eliminate all the unhappy guests, you can have a fairly high park rating regardless of park conditions. The rules of the game allowed that little anomaly, and these middle school kids quickly took advantage of it. They weren't really thinking about killing a person; they were thinking of how to get the highest satisfaction rate. It was a little disturbing to me, but to them it was part of the game.

Figure 5.2. Improving the Customer Satisfaction Rating Should Not Include Drowning Unhappy Guests.

Source: Reprinted with permission of the artist, Kristin Longenecker.

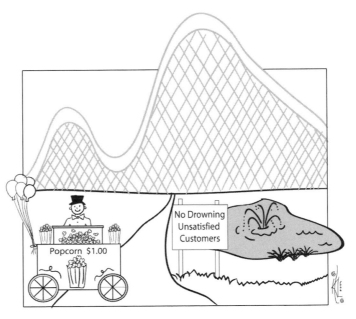

That wasn't the only step they took to game the system. They also took advantage of the fact that they could place "Do Not Exit" signs near the end of rides and force patrons to ride the same ride again and again each time, paying full price. These kids were scary clever, sort of like a horror flick titled *Death at the Amusement Park.*

Because of occasional flaws in the logic of games and the ability to manipulate most aspects of a game, gamers have developed a mentality of working the
system. To my son, changing the ability of the other team's goalie wasn't a big
deal, and neither was driving an airplane like a car. He wasn't using a cheat code.
He was doing what was allowed by the game. He was playing by the rules—by
the letter of the rules and not the intent, but by the rules nevertheless.

Help Codes

The concept of cheating and cheat codes can be a source of conflict between
boomers and gamers. Boomers tend to want to work their way through a
game and progress one level at a time. They view the use of cheat codes as
wrong and unfair. They weren't allowed to use cheat sheets in school, so the
use of cheat codes for games should not be allowed. To the boomers, it is as
simple as that: no cheating.

But to gamers, cheat codes are not cheating. They are more like help
codes. These codes help gamers get through the game in a quick and easy format without interference from some conventions of the game, like running
out of ammunition or getting killed too many times on a level. For a gamer,
it is okay to work with codes designed to make game play more fun, because
they are resources to help win the game. It is okay to use a cheat code.

The habitual use of cheat codes bears on how gamers view the workplace and the rules governing the marketplace. They see the rules of the
workplace and the marketplace as boundaries to be pushed. Remember the
dot-com phenomenon. The mantra was the "new economy" versus the "old
economy." The prevailing thought among those gamers-turned-entrepreneurs
was that the old rules didn't apply. It turned out that they did apply, but the
gamers were able to push those rules to the limit and drive a financial phenomenon. They were working at the edge of the rules of the economy.

Many of the ideas of the new economy that didn't seem to work in the
late 1990s are now working. Sites like Google receive a tremendous amount
of revenue by providing a "free" service to end users and then charging advertisers for the aggregated eyeshare of the marketplace. The eyeshare concept is
the marketing concept that prompted many dot-com companies to give away
applications in hopes of capturing enough site visitors to convert that traffic

to dollars. The eyeshare business model does work; Google has a market value of about $4 billion. The gamers worked at the edge of the rules of commerce and made it work. This is only the beginning of how much they are going to push conventional rules.

Workplace Implications

To work with gamers and their affinity for cheat codes, boomers need to keep in mind certain concepts and ideas that gamers have about cheat codes. For their part, gamers need to understand that cheat codes are not always appropriate.

Even in the gamer universe, cheat codes have limits. In massively multi-player online role-play games (MMORPGs), cheat codes are forbidden. On-line games with hundreds or thousands of other players need to ensure a level playing field for the fair exchange of goods, money, and trinkets. If someone incorporates a cheat or hack into a MMORPG, the game no longer becomes fun for the honest players.

To help keep a level playing environment, companies have created programs to prevent cheating in online games. One well-known program is Punk-Buster, whose motto flashes at the top of its Web site "If you cheat, you're a punk."[8]

Even Balance, the Spring, Texas, company that created PunkBuster, works hard to ensure that players in all types of MMORPGs have equal opportunities within the world of the game. This keeps it fair and fun, and the players in the MMORPG appreciate and value the idea of fair play in those environments.

Gamers understand that using cheat codes all the time and in every situation is not appropriate. They are not out to unfairly or maliciously exploit every flaw or take advantage of every situation; instead they are looking for opportunities and fair advantage over the competition.

So when gamers enter the workforce, the challenge to boomers is to find a way to manage the gamers so they retain their drive to work at the edges of convention—allow them the freedom to look for opportunities in unusual places. At the same time, boomers must help ensure that working on the edge does not include illegal or unethical activities or behaviors. This is a difficult line to straddle, but it must be maintained.

Gamers must understand that working at the edge is not always the right answer and that boomers have created some boundaries for very good reasons. Both boomers and gamers need to proceed with caution in the areas of cheat codes and working at the edge, but they need to proceed nevertheless.

For Boomers

Since gamers want to work at the boundaries of what is allowed by the rules, there are certain steps that should be taken to clarify those rules and boundaries:

- Be clear about the parameters of the work environment.

- Realize gamers will work at the edge of those parameters.

- Create cheat sheets for procedures, policies, and interactions with clients. Create bulleted lists that can be picked up and used quickly by the gamers. Consider creating a kind of "ABC Corporation for Dummies" book.

- Ask gamers to inform you of rules they think are weak or "stupid." You can either agree with them or explain something they might not see or realize.

- Make implicit rules explicit. Create a list of rules that cannot be broken for any reason.

- Expect to become frustrated when gamers challenge the system and convention.

- Remind gamers that sometimes in some situations with some co-workers there is value and respect in "paying dues" and that just because a rule could be exploited or bent doesn't mean it should be.

For Gamers

Gamers need to realize that certain aspects of the workplace and the marketplace require adherence to rules and that many rules are in place because the alternatives have been tried and were found wanting. Gamers need to consider a few guidelines and conventions when it comes to working within an organization with rules, policies, and procedures:

- Boomers may resent the fact that you are trying to game the system.
- Learn the rules and their implications before deciding to break a rule.
- Learn what rules can be broken and what rules should be left intact.
- Understand that you will meet with resistance when you try to break a rule or decide to work at the boundaries or edges of existing systems.
- If no cheat sheets have been created for you, start your own, and share it with your coworkers.
- Cheating is not always a good thing, especially when it will hurt others or is unethical.
- Boomers have a wealth of information about what works and what doesn't. Seek their advice before taking action.

SUMMARY

Organizations can take advantage of gamers' love of cheat codes by designing training forms, company manuals, and online search systems around the cheat code concept. Organizations can actually encourage a certain level of cheating to help their employees achieve success. Rethink the term *cheat codes,* and exploit gamers' tendency to work at the edges of systems, which can be advantageous as organizations seek a competitive advantage. The role of boomers will be to police those cheat codes to make sure they are helpful and not violating ethical or legal parameters.

Organizations also need to take advantage of the gamers' fondness for search engines. When gamers have questions, they don't seek the encyclopedia; they seek a search engine. Learn in the next chapter how this can be helpful to organizations.

Searching for the Ideal Learning Event

M Y ELEVEN-YEAR-OLD SON researched the history of the saxophone for his music class by "googling" it. He never went to the library or even opened a book. A pharmaceutical sales representative sitting in a doctor's office—waiting to give her five-minute sales pitch—"googles" a competitor's product. An inventory control manager "googles" the terms *Lean* and *Six Sigma* after vaguely hearing something about those concepts in a meeting. Before a big Saturday night date, a young woman "googles" her date's name. She wants to make sure he is not some deranged lunatic (Figure 6.1).

Gamers are constantly typing terms and phrases into the simple, ubiquitous search engine named Google and impatiently awaiting results. Connected gamers want information, and they want it now, or in at least 2.3 seconds, faster than most employees can log into a learning management system. This is the generation that puts instant coffee in the microwave and wonders what takes so long. They don't want an entire lecture, book, or class; they

Figure 6.1. Googling a Date's Name Can Bring Interesting Results.

Source: Reprinted with permission of the artist, Kristin Longenecker.

want just a single nugget of information and are happy with 1,490,000 hits from which to choose.

Google, the company with the motto "Do No Evil," is an integral part of the gamers' approach to information, learning, and knowledge. Gamers turn to Google to learn about everything from Cox2 Inhibitors to quality improvement methodologies to murder suspects.

It didn't start that way. In the 1990s, Google was just another search engine. Its simple interface and ability to find information in the nooks and crannies of the Web almost instantaneously propelled its rapid growth and acceptance. In fact, the accounting and consulting firm Deloitte and Touche named Google the fastest-growing company ever. Google's initial five-year revenue growth exceeded 400,000 percent.[1] It is predicted that search engines will displace e-mail as the most used digital application.[2]

This rapid growth has morphed the company and its name into a part of the English language. *Google* is now a verb meaning "to search the Internet for information on a person or thing" as in "let's google 'iPod accessories' to find better headphones." The American Dialect Society chose the verb *to google* as the "most useful word of 2002."[3]

The convenience and speed at which millions of pages of information can be searched has created an expectation of instant information. This expectation has a direct impact on how gamers seek and view information. They are not looking to learn in a formal environment with information spoon-fed to them at the instructor's rate of delivery. They have little patience for "lectures, step-by-step logic, and 'tell-test' instruction."[4] They seek that single nugget of information, a small paragraph explaining that Adolphe Sax patented the first saxophone in 1846. Nothing more, nothing less.

Learning at Work

A gamer who waits for instructions or information while playing a video game fails. Decisive action must be taken immediately. Gamers have learned this and expect speed in answers and learning. A gamer who needs information inputs a question into a search engine and then demands accurate, up-to-date results. Gamers seek rather than wait for information.

In contrast, boomers are used to receiving information in a formal, hierarchical sequence. Television, the medium of boomers, is linear, one way, and delivered in thirty- or sixty-minute chunks. Books are divided into sections, chapters, and parts. Academic classroom sessions last anywhere from one to three hours. Corporate training classes are often six hours long. Content is provided in a formal context with introductions, carefully parsed lessons, and all-encompassing summaries.

Gamers have a different expectation. They desire instant (or almost instant) learning delivered in an informal manner. They do not want to log into the corporate learning management system, navigate to the desired course, and then page through forty screens to find that one desired piece of information. It takes too long. Nor do they have the tolerance to sit in a classroom and be lectured at for hours on end about information they might need later.

The gamer expectation of instant learning may explain why dropout rates for e-learning courses are as high as 50 to 60 percent.[5] Boomers have lifted the classroom paradigm of long hours of instruction and simply placed it online, assuming the paradigm will work in this digital format. Many e-learning courses are as long as four hours, require the learner to progress screen by screen, and provide little interactivity. These long, linear e-learning events are too boring and tedious for gamers.

Transferring knowledge from boomers to gamers requires a rethinking of how corporations and academic institutions present learning opportunities to gamers. The fondness for searching and the informal nature of the gamer approach means the paradigms currently in place for online and classroom instruction need to change.

Embracing Informal Learning

In any organization, 70 to 90 percent of learning is informal.[6] Yet the majority of the learning dollars are spent on formal courses. If organizations are going to transfer knowledge to the gamers, they need to tap into this informal network of learning. Gamers are masters of informal learning. Monies need to move from formal training interventions to informal learning opportunities.

Learning needs to be built into the fabric of the gamer's day. It cannot be event driven: stop work, attend learning, return to work. Learning opportunities should be as ubiquitous as e-mail, instant messaging, and conducting searches on the Web. Employees already build learning into their days in unstructured, informal exchanges with colleagues. They ask questions, seek answers, and learn new information from manuals, Web sites, and books. Corporate training efforts are not competing against nothing; they are competing against technologies and paper-based resources independently referenced by employees. Because these learning events are unmonitored, it is not known if the senior employee mentoring the new account manager is providing the right information. He or she needs tools provided by the training department to ensure the right information is transferred.

One organization weaving formal learning opportunities into informal daily processes is Cisco Systems, the company that supplies Internet devices for networking. Cisco's Internet Learning Solutions Group has created a service to provide employees with knowledge, ideas, and training on a regular, informal basis. Members of the sales force can subscribe to a service called News Clips. First, employees complete an interest profile describing what types of information are of interest to them. After subscribing and completing the profile, the employee receives a daily e-mail containing information relevant to his or her sales responsibilities based on this profile. Each e-mail summarizes six, eight, or ten different things related to the person's indicated areas of interest. Each item has a three-sentence descriptor, plus a headline and a URL link to the entire article, white paper, or video. Cisco is using e-mail as a training distribution mechanism. It is an integral part of its e-learning strategy.[7]

Organizations must develop processes and procedures for capturing and distributing the learning that occurs informally within their organization. Much of what will be transferred to gamers from boomers will be informal, with no mechanism of checking the veracity of the information or duplicating the captured knowledge to share with others. Creating collaborative online learning spaces for boomers and gamers to share information, the use of captured instant messaging discussions, and creating small chunks of knowledge to be quickly digested by interested gamers will all help in this process.

Instant Messaging

Instant messaging (IM) is a powerful method fostering informal learning. Instant Messenger is a program that allows two or more computers on a network to communicate with each other in real time. It has several advantages over e-mail. It is real time, allows you to see if the person is online and open to receiving messages, and provides a quicker response than e-mail. In fact, gamers are beginning to call e-mail the new snail mail.[8] And one focus group of gamers defined e-mail as "something you use to talk to 'old people,' institutions, or to send complex instructions to large groups."[9]

Seventy-five percent of online teens, or about two-thirds of all teenagers, use IM, compared to 42 percent of online adults, and of the teens who use IM, 48 percent say they exchange IMs at least once every day.[10] They even have their own language, as shown in Table 6.1.[11] The goal seems to be the shorter the better; my Gamer 4.0 son asked me one day why we need the *H* in *the*.

Table 6.1. Instant Messaging Words and Their Standard Equivalents.

IM Word	Standard Equivalent
gr8	Great
lol	Laugh out loud
omg	Oh, my goodness
nvm	Never mind
np	No problem
ppl	People
r	Are
thnx	Thanks
ttyl	Talk to you later
ty	Thank you
yw	You're welcome
wat	What
w/e	Whatever (emphasis on *ever*)

One key advantage of the IM system is that it allows gamers to see who is online and accessible. Gamers can always know who is connected or present and who is not. Most are comfortable with the idea of letting others know when they are online and with being constantly accessible. Boomers are not always comfortable with the idea and don't want others to know when they are online and when they are not.

In this information age, the idea of instant availability and presence is important to gamers. They often reach out to friends and colleagues outside their organization for essential information via instant messaging. IM enables one-on-one informal learning that cuts across organizational boundaries. When you see a gamer with an IM window open, it does not mean he or she is engaged in idle chitchat with a friend. Most likely, he or she is seeking information.

IM also enables groups of gamers to exchange information. A person can speak to a colleague anywhere in the world and create an ad hoc chatroom where several people can get together and discuss a sales meeting, upcoming proposal, or any other group project.

Informal learning occurs any time two or more people exchange ideas, test concepts, or think through processes. All of that thinking and exchanging of ideas occurs with IM all the time. Corporations need to learn how to capture that knowledge and use it for future learning opportunities.

But corporations are not capturing this informal knowledge. One study revealed that while 50 percent of employees within corporations are using some form of IM, 76 percent of those corporations have not deployed a formal IM solution.[12] This means that gamers and others are downloading their own versions of IM and using them to communicate with each other outside corporate guidelines, control, or monitoring. In addition to a huge security concern with these downloads, corporations are losing out on an opportunity to capture informal learning.

One advantage of IM over a technology like the telephone is that IM conversations can be easily captured and recorded. Telephone conversations can be recorded, but the technology is awkward, and there is no expectation that the conversation is being recorded except on customer service or help desk calls, and those are not typically internal conversations. They are discussions between a customer and the business.

With IM, recording the conversation requires little space, no additional equipment, and an expectation that the discussion is being recorded. It is well known that organizations can retrieve e-mail even when it has been deleted. Thought processes, relevant tangents leading to insights, and other subtle problem-solving elements can all be recorded and codified during the conversation itself. If handled correctly, IM transcripts can be made available for search by others looking for similar ideas or dealing with similar issues.

In fact, one AOL blog is already tapping into IM conversations and making them permanent and available to a wider audience. The blog site, called The Cooler, has a simple statement at the top of its page: "We gather at *The Cooler* to chat up the day's top entertainment headlines and rumors, then we cut and paste our chatroom conversations straight to the blog."[13]

This can be a great method for sharing knowledge and transferring ideas. Imagine scientists or technicians gathering on an IM chat to discuss an issue and then posting the most important parts of the discussion on an internal company blog to share the best ideas, concepts, and thoughts.

Given gamers' fondness for IM, it makes sense to get senior technicians, scientists, salespeople, and others on Instant Messenger to facilitate the transfer of knowledge within the organization. Being connected by IM allows them to communicate with gamers in real time and on the gamers' favorite communication medium. The transition to IM can be a culture shock for many boomers. Most boomers prefer face-to-face communication, while most gamers consistently choose IM over e-mail in a wide array of contexts.[14]

When an IM communication channel is established between gamers and boomers, a manager can reach out to a geographically dispersed team and have a conversation or work on a problem with ease and quickness not available with other types of communication. The use of IM can be a great way for a boomer to mentor a gamer on a particular topic or area of expertise.

Blogs

In contrast to the one-on-one or small group discussions possible through IM, a Web log, or *blog,* as it is commonly known, can broadcast boomer knowledge across an entire organization or across the world. In a blog, the author enters his or her thoughts onto a Web page, and the postings are displayed in reverse chronological order on a Web site, available to anyone who has access (Figure 6.2). According to Technorati, a Web site that tracks blog information, "There are about 75,000 new blogs a day. Bloggers—people who write Weblogs—update their Weblogs regularly; there are about 1.2 million posts daily, or about 50,000 blog updates an hour."[15]

Figure 6.2. Example of a Blog.

Readers of a blog have a chance to post comments and thoughts but cannot change the original author's contribution. Blogs have become well known as online personal diaries available for the entire world to view. These personal thoughts and comments have gotten bloggers in trouble and, in some cases, even fired. In 2002, Heather Armstrong lost her job because of negative comments she made about her employer and coworkers on her blog www.dooce.com. Since that time, the term *dooced* has become synonymous with "the act of getting fired because of one's blog or Web site."[16]

A Delta Air Lines employee calling herself "Queen of the Sky" was dooced because her "Diary of a Flight Attendant" blog contained information and photographs Delta felt were "inappropriate."[17] Other companies that have dooced employees or contractors include Microsoft, Google, and the online social networking site Friendster.[18]

These incidents and the idea that blogs are simply a tool of political pundits and brooding, lonely teenagers have given blogs a somewhat negative connotation in the mass media and within a few corporations. Nevertheless, blogs can be used for good.

Blogs are a bottom-up approach to communication and knowledge management. They can be mined for information and provide a spam-free way of gaining it.[19] A boomer can write his or her thoughts in a blog concerning a particular issue, and then anyone within the organization can access the information, ask questions, make comments, or contact that person directly for more information. A blog allows others to "see" what is inside a person's head. This can be a great tool for transferring knowledge. The value of blogs is accelerating their adoption in many companies and organizations. Dr. Pepper/7 UP, Verizon, and Hartford Financial Services Group all have internal blogs.[20]

Blogs are an effective tool for an expert to contribute knowledge to the organization. A boomer expert can input his or her knowledge, and gamers can access that knowledge and make comments or seek additional information. Internal corporate blogs provide a place that gamers can visit to find out key information.

At some DaimlerChrysler plants, managers use blogs to discuss problems, share information, and keep a record of solutions. At the Dutch technology company Macaw, up to 90 percent of its employees blog to share knowledge about technical issues and resolutions.[21]

At IBM, blogs are used to discuss software development projects and business strategies. A blog's inherently open, anarchic nature may be a bit unsettling for some boomers, but their simplicity and informality have given them appeal and widespread use. The idea of simplicity and informality is what appeals to many gamers. They often turn to internal blogs before looking for more formal channels of information.

Blogs can be used to track the progress of a project, gather and post information about competitors, and share ideas among geographically dispersed individuals. Internal blogs provide a written, time-stamped version of research and development programs. Organizations can track the growth and development of ideas in a single location, thereby recording the development of a patent or the history and progress of research projects.

Wiki

In contrast to the single contributions of a blog, collective knowledge can be gathered and distributed using a wiki. If a blog is a monologue, then the wiki is a discussion. In their quest to quickly exchange information, gamers have embraced the technology of wikis.

A wiki allows the reader of a Web site to instantly edit and add content directly on the site. There is no need to create code in HTML or use any type of external editor, and the process is fast.

The word *wiki* is a Hawaiian term meaning quick, fast, or to hasten.[22] The term *WikiWikiWeb,* shortened to *wiki,* was coined by American programmer Ward Cunningham in 1995 as an alliterative, rhyming substitute for the word *quick.*[23] Cunningham came up with the name after being directed to the "Wiki Wiki" line of buses at the Honolulu International Airport. He learned that *wiki* meant quick and that doubling a word in the Hawaiian language added emphasis. Cunningham felt that since his new technology allowed the quick exchange of information, it should be given a name that reflected that sense of speed.[24]

Wikis work well for the collaborative sharing of knowledge between boomers and gamers because their content can be updated easily. There is no need for technical know-how; a person just needs the ability to operate a basic word processor.

Perhaps one of the most dramatic examples of a wiki in action is the Web site Wikipedia (www.wikipedia.org). Wikipedia "is an encyclopedia written collaboratively by many of its readers. Lots of people are constantly improving Wikipedia, making thousands of changes an hour, all of which are recorded on article histories and recent changes. Inappropriate changes are usually removed quickly"[25] by one of the thousands of daily visitors to the site.

The process works as follows. Someone notices an inaccuracy in an entry and makes the change immediately. There is no need to notify an editor, wait for verification, or even check sources. Because entries are tracked and changes recorded, people tend to make accurate changes and corrections. Even if an entry is not correct, inaccuracies are quickly addressed and remedied because of the volume of visitors and ease in changing the information. Wikipedia is basically a collective encyclopedia written by volunteers with over 3.5 million articles in two hundred languages. Anyone who visits the site can become an author or an editor, changing or adding entries.

Boomers and others have called into question the veracity of data contained in Wikipedia since anyone with access to the World Wide Web can add, edit, delete, or change any information in it. Can a collective effort of creating knowledge be trusted to be correct? The answer appears to be yes— or, more precisely, as accurate as a printed encyclopedia.

The British journal *Nature,* a top scientific journal first published in 1869, published a peer-reviewed article examining a range of scientific entries in both the *Encyclopedia Britannica* and Wikipedia through a rigorous peer review process and found few differences in accuracy: "The average science entry in Wikipedia contained around four inaccuracies; Britannica, about three."[26] The researchers found eight serious errors, such as misinterpretations of important concepts, in forty-two reviews; four such errors were found in each encyclopedia. In addition, the reviewers found factual errors, omissions, or misleading statements in both. Wikipedia had 162 of these types of errors. The *Encyclopedia Britannica* had 123.

Essentially the accuracy of the paper-based encyclopedia created by paid editors and researchers was about the same as the collective encyclopedia created by visitors to the Wikipedia site—volunteer writers and editors.[27] The implication is that collective knowledge is as accurate, reliable, and helpful as edited and carefully reviewed knowledge. The openness of Wikipedia and wikis in general helps to ensure accuracy. A person browsing the site who sees something he or she believes is wrong updates it. The openness of the information ensures its accuracy. This concept has taken freedom of the press to the nth degree, and it works.

Not only is Wikipedia as accurate (or inaccurate) as its land-based competitor, its primary advantage over print media is that it's quick. If your content has a need for speed, the wiki is the answer. A wiki is instant and can be updated without production or printing delays. If an expert within a company or a scientist working in a lab discovers something interesting, he or she can share it immediately, with no delay. More important, he or she can receive feedback and comments just as quickly.

This reminds me of the old saying, "If I have a penny and you have a penny and we exchange pennies, we each have a penny. But if I have an idea and you have an idea and we exchange ideas, now we each have two ideas"— and maybe even a third or fourth if the ideas spawn other thoughts and ideas.

The speed and ease of updating wikis has accelerated their adoption within several organizations. They are now commonly being used as a mechanism for transferring knowledge from the boomer generation of scientists, researchers, and others to the incoming gamer generation.

Fighting Cancer. The Leukemia & Lymphoma Society, the world's largest voluntary health organization dedicated to funding blood cancer research, education, and patient service, is employing a wiki to share best practices. With sixty-six chapters spread across the United States and Canada, the society has unique opportunities and issues in the dissemination and implementation of best practices. In addition to geographical dispersal of its operations, the society also faces staff turnover, varying levels of computer expertise, and the need to disseminate information in a manner compatible with existing computer systems.

The society's e-marketing team, which consists of staff ranging in age and abilities from gamers to baby boomers, worked together to employ a wiki to share best practices among chapters. The wiki provides a central location for best practices and an easy-to-use interface that anyone with typing and some minimal search capabilities can master. It is paying off in terms of building a knowledge base and the ability to provide best practices and training rapidly, according to Marty Siederer, the society's senior director of training and customer service. Siederer provides training for the organization's content management, mass e-mail distribution, and online fundraising systems. "The wiki gives us a method to connect our staff to best practices and much needed resources. Staff can share feedback and techniques," said Siederer. "We can instantly post and share best practices or training information to all of our staff members simply and easily. With the implementation of the wiki, we are able to post our resources electronically and reallocate the funds that would have been used to print manuals and training materials toward the Society's ultimate goals: cures for leukemia, lymphoma, and myeloma and improving the quality of life for patients and their families."[28]

Do I Know You?   One of the challenges of large, scientific-based organizations is the sharing of knowledge between boomers and gamers. How do you share knowledge across an organization with over seventy-five thousand employees? It is difficult sometimes even to know who knows what. Finding an expert or individuals within the company with similar interests can be difficult. You might meet a lot of people, but how do you know they have similar knowledge needs or have knowledge you require?

A large global pharmaceutical and health care company with decentralized training organizations is dealing with that issue. Their answer is to create an environment to foster an informal knowledge network—a linking together of expert wikis. This informal knowledge network connects learning professionals within the organization with peers, potential mentors, and other experts. The initiative involves the combination of social networking and wiki-based software, which provides learning professionals with the ability to identify, locate, and call on experts while fostering an environment for knowledge exchange and sharing within the organization.

The informal knowledge network is created by individuals who self-identify their expertise by way of knowledge profiles. The profile includes information about the person's line of business, area of expertise, areas of interest, and level of knowledge (novice to expert). The individuals and their knowledge profiles are mapped on a graphical configuration that resembles a target. Each person in the group is represented on the target by an individual pushpin. Each pin, or person, is arranged around the target in four quadrants: expertise, interest, work focus, and help sought (a generic example of the concept is shown in Figure 6.3). The software is supplied by introNetworks, a company located in San Barbara, California, that creates the social networking software for conferences, corporations, online communities, and organizations.

Figure 6.3. Social Networking Tool.

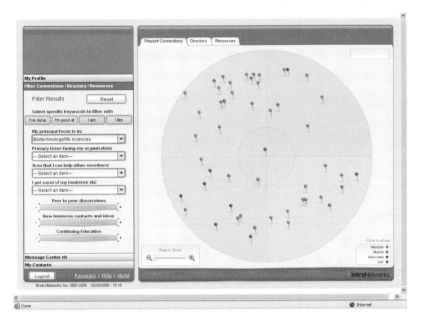

When a person within the network accesses the organizational knowledge map, he or she is represented in the middle of the target. The proximity of the pins within the four quadrants represents an affinity-mapping relationship, which individuals can use to seek each other to solve business problems, collaborate, and learn from each other. The pushpins can also represent articles, templates, vendors, events, and tools, thereby associating individuals with a variety of knowledge objects. In this framework, individuals are considered learning objects themselves, and once a user accesses the map, he or she can look for peers, references, and other resources across the network by filtering specific data within the network.

A member seeking expert information can link directly to the expert's information. The expert publishes information such as work instructions, concepts, policies, and work samples to the wiki-based software, the other technology used within this initiative. This content provides useful information to those who seek the knowledge from the expert, yet the expert does not need to be interrupted. Also, placing this knowledge on the wiki frees up the expert to pursue new ideas and continue to supply this community of practice with information and new opportunities for informal learning. The visitor can also post questions and add examples.

The designer of the system says the goal is to create a virtual community of practice that serves to achieve greater standardization and process among the company's global training organizations. This entails a virtual hub for the gathering, distribution, and creation of its training-related materials, such as process guides, instructional guidelines, best practices, and resource tools and templates. This community of practice will foster growing collaboration among the company's training and affiliate groups that will be the driving force in aligning training initiatives globally and reducing inconsistencies and duplication of work efforts.

Can You Hear Me Now? The National Center for Telecommunication Technologies (NCTT) was established in 1997 as a division of Springfield Technical Community College in Springfield, Massachusetts. Its mission is to provide community college educators in the area of information and communications technologies (ICT) with resources to stay current, relevant, and up-to-date in an ever-changing field. The NCTT is one of fourteen Advanced Technological Education Resource Centers of Excellence sponsored by the National Science Foundation.

NCTT disseminates information about fiber optics, wireless protocols, voice over Internet protocols (VoIP), television over Internet protocols (TVIP), geographic information systems (GIS), and other cutting-edge technologies to help community colleges across the country train tomorrow's ICT technicians and technologists. For companies to roll out these technologies, they need technicians trained in these areas. Much of that training of new workers and retraining of incumbents is done through community colleges.

The organization has authored a number of traditional textbooks but has found that almost as soon as the textbook is published, it contains obsolete information. To remedy this problem, the group is creating a wiki textbook around the topic of standards and protocols. The five-hundred-page book is already written, it will be posted online rather than published in the usual way. The book will be maintained by experts across the country and will be accessed by both community college educators and corporations that want to keep their technicians up-to-date. In fact, a major telecommunications company in New England is paying the authors responsible for the various chapters of the wiki book a monthly retainer to facilitate the collaboration process among the various authors of the chapter.

Gordon Snyder Jr., the executive director of NCTT, states, "The wiki will allow us to keep our classroom content up to date with the constant changes occurring in the Information and Communications Technology disciplines."[29] NCTT had no choice: if it wanted an up-to-date textbook, it had to publish in a format that allowed quick, easy access. It therefore needed to avoid the six to twelve months or longer that traditional publishing takes.

Really Simple Syndication

Gamers like to search for and find information on their own, but one problem they encounter is that they do not always know what to search for. It is the classic case of "you don't know what you don't know." Boomers who have been working within an organization for a while have knowledge of the context of the industry. They know what types of information are of value and what are not. New employees or individuals not familiar with the industry have no idea what is worth searching for and what is not. A common complaint among new employees is they are overwhelmed with the amount of information confronting them on the first few days of work.

An answer to this problem is the use of one or more RSS feeds. RSS represents the term *really simple syndication.* This Web technology allows a person to subscribe to a feed from a Web site and receive new information or content only when the original information is updated through a portal called an RSS aggregator. An RSS aggregator provides a consolidated view of the content in a single browser display or desktop application. One example is www.my.yahoo.com where you can establish your own page, complete with links to any RSS feed you desire. Instead of your searching for information, the information comes to you.

This is a pull technology rather than a push technology. The information is pulled to your desktop or customized Web page when updates occur based on your specific request. With push technology, information is delivered without your expressed consent. A good example of a push technology is spam e-mail. You don't request spam; it is pushed to your e-mail in-box.

RSS feeds can be effective for consulting firms, professors seeking to stay up-to-date, law firms, and government agencies like the Food and Drug Administration. Any organization or individual that deals with large amounts of constantly updated information can benefit from an RSS feed.

Government organizations are a prime example of continually changing rules and regulations: every time a law or policy is changed or reinterpreted, rules change. Government workers are constantly receiving e-mails about updated, changed, or clarified policies. RSS feeds can be established so changes, deletions, or additions to policies can be provided directly to subscribers who need the updated information, and not to everyone on the e-mail list.

For new employees, an organization could establish a Web page with RSS feeds from the departments relevant to that employee's role within the organization. A new employee working in the inventory department of a manufacturing firm, for example, could receive feeds from the shipping, inventory control, and human resource departments.

RSS can be used throughout the organization to transfer knowledge from one group of employees to another. Since just about any universal resource locator (URL), or Web address, can have its own RSS feed, the internal home page within an organization could consist of a number of RSS feeds to which employees subscribe. RSS has an advantage over e-mail distributions because it does not have any spam, can be organized by topic, and is easy to search.

It is even possible to create query-based searches on certain key information and receive the RSS feed only when it meets prespecified criteria—for example:

- Provide me with any feed from the Learning and Development department that contains the words "Lean" or "Quality" or "Six Sigma."

- I am not interested in everything that my instructional designers record about their projects, I only want to see any log entries containing the words "late," "deadline," "behind," or "delay."

- Send me the feed from the research and development department when the words "patent," "trademark," or "copyright" are included.

- Send me the information from the environmental health and safety department ONLY when the terms "violation," "problem," or "unmet certification requirements" appear.

This searchability can be critical when working in an organization producing a great deal of information. The proper use of an RSS feed can allow a person to glean just the information needed and not be overwhelmed with the hundreds of thousands of other pieces of information created within the organization on a daily basis. RSS feeds can be linked to blogs, pulling only the information indicated by the employee. The employee can always go to the internal blog and retrieve additional information.

Text Messaging

Text messages are short bursts of text sent from a computer or a cell phone directly to a cell phone. Once a text message is sent, information can be sent back or a text conversation can take place. Text messages can also be broadcast to a large number of people but are limited to 160 characters. "Texting," as it is called, has become so popular that the *Guinness Book of World Records* has set a standard that must be met to be deemed the fastest text messenger in the world. To be deemed the fastest in the world, you must send the message, "The razor-toothed piranhas of the genera Serrasalmus and Pygocentrus are the most ferocious freshwater fish in the world. In reality they seldom attack a human." You must use proper case with no predictive text. (Predictive text is when the digital phone completes common words for you.) A twenty-three-year-old Singapore woman named Kimberly Yeo Sue Fern received worldwide attention when she typed in the prescribed message in 43.2 seconds.[30]

Text messaging, or short message service (SMS), as it is sometimes called, is becoming increasingly popular among the gamer generation. It is particularly popular in Asia and Europe, with over 78 billion text messages sent every day in the United Kingdom alone.[31] In the United States, which is behind the rest of the world in text messaging, almost two out of every three cell phone subscribers between the ages of eighteen and twenty-seven use text messaging. This is in contrast to those over sixty years old: only 7 percent of cell phone subscribers send text messages.[32]

News services are also getting in on text messaging. Gannett, the publisher of *USA Today* and other print-based media, makes it possible for readers to get information such as weather reports, stock quotes, and flight information by sending a certain text message contained in the paper.

Google calls its service Google Short Message Service, or Google SMS. A cell phone user can send a message over a mobile phone and receive information back on, for example, dictionary definitions, driving directions, and answers to straightforward questions.

The advantages of using text messaging in a corporate environment are many. Text messages can be sent in meetings or in places where a conversation on the cell phone is not practical because of noise or other distracting working conditions. Text messaging is a convenient way of communicating with fellow employees and even customers. Text messages can be used to recruit for a new internal job or send an enterprisewide message from the president or a request for help in a particular area or to assemble a flash team. Text messaging can be used for transferring knowledge to gamers who could text-message questions and receive answers.

Searching What Is Searched

In addition to its search features, Google has another powerful tool, the Zeitgeist. It is "a tool that summarizes search terms that are gaining or losing momentum during a particular period of time. By watching and counting popular search terms, Zeigeist provides a fascinating summary of what our culture is looking for or finds interesting, and, conversely, what was once popular that is losing cultural momentum."[33]

Another site tracking favorites is http://del.icio.us, a "social bookmarking service that allows users to tag, save, manage, and share Web pages from a centralized source," which is helpful in building a community.[34] The real power is in finding out what Web sites and digital information others have bookmarked. The users of the site are building "a collaborative repository of related information, driven by personal interests and creative organization" visible to anyone on the Web.[35] The idea is that you can see what people think is popular or important by viewing what they have collectively bookmarked on the site.

Search terms and Web sites are not the only information tracked on the Web. Technorati tracks blogs: over 45.6 million blogs and over 2.6 billion links.[36] You can see the most popularly blogged terms, top tags, and most frequently visited blog sites.

Imagine tracking these areas within the corporate intranet. You could see what terms or tags are receiving the greatest number of search hits or what information is being discussed on the corporate blogs. You would know what was on the minds of employees. You would know what was of value to them as they went about their daily business. Is it the term *compliance, profits,* or *time off?*

Knowing the most frequently searched or tagged terms offers opportunities to provide additional information or training on areas of interest and need to employees. Proactive learning solutions could be offered to employees. The learning and development department wouldn't need to wait for requests or guess what areas need additional training or attention. In a pharmaceutical firm, if the term *oncology* had the most hits, a course or game could be developed to teach about oncology. If the term *inventory control* received the largest number of hits in a manufacturing firm, a class on the topic might be created.

The learning and development department would have a "database of intentions."[37] It would list every term, concept, topic, and expert perceived as having value to someone within the organization. The informal inquiries of the employees would be mined to create formal requests for learning interventions. The need would be identified and addressed.

The Ideal Learning Event

The best time to learn something is right before you need it. This is exactly the opposite of how most training programs work (for boomers and gamers). In many corporate training programs, you learn about a subject or topic in January, with the hope that you will recall that information in, say, June. In fact, the ideal learning event is quick and timely.

Gamers want to find the answer and quickly move on. One executive described the ideal learning event as occurring within five to ten minutes of realizing the need, customized to the situation, and providing just the right "trick" or insight needed to perform a specific task. Learning would thereby be embedded in the work flow.[38] The goal is to reduce learning to its smallest, most useful increments. Put the learner in charge of the entire process. Elliott Maisie, an e-learning industry analyst, calls this "nano learning."[39] Smaller learning chunks are being put into place in many organizations. One example is Novartis, a health care firm working in the areas of pharmaceuticals, consumer health, generics, eye care, and animal health. The learning team at Novartis has created a series of eight- to ten-minute modules to provide sales representatives with just the right knowledge at just the right time.

One of the uses of this approach is to help sales representatives interpret graphs contained within clinical studies. Often the graphs are rich with information but difficult to explain and understand without some training assistance. The training and development team at Novartis creates modules of no more than seven or eight screens, complete with a quiz, to provide instruction and assessment of the ten-minute module. The feedback the team receives is positive, with nearly 90 percent of the learners indicating that the ten minutes of learning was just what they needed.[40]

Cisco has set an upper limit of twenty minutes for its learning chunks. They have found that almost anybody will stay for ten to twelve minutes of content, no matter how mediocre it is; if it's bad, learners start to drop off at ten to twelve minutes, and even if it's really good, there is still a significant drop-off at twenty minutes. Cisco guidelines are twenty minutes, and there are very few things that exceed the twenty-minute chunks except for a reading like a white paper, which may take longer.[41] Whether it's video or audio or even text, it can be chunked into twenty minutes.

Learning events in a gamer-infested corporation need to be short, quick, to the point, and not necessarily linear. There is little desire among gamers to sit through a long classroom session or even long online session to learn one or two pieces of valuable information. And they don't want to go through information sequentially just because that is the way it is organized.

Gamers need systems to quickly and effectively provide information and knowledge. They want the site map or the index or the search feature so they can quickly access what they need and get back to work.

Perhaps the best way to think about providing information to gamers is in a just-in-time format with the learner accessing information exactly at the moment of need, learning all he or she needs at that instant, applying that information, and then subsequently forgetting that information. These gamers want a corporate YouTube where they can find the exact piece of video-based training they desire, view the training clip, and move on.

Workplace Implications

Although most gamers are comfortable with wikis, blogs, IM, nano learning, and other methods of informal knowledge transfer, many organizations do not have the infrastructure or culture to support these types of knowledge transfer channels. Boomer-controlled organizations are typically hierarchical in how they dispense and guard knowledge. Information comes from the top, knowledge is held in discrete departments or divisions, and people are informed on a need-to-know basis.

Informal channels need to be embraced for information to truly transfer to the incoming workers. Creating multiple channels to information will increase the transfer of knowledge and help foster a culture of sharing. Another critical step is to take the time to teach boomers, and even some gamers, how to use the tools of search engines to find the critical information. With information doubling and tripling yearly, the need to use search tools effectively is becoming increasingly critical for employees and students alike.

Creating Informal Learning Channels

The first step in creating informal learning channels is to define the type of information that will be searched for. Instead of trying to develop training objectives or carefully considering what every person needs to know, start with capturing and cataloguing everything about an application or business process and making the information searchable.

Next, interview boomers to find out what information they need to perform for their job. It is surprising how much information is missing from work instructions, policies, and procedures. Ask employees the following types of questions to see what information they would want to search for. Remember to ask veteran and newer employees. Sometimes new employees have great insights into what should have been taught to them but wasn't:

- What do you know now that you wish you had known earlier?

- What area of your job is causing you the greatest frustration?

- Have any coworkers taught you some tricks of the trade?

- What advice would you give to a new employee?

- What is the hardest thing to learn in this job?

- What causes you to make the most mistakes?

- Are there activities that you do infrequently and, therefore, are forced to look up the proper procedure for each time?

- What information do you find yourself looking up over and over again?

- What job aids or notes do you have by your workstation to remind you of actions that you need to take?

Asking these types of questions will help to clarify the types of information that people need to learn quickly and that are going to be referenced quickly.

The next step is to decompose the information into its smallest components. This step is so that you can meta-tag the information for a quick and easy search. When retrieving online data, gamers don't want pages and pages of text. They want just the piece of information they are looking for at that moment. Effective meta-tagging and indexing of information can be helpful in supplying the right information at the right time. Break the knowledge into easily digestible chunks. The most appropriate size seems to be about a page, although short paragraphs or sentences can be valuable as quick providers of information to an employee while he or she is working.

After that step is completed, decide on the best method for making the information available. This could be on an internal Web site with hyperlinks and site maps pointing to the right direction. It could be contained within the help system of an application. Some help systems have multiple levels of help that can be populated by the owners of the system.

I worked with an ERP system that had three levels of help. The first level was created by the software manufacturer and could not be changed. This was basic information about a particular field or other piece of information on the screen. The next level of help was company-level help, customizable by the organization that purchased the software. This was the place to input company procedures, policies, and recommended methods of processing information. The third level of help was individual help, which meant the employee could input his or her own information and reminders. It was basically an electronic sticky note placed inside the computer application rather than stuck on the monitor. Many systems already have these three levels of help built in or could have them added with relative ease.

Once the best method is determined, employees within the organization need to be taught the best methodology for retrieving the desired information. Often, creating more than one path to the information is the preferred method. You can create a site map, embed links into other programs, and provide an electronic job aid. The goal is to make the information easily and quickly accessible throughout the organization. This will enable the gamers to locate the information they need quickly, while keeping the original information in one place.

Teaching Tools

Just because information is available and searchable doesn't mean that everyone understands how to conduct a proper search. One task among developers of instruction is to create instruction on how to use information retrieval tools. Although gamers go to search engines, they are not always the most efficient searchers. John Batelle in his book about Google, *Search,* makes the following observation about how most people search: "We are incredibly lazy. We type in a few words at most, then expect the engine to bring back perfect results. More than 95 percent of us never use the advanced search features most engines include. . . . A quick study of common advanced search tricks will yield significantly better results. Most engines offer the ability to narrow a search by phrase, domain, file type, location, language, and number of results."[42]

Gamers taught how to use the tools effectively will be successful in applying those tools. The boomers must be taught the value of using tools. The boomer paradigm is geared more toward knowing content than knowing tools. For example, I frequently get calls from boomer clients who want to know a certain piece of information and call me hoping I will have that piece of information at my fingertips. They might want to know the different types of e-learning awards that can be won by an excellent e-learning course they are developing.

When I get that call, the first thing I do is access an online search engine and find what I need. My boomer client could have performed the same search, but the concept of searching for the information online doesn't occur to him. It is not ingrained in his thought pattern for information retrieval; instead, he is more comfortable and familiar with looking up a telephone number and calling someone who might know. Think of the time and effort he could have saved himself and me by simply conducting his own search.

An important element in providing information to employees is to teach them how to access the necessary information. It is impossible to teach employees everything that they will need to know to complete a job in an environment that is constantly changing, so teach them how to maximize their existing systems. Gamers know this and seem to spend more time learning the structure, that is, architectural elements of a software application, than the content. You can always look up the content.

Corporations need to take time to teach the layout of a job aid or help system and how to use it properly. This time will repay itself over and over again to the organization. The content in the help system may change, but the basic tenets of the system usually remain the same—something that organizations often overlook. For example, in one insurance agency, employees complained that although the release notes for the software were available for all new releases of the customer relationship management (CRM) software, the notes were too numerous and poorly laid out to be of much value to them. The employees did not like scrolling through 100 to 150 notes to find the one specific to their department. They had been using the scrolling technique for about a year and for the most part had abandoned the process of looking up new items in the release notes.

One day a representative from the CRM software company was visiting for another reason and noticed one of the employees scrolling through the long list of release notes. She was impressed that an employee was looking over all the notes and reading about all the changes. When she complimented the employee on her interest in the software and her commitment to reading all the notes, the employee replied that she had no interest in reading all of the notes and was looking only for notes that pertained to her department.

The representative from the software company showed her how to search and sort the release notes by department and by subject. She was grateful and spread the news to her coworkers. The number of hours that must have been wasted by that person and company looking through release note after release note must have been in the hundreds of hours—time they could have spent far more profitably on other endeavors.

While software functionality changes with each release of an application, the functionality of online help or searching and sorting conventions rarely changes. Once an employee knows how to use an online help system, he or she then has a new and powerful tool to retrieve information. Most gamers are familiar with the concept of these tools and need to know only the nuances of an organization's particular tool.

This is similar to how a gamer is able to pick up a particular genre of game and know exactly the goal of the game and how to play. He or she can pick up a first-person shooter and tell you what you need to do: shoot everyone in sight. Or tell you how to play an online role-play game. You need to find clues hidden around the game world and then solve a problem to move onto the next level. The gamer can tell you what you need to do in a simulation game like *Roller Coaster Tycoon*. Gamers understand the genre and the basics, even though the simulation might change from building an amusement park to building a school or a zoo.

Just as gamers know the general parameters of certain game types, employees need to be taught the general conventions of help systems and search tools. This knowledge is transferable from one situation to another. Once they learn this skill, they can apply it to seeking information from a variety of informal learning sources such as wikis, blogs, and archived IM chats. The ability to find the right information at the right time is a critical skill.

■ ■ ■ ■

SUMMARY

The convenience of search engines and the speed at which millions of pages of information can be searched have created an expectation of instant information. Blogs, wikis, and instant messaging can make information available in a few seconds. Organizations that want gamers to tap into these knowledge sources need to find methods of integrating them into the fabric of the everyday lives of their employees. When gamers need information to do their jobs or homework, they expect the information to be at their fingertips. Organizations that do not supply this type of information access will have trouble surviving.

In addition, methods need to be developed to codify boomer knowledge into systems and machines so that the machine or system actually teaches the operator. This will eliminate the gamers' need to look up information, because it will already be embedded in the work flow process. Learn in the next chapter how this can be done.

Replace Education
with Automation

I WAS GETTING DESPERATE for some money the summer between my freshman and sophomore years in college. I couldn't find a job anywhere. Rent was due, and there was no food in the fridge. I even considered canceling my cable subscription. Finally I learned of an opening for a cashier at a branch of a national drugstore chain. It was my last resort.

Securing the position was not easy. The interview process was intense. It involved a battery of tests: psychological, drug, and mathematical. I did satisfactorily on all three and was hired. Finally I had a job. It lasted three days.

After the end of my shift the first day, the amount of money in my drawer compared to the amount indicated by the register tape was off by five cents. Not bad for a beginner. The second day it was $2.50, and the third day it was closer to $5.00. I left voluntarily.

The problem was doing math under pressure. Sure, I could do the math on a paper-and-pencil test when I didn't have fifteen people in line waiting to buy lottery tickets and toothpaste without exact change. But calculating change in a pressured situation, I got flustered and gave the wrong amount. Some people told me, and some people kept the extra change.

Today I walk into a drugstore and hand the clerk a fifty-dollar bill for a can of soda (Figure 7.1). The clerk doesn't calculate the change; the cash register does. For that matter, the clerk doesn't need to know any math or psychology; I doubt he or she even takes a math test to qualify for the job. The need for education was replaced by an innovation: an automated cash register that calculates change correctly every time. It never feels the pressure of a line of ten people waiting to buy a lottery ticket before their lunch hour ends.

Figure 7.1. The Cash Register Makes Change So the Clerk Doesn't Need To.

Source: Reprinted with permission of the artist, Kristin Longenecker.

If you look at what is happening in airports, supermarkets, hotels, and convenience stores, you will notice a shift toward customer-automation interfaces. At the airport, you can use a kiosk to check in for your flight, check your baggage, and receive a claim ticket and boarding pass. Customers themselves now do the entire process of checking in at the airport. The kiosk is so easy to use that you don't require any training; you just follow the instructions on the screen.

At the supermarket, you can check yourself out after you have gathered all your groceries. There is no need to train teenage or older workers how to use the cash register. Customers are learning how to do it themselves and in half the time. At many convenience stores, you can order your own sandwich at a kiosk, and the clerk behind the counter gets an automated printout of the order, with no need for training on how to take an order or ensure accuracy.

Innovation Trumps Education

It doesn't always make sense to teach people. Sometimes it is better to automate the process and eliminate the need for training. Training is time-consuming, expensive, and not always effective. In fact, many software training programs, classes, and manuals are necessary because the designers of the software did not take the time to think through how it would be used.

One time we were called into a public welfare agency to address the problems of training new caseworkers how to use the automated client tracking software. We took one look at the software and said, "First, you need to redo the interface. This will cut your training time in half." After the officials from the welfare agency got up off the floor from laughing so hard, they said, "No, really, what kind of training classes can you provide?" The problem was that they had no control over the software interface, which was hard to use; it had obscure data labels, no logic behind the grouping of fields, and no thought to how caseworkers interact and relate to their welfare clients when meeting with them face-to-face or speaking with them over the phone. Caseworkers had been consulted only once during the entire software development process.

While the baby boomer caseworkers begrudgingly dealt with the system, the newly hired gamers were appalled. They had never seen software this difficult to use. The agency had to update the interface; there was no way they could spend the amount of time or energy necessary to train all the new employees. It is amazing how much organizations spend on training and education to help employees cope with poorly designed hardware and software.

The national drugstore chain obviously went to great lengths—three tests and an interview—to determine if a potential employee had the right skills, but even then the results weren't perfect. From an overall perspective, it is much less expensive to invest in change-calculating cash registers than in a course titled "Making Change Under Pressure" for every new clerk. Even an expensive, elaborate employee selection process can still put an unfit or unproductive employee behind the cash register.

The same thinking needs to be applied to workforce learning needs. What can be done to automate the simple, error-prone processes that require a high level of training? What can be done to automate complex processes that require intensive training? Too often organizations spend time and money conducting training or providing e-learning events because the system is not smart enough to handle mundane, repetitive, non-value-added tasks. Look at your organization's processes, and identify opportunities to replace training with automation. It is being done all around you.

Are We There Yet?

In high school, I literally had a lesson on how to fold a map, part of a six-week class on how to read and use maps. I vividly remember the lesson because it confounded me how refolding a simple piece of paper could be so frustrating. I always had the last flap inside out. Instead of the nice map cover, I had an obscure piece of Pennsylvania highway on the front. I did not do well folding a map and only a little better reading it.

When I got older, all of my jobs required me to travel (someone has a warped sense of humor). Therefore, various types of maps in various stages of being folded were shoved into the glove compartment of my car—just enough so it would close. The maps had highlighter all over them from my efforts to determine the quickest route to my destination. Then one day, after being forced to take my car because hers was in the shop, my wife bought me an atlas. It had all the maps neatly in a book I could keep on the front seat. It was a great improvement for the aesthetics of my car.

Then a few years ago, I started to use automated directions from the Internet: all I needed to do was type in my home address and the destination address. My printer would instantly provide turn-by-turn directions and even small pictures of the route highlighted in purple. I received a printed set of instructions guiding me to my final destination. I could throw away my atlas.

Whenever I traveled, the electronic directions provided pinpoint accuracy for about 99 percent of the trip, but the last 5,280 feet were always wrong, leading me to believe that gas stations created the Web-based directions so drivers would stop in and ask for directions. It was also a little daunting trying to read the directions at sixty miles an hour to determine whether I should get off at the upcoming exit, which inevitably was three lanes over.

Another unfortunate side effect was that my car now had dozens of sheets of paper scattered about. Every trip required one set of directions for my destination and one set for the return trip. If I wanted to take a side trip, I needed to print directions for that jaunt as well. These directions were a definite improvement over maps, since they didn't need folding, but my car was back to being a mess.

Enter global positioning system (GPS) technology. I now have a small device that looks like a tiny television monitor stuck on the inside of my windshield and plugged into the outlet of my car. This GPS receiver, no bigger than six inches, displays a map showing the route I need to follow and providing a visual image of my car on the highway. It also gives me verbal turn-by-turn directions from a female voice named "Jill." It has eliminated both my need to print directions from the Internet and the danger of trying to read instructions while flying down the road. Technology has replaced the need to teach people how to read (and fold) maps, and it made my car neater (Figure 7.2).

Figure 7.2. Evolution of Getting from Point A to Point B.

Source: Author.

The next step may be intelligent vehicles that guide themselves. The U.S. Department of Transportation is working on the Intelligent Vehicle Initiative, a program that will create smart cars with the abilities to "give route directions, sense objects, warn drivers of impending collisions, automatically signal for help in emergencies, keep drivers alert, and may ultimately be able to take over driving."[1] Eventually we won't even need driving lessons. Automation will replace education.

Don't Educate, Automate

With training programs becoming more and more expensive for both stand-up and online delivery, a faster, more efficient remedy is to replace educational requirements with automation. As boomers start to retire, their knowledge and know-how need to be automated into devices and software applications for internal employees and customers.

Most automation projects focus on streamlining processes, integrating two or more existing systems, removing humans from danger, or eliminating redundant data entry. These are all good reasons for automation, but they are not enough to bridge the gap between boomers and gamers. The designers of software applications and hardware devices must team up with learning and development professionals to incorporate education into software, hardware, and other human-device interfaces and designs.

The next generation of software and hardware devices must not only perform its desired function from an operational standpoint; it must also teach the humans using it how to do their job. Learning must be built into systems so humans do not have to learn what the hardware or software can do for them. They need to learn as they are using the software or device in a type of just-in-time learning. The device or software must do its job automatically and coach or teach the human when and how it wants information, feedback, or data.

In manufacturing, there is a technique called "poka-yoke," which means mistake-proofing a process. The idea is to create a method that prevents the wrong activity from occurring. It could be that a piece of metal to be cut can be placed on the cutter machine in only one way because of the placement of guides and the measurements of the metal. Or it could be that a sensor on an assembly process shuts down a machine if the material in it is out of spec. The idea is that potential mistakes made by a new employee or someone else unfamiliar with the process cannot be made because the process itself has built-in safeguards.

Replacing education with automation requires knowing what is possible. You need to examine technologies used in other industries and within the consumer electronics realm and determine what can be applied to your situation. Begin with these questions:

- How do you currently interface with the computer? Is it the best way?

- Can you get away from using the keyboard or mouse?

- Can you use natural human movements or voice?

- Can the computer figure out what you already know and then just give the information you don't know?

- Can the computer act more like a person in both looks and language?

- Can you make the interface with your gadgets better?

- Can you create a virtual but realistic environment in which you can do both realistic activities and fantastic activities—like flying over a "sea" of stocks color-coded to indicate price increases or decreases.

Let's try to answer some of these questions by looking at what is possible.

Is It Hot in Here?

In a manufacturing plant, the operations manager conducted the same training class about every six months to teach his oven operators how to read a series of temperature gauges on an oven. There were four gauges that had to be read and interpreted to modify and adjust the baking temperature. After six months, everyone forgot how to read the gauges.

The ovens baked porcelain insulators for use on high-voltage power lines. If the temperature was too low, the insulation factor wasn't high enough, and if it was too high, the porcelain insulators cracked. The ovens were extremely large and took a long time to cool down and heat up. Maintaining a constant temperature was a key productivity factor.

Finally, the operations manager hired a training and development firm to create a training class. He figured that maybe his instruction wasn't good enough and that that was the reason the operators began misreading the gauges after every six months.

The team came in and designed an elaborate training program with multimedia elements, hands-on instruction, and a variety of other learning strategies to ensure that the operators knew how to read, interpret, and adjust all the gages. The class was well received.

After about six months, performance dropped. Gauges were misread, insulators cracked, and productivity slowed. Desperate, the operations manager called another training and development firm. He was not happy with the first one since performance once again had dropped after six months.

The second firm conducted an extensive needs analysis of the learners, the environment, and the skills gap. They determined that the operators of the oven work cell had a high rate of turnover and that one-third of all operators in that area had been on the job only six months. It was hot, difficult work, and whenever another position opened up in the plant, the operators bid on that new position.

The learning and development firm decided not to create training. Instead, they told the operations manager to invest in a digital readout system. The new system would have temperature sensors placed on the oven and would provide both a number reading of the temperature and a red, yellow, and green indicator light to let operators know when the temperature needed to be adjusted. The new system eliminated the need to invest in a difficult training process; in fact, the operators now needed only fifteen minutes of instruction on how to read the gauge and what to do for the various colors of the indicator light. The automation of the temperature gauges eliminated the entire problem.

That Ain't Fast

I was doing some work in a plant that makes breakfast pastries. Each line made about fifteen hundred pastries a minute, and there were bins of discarded pastries everywhere. You could put on fifty pounds just nibbling on scraps.

Several years ago, the plant had three people sitting at the end of the machines looking for bad pastries. A bad pastry doesn't have a problem with the taste or flavor; it is visually unappealing. The filling is leaking or the topping is not centered or there is a visible tear or dough on the pastry. Literally dozens of things could cause a bad pastry, which was then identified and removed from the line by one of the three workers. To do this job, a person needed at least five years of experience, sharp eyesight, and some self-motivation to stay focused on identifying the bad pastries. If one was missed, it would be packaged and sent to a consumer, who presumably would be unhappy with the visually repulsive pastry.

At some point, the plant implemented a machine that photographs the breakfast pastries as they are coming off the production line and compares the photographs with images of good pastries: a pastry deemed bad is eliminated. The knowledge of how to identify a bad pastry was transferred from the three people sitting at the end of the production line to an innovative system. The goal of eliminating education with innovation was achieved. We can all rest more easily knowing that our breakfast pastries will be visually appealing.

I told this story to a person working in the medical device industry once and she said, "Fifteen hundred a minute scanned, photographed, and compared to an ideal. That ain't fast; we scan thirty-five hundred tubes a minute."

iPod's Wheel

How are the controls for your machinery configured? Are the tools you use to conduct your business easy or complicated? Can rethinking the human-device interface of your gadgets increase productivity and knowledge transfer?

One reason Apple's iPod technology was so popular compared to other MP3 or digital audio players (DAPs) was its interface. Apple was not the first company to produce a DAP player. In fact, several companies already had DAP players on the market and were doing reasonably well with the technology. One was Compaq's Personal Jukebox-100 (PJB-100), introduced in 1999. It was a 30 gigabyte portable music player that weighed nine and a half ounces, could fit in a pocket, and had ten hours of battery life.[2] Compaq even received a patent on the item, but it never took off.

In 2001, Apple released the iPod, which immediately took off. The difference? The iPod's intuitive interface wheel and the hierarchically ordered graphical user interface available on the device. Apple has filed patent number 20040055446 to protect the hierarchically ordered graphical user interface. The wheel and interface allow quick scrolling with one hand through the playlist of songs. This simple design helped to fuel the popularity. There were no buttons to push for volume or selection, and no manual was needed to explain how to play your favorite songs.

Let the Music Play

Computer interfaces are historically difficult to use. The graphical user interface everyone talks about isn't graphical at all. Liveplasma.com (http://www. liveplasma.com) is an exception. This software is a musical database of popular singers and bands that has an intuitive, easy-to-use interface. It is completely visual, with three simple elements providing the user interface: color, size, and proximity.

Bands or singers are grouped according to interest, style, and other criteria that indicate how much someone would enjoy one band as compared to others. Each band appears as a colored sphere shown on a map of linked spheres. Color indicates how much a band influenced other bands or how related one band is to another. Bands shown in shades of the same color indicate a relationship between those bands. For example, the Beatles are in one shade of yellow and, as separate artists, John, George, Paul, and Ringo are in slightly different yellow shades. Roy Orbison is shown in a shade of green.

Since both George Harrison and Roy Orbison played in the Traveling Wilburys, that group is shown as a yellowish-green sphere, indicating a relationship with both artists.

The size of the sphere indicates the popularity of the band. The sphere for the Beatles is extremely large compared to the four individual members and to other groups like the Traveling Wilburys or singers like Britney Spears.

Another level of information is contained in the proximity of one sphere to another. The closer one band or singer is to your favorite band, the greater are the chances of your liking that other band; the farther away, the less similar the musical styles are. Britney Spears is shown in close proximity to Christina Aguilera and Jessica Simpson but farther away from Sheryl Crow and Alanis Morissette.

This type of interface is easy to learn, contains critical information available at a glance, and can be applied to a variety of content types. It could be used to look at sales data, production information, or organizational expenses. Once the principles of the interface are learned, they can be applied to a variety of content, virtually eliminating the need for training on how to use the software.

Do You See What I See?

Do we always need to type information into a computer? Isn't there a better alternative? One small item enabling a unique human-computer interface is Sony's EyeToy, a small camera that connects to the PlayStation 2 game platform and picks up audio and visual signals. The camera sits on top of the television or on the floor and tracks movements of anyone standing in front of it. The movements are broadcast through the PlayStation 2 to the television screen. Every movement done in front of the EyeToy is reflected on the screen. The "game" part comes into play when the system overlays images on top of your image and the two interact (Figure 7.3).

There is a Kung Fu game where you battle cartoon ninjas. Your feet and hand movements are tracked, and when the EyeToy detects the proper movement in the proper area, you score a hit against your cartoon foe. Other games

Figure 7.3. Author's Gamer 4.0 Son Playing Fun EyeToy Game.

Source: Author.

allow you to hit soccer balls, box a robot, or even catch the snitch with the EyeToy-enabled game *Harry Potter and the Prisoner of Azkaban.*

One game, *EyeToy: Operation Spy,* contains a storyline in which you are an agent working for Strategic Intelligence Agency (SIA). In the mission, you skydive, break codes, and search city neighborhoods for criminal masterminds, all while interacting with combined images of yourself and the virtual environment on the television screen.

It seems like just another interesting toy until you realize that EyeToy and the spy game can be used to record movements within the room when the television appears to be turned off. Crude but effective facial recognition software allows you to set a security code so that the game will recognize only the person who set it up. Anyone who enters the room will see a blank screen and not realize that the elements of the game, including alarms and the ability to covertly record anyone not recognized by the system, are being employed. It's pretty sophisticated stuff for a child's toy.

Another game for the EyeToy shows even more potential for transferring knowledge from boomers to gamers. *EyeToy Kinetic* is designed to provide at-home exercises with all of the benefits of working with a professional trainer. The game puts you in instant contact with a professional, private virtual trainer who guides you through one of twenty-two workouts. You determine the sequence and level of difficulty for the workouts, and the trainer then walks you through the process. Each workout provides verbal instructions as well as images on the screen with which you interact. With games like *EyeToy: Kinetic,* the EyeToy camera moves from a child's plaything to a tool for general fitness. It basically provides a mentor who can provide you with instruction, evaluate your actions, and give real-time targeted feedback.

Taking the concept further, organizations could create EyeToy interactions for any type of physical movement that had to be learned. Classes on the proper method of lifting heavy objects could be placed into an EyeToy type of environment to track movement and provide feedback on whether you were using the proper technique. You could work on a virtual piece of equipment with the controls overlaid on the screen. If you operated the controls incorrectly, you would receive corrective feedback. The advantage over the standard keyboard interface for simulation or equipment emulation is that you would be doing the same kinetic motions as you would do on the actual piece of machinery. You would build muscle memory as well as learn the proper techniques.

Other nonkeyboard interfaces are catching on as well. One example is Dance, Dance Revolution, a game series developed by the Japanese company Konami that features a dance mat linked to a game console. The mat has four squares, each with an arrow indicating up, down, left, and right. The player observes the arrows on the screen, which indicate which arrows they should land on with their feet. The game is typically set to music, and the steps are reminiscent of the shoeprints that were put on a dance floor to teach novices how to dance. The game has evolved to teach complicated game moves and multiplayer online versions where dancers meet virtually and compete against each other.

Another example is the biofeedback game *Journey to the Wild Beyond* (which can be found at www.wilddivine.com). To play the game, you hook up your fingers to three biofeedback sensors that measure heart rate variability and skin conductance. You progress through the game by eliciting certain reactions from your body. Sometimes you are required to relax and focus your breathing, and other times you are encouraged to breathe faster or to laugh. The idea is to teach you how to connect your body and spirit through interactions throughout the game, all the while learning breathing and meditation techniques in a rich multimedia environment.

Anthropomorphics Are Your Friends

A project under development at Florida State University and funded in part by the National Science Foundation is creating anthropomorphic interface agents called avatars, or in lay terms, virtual trainers. The concept is to create online pedagogical agents or avatars that can act as an instructor or trainer providing guidance and motivation when the learner needs it.

These animated trainers provide learners with assistance through gestures, voice, and image. They guide learners through the information in the same way a trainer or instructor assists a learner in the physical world. But because they are computer generated, each virtual trainer can be chosen by the learner to be the gender, age, or ethnicity that the learner desires. Amy L. Baylor, founder of the Center for Research of Innovative Technologies for Learning, which is creating these virtual trainers, has found that learners tend to choose virtual trainer types similar in ethnicity to themselves. She has also found that female avatars seem to be better than male versions at motivating learners.

The customizability of the avatars means a learner can choose to learn from a wise old mentor or a hip young person. Gamers, who are used to building their own players in video games, can now construct their own on-line trainers, tutors, or mentors. These trainers can assist learners to learn new information or be available from time to time when they detect that the learner needs help.

The concept of providing virtual help in the form of a computerized assistant is not new. Microsoft Word has several virtual trainers who can help users through the ins and outs of the word processing program. They are known as the Office Assistant. None of them are in the form of a customizable person but they are in the form of paperclips and a cute dog (Figure 7.4). The Office

---

Figure 7.4. Microsoft Word's Office Assistant.

Source: Screen shot reprinted by permission from Microsoft Corporation.

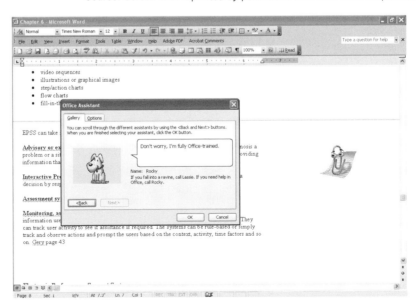

Assistant (if you have it turned on) appears with answers and suggestions whenever you ask or whenever it detects you are trying to perform a particular function, like writing a letter.

Combine the context-sensitive help features of the Office Assistant with the humanlike qualities of a virtual person, and you can have a powerful tool for transferring knowledge. Virtual assistants can eventually behave like actual mentors. They can "get angry" if you make the same mistake over and over again, add some humor, or even provide stress relief while you perform a difficult function.

It is even possible to create virtual trainers that look like influential people from a person's past. A customizable trainer who has the wisdom of a boomer but the looks of a gamer might be an effective method of providing information from the boomers to the gamers. Adding a virtual human to a computer application can make the application seem more comfortable and fun for people who have grown up with games and virtual players.

There is one caution about avatars and online mentors. Avoid the uncanny valley, the phenomenon put forth by Masahiro Mori, a *Japanese* robotics scientist noted for his pioneering work on the emotional response of humans to nonhuman entities, in the 1970s. The theory states that as a robot or other animated figure becomes more humanlike in its movements and appearance, the emotional response to the figure becomes more favorable, but only up until a certain point.[3] People can relate easily to explicitly nonhuman characters like an animated dog, cat, or ninja turtle because when we interact with a highly stylized or abstract avatar, we are not "so much eliminating details as we are focusing on specific details."[4] By stripping down an image to its essential meaning, a designer of an online avatar can allow the learner to feel comfortable interacting with the avatar, because the basic human elements are there and the learner fills in the rest. At a certain point, however, the theory argues, the animated figure becomes too humanlike to be considered nonthreatening but not human enough for us to feel comfortable with. If a designer attempts to create a 100 percent realistic avatar and the technology isn't there yet, the learner becomes "creeped out" by the avatar and can't relate. The figure will have certain human attributes but not enough.

Eventually the technology will allow avatars to move past the uncanny valley and become so humanlike that interactions with the avatar or animated figure can again be favorable, like the android named Data from *Star Trek: The Next Generation.* This is the goal of the developers of avatars: a humanlike mentor that can act, speak, and interact like a human. Currently, we are climbing our way out of the uncanny valley but haven't done it yet.

You Should Know Jack

Did you ever try to carry on a conversation with an avatar? It's impossible. They're distant, drift in and out of the conversation, speak off-topic, and generally don't pay attention to a word you say. Verbally interfacing with computers always seems forced, unnatural, and stilted. The illusion of talking with a person is just not there; you always know you are speaking with a computer.

One notable exception is the game *You Don't Know Jack,* first released in 1995 (Figure 7.5). It is a trivia game in which an announcer interacts with the players of the game as if they were all in the same room or studio. The announcer uses a combination of humor and direct-response interactivity. He remembers whether you got the last answer correct and encourages you to "hurry up and pick an answer" if you hesitate too long. He talks to you as if he was standing right in front of you watching what you are doing.

Jellyvison, the developers of the game, purposefully set out to create a computer-human interface that is realistic and fun. It calls its interface the Interactive Conversation Interface (iCi for short, pronounced "icky"). Using the "iCi interface, Jellyvision seeks to give every digital device the ability to communicate information and ideas with such seamless pacing and awareness, such personality and wit, that it feels like a real person is just behind the machine" (Figure 7.6). When you play the game, you know they've succeeded.

Figure 7.5. User Manual Cover from 1995 *You Don't Know Jack* Game.

Figure 7.6. Using iCi Interface Conventions to "Talk" to a Person Through the Data Entry Process.

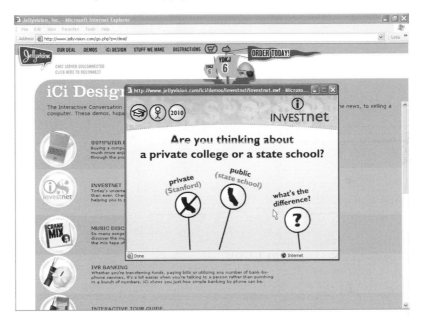

An enabler of the iCi interface is a set of guidelines known as the Jack Principles:

- Maintaining pacing
- Creating the illusion of awareness
- Maintaining the illusion of awareness

These principles need to be in any software program trying to create the illusion of conversation or interaction with the person sitting in front of the computer.

Maintaining Pacing. Pacing is the flow of the program, that is, how closely the program follows what the learner is doing. It means paying attention to the timing of events. Eight ideas are contained in the principle of pacing:

1. Give the user only one task to accomplish at a time.

2. Limit the number of choices the user has at any one time.

3. Give the user only meaningful choices.

4. Make sure the user knows what to do at every moment.

5. Focus the user's attention on the task at hand.

6. Use the most efficient manner of user input.

7. Make the user aware that the program is waiting.

8. Pause, quit, or move on without the user's response if it doesn't come soon enough.

Creating the Illusion of Awareness. The goal of the interaction between the person and the computer is to provide the illusion that the computer is aware of the person sitting in front of it. This illusion of awareness can be created by responding to the person's actions with human intelligence and emotion. Specifically, the computer responds to:

1. The user's actions

2. The user's inactions

3. The user's past actions

4. A series of the user's actions

5. The actual time and space that the user is in

6. The comparison of different users' situations and actions

Maintaining the Illusion of Awareness. The final main principle is to maintain the illusion of awareness. It is one thing to create the illusion up front; the goal is to continue the illusion throughout the interaction with the person. This can be accomplished in the following way:

1. Use dialogue that conveys a sense of intimacy.

2. Make sure characters act appropriately while the user is interacting.

3. Make sure dialogue never seems to repeat.

4. Be aware of the number of simultaneous users.

5. Be aware of the gender of the user.

6. Make sure the performance of dialogue is seamless.

7. Avoid the presence of characters when user input cannot be evaluated.

These principles have been applied to far more than games. The folks at Jellyvision have used the concept of iCi design to create programs to help a person choose the right computer, learn about investing, and participate in a virtual tour guided by a friendly voice using a cell phone.[5]

Just Tell Me What I Need to Know

The traditional classroom environment is based on a one-size-fits-all paradigm. Anyone who needs to learn a topic is marched into a classroom, and regardless of previous knowledge, everyone receives the same lecture.

Back in the early nineteenth and twentieth centuries, if you wanted truly customized training, an apprenticeship was established. The learner would receive one-on-one instruction tailored specifically to his or her needs. This provided an excellent learning environment. The learner did not spend time covering already known information, because the focus was on new information and specific content. A mentor who had two people serving as an apprentice would provide slightly different information to each based on what they knew or did not know. Unfortunately, apprenticeships are not feasible for large numbers of people; they are too labor intensive. If you have five thousand people in an organization or attending a college, all five thousand could not have a one-to-one or even two-to-one apprentice-mentor model. It would be too expensive.

When the Internet was introduced as a tool to deliver instruction, the boomer paradigm of providing everyone with the same course materials was continued. If you needed to take a course on something like basic accounting principles, you logged onto a learning management system and took the same course as everyone else, even if you already had some knowledge of accounting. There was no customization. The ability of technology to adapt to the learner was not exploited.

Organizations need to take advantage of the ability of technology to create adaptive learning systems, which provide learners with only the information they do not know. These systems provide customized instruction in the same way a mentor provides customized instruction to his or her apprentice. Figure 7.7 shows the different types of instruction and the number of people that each can effectively instruct. It is possible that with the advent of databases and logic trees, the Internet can be applied as a delivery mechanism to provide customized instruction to thousands of people.

Figure 7.7. Types of Instruction and the Number of People They Instruct.

Source: Author.

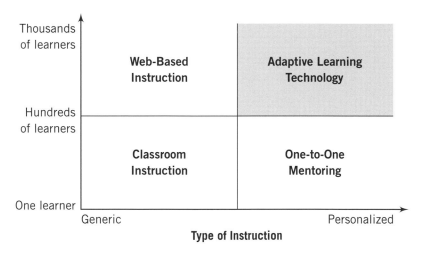

One method of providing this customized instruction is to pretest the learner on the content to be presented. At the beginning of a lesson, the learner answers a series of questions, each linked to a specific topic. When the learner answers a question correctly, the material that question encompasses is not presented in the lesson. Therefore, the only content presented to the learner during the lesson is that related to questions missed during the pretest. Using this method, personalized instruction can be provided quickly and easily to thousands of employees or students.

Another method is for the learning system to be tied into a mission critical software application like a customer relationship management system. The system could be programmed to detect a user's errors or mistakes and then, based on those mistakes, it could provide instruction. This is a more advanced system and requires tying the learning system into a mission-critical system, but it provides the type of just-in-time learning that can be of benefit to new gamer employees.

Work Flow Learning

In the training field, one of the tools for replacing education with automation is called an electronic performance support system (EPSS). These systems are designed to provide guidance, help, and assistance to people performing their job duties. This concept has also been referred to as work flow learning, meaning that the learning occurs within the natural flow of work and is not separate from a person's daily work tasks.

The pioneer of the concept of EPSS is Gloria Gery, who wrote a book titled *Electronic Performance Support Systems: How and Why to Remake the Workplace through the Strategic Application of Technology.* In that book, she defines the goal of an EPSS as providing "whatever is necessary to generate performance and learning *at the moment of need.*" She points out that the common "denominator that differentiates an electronic performance support system from other types of systems or interactive resources is the degree to which it *integrates information, tools, and methodology* for the user."[6]

One such system is a Web-based if-then chart. The chart is used when a sales representative is on the telephone with a customer. When the sales representative is attempting to sell a product and encounters an objection, the table contains the objection and a link to another page indicating what the sales representative should say in response. This means that the sales representative does not need to learn all of the possible objections and responses in a class six months prior to ever encountering a particular objection. The sales representative simply needs to be taught how to use the if-then chart. He or she can quickly navigate the chart and respond to inquiries, sales objections, or other information required by customers, all without ever having to learn or memorize the information, as shown in Figure 7.8.

Figure 7.8. Web-Based If-Then Chart for a Customer Sales Representative.

Source: Author.

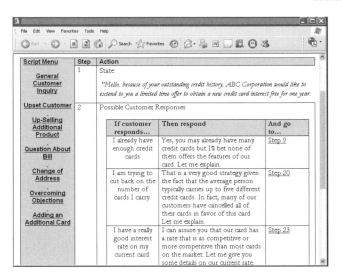

Another example is the help that appears as you are completing a form, as shown in Figure 7.9.

The goal of any EPSS is to support the person in his or her job and replace education with automation so the level of training is reduced or eliminated. EPSS can take many forms, and many systems are a combination of several of these systems:[7]

• Advisory or expert system. This is a system that walks the user through steps to diagnose a problem or a situation. It can lead the user through a process of completing a form or providing information that is required for an

Figure 7.9. Online Assistance for Properly Completing a Form.

Source: Author.

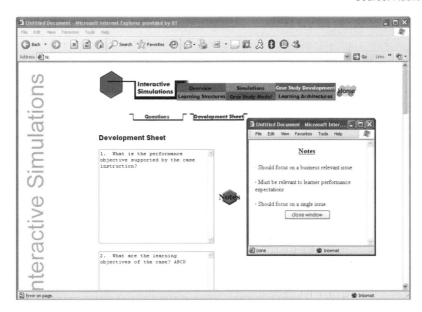

activity. Increasingly, these systems are taking the end user through the system. For example, *TurboTax* provides step-by-step instructions needed to complete complex tax forms. In the past, many people hired accountants to help prepare their tax return; today many people do this work using *TurboTax.*

• Interactive productivity software. This includes online tools that help users make a decision by responding to a series of questions or troubleshooting a problem. This is the online guide that helps you troubleshoot your printer or router by asking you a series of questions, each question drilling down into more specific questions until the system ultimately solves the problem or instructs you to call the support desk.

• Assessment system. This system assesses the user's proficiency. This is the adaptive learning technology process explained previously in this chapter.

• Monitoring, assessment, and feedback. These systems observe user activity and can give information to users about the appropriateness of their actions with the software or device. They can track user activity to see if assistance is required. The systems can be rule based or simply track and observe actions and prompt users based on the context, activity, time factors, and so on. An example of this type of EPSS that many people are familiar with is the Office Assistant in MS Word.

Workplace Implications

To replace educational needs with automation, look at existing processes and identify those with a high potential for return if automated. Several elements can indicate if a process or a device is ripe for replacing education with automation:

- Calculations or formulas. Computers were made for calculating information and working through formulas. Computers are fast, efficient, and accurate. If you find a process that requires an individual to add, subtract, multiply, or divide, chances are that the process can be embedded into the software application or device, and the educational burden can be taken off humans.

- High degree of choice. The best examples of these types of systems are the kiosks at airports and convenience stores. These types of arrangements can also be found at financial Web sites. The visitor to the site answers questions about risk tolerance, allocation choices, and other information, and a model profile is created. The visitor can then arrange his or her assets to match the recommended portfolio.

- Requires trained observation skills. This suggestion may seem counterintuitive, but it is not. If you are involved in a manufacturing process and the correctly manufactured items must look just so, a system can be put into place to scan the product, compare it to an ideal, and eliminate any product not matching the ideal, all within a few seconds. This is done frequently in the manufacturing of food items and precision tools.

- High transactional volume. Sometimes a process that is performed over and over again is an excellent candidate for automation. A good example is self-service gas station pumps. The idea is that the gas pump instructions walk the driver through the process of pumping gas. This helps to expedite the process and removes the need to hire and train a gas station attendant.

- Infrequently used information. If an application or a device is used infrequently, the process should be embedded in the device.

■　■　■　■

SUMMARY

When designing systems in which knowledge is transferred through the interface between a human and a machine, business managers, educators, and trainers need to think about embedding the knowledge into the work flow process. Too much time is spent teaching and training employees when the time would be better spent designing and implementing more automated learning processes.

Automating education processes is not the only issue facing boomers as they try to integrate gamers into the workforce and academic systems. Being the supervisor or boss of gamers can be tricky. Next, we explore what it means to be a boss or teacher of a gamer.

8

Trust Me; You Don't Want to Be the Boss

HERE IS A LITTLE QUIZ:

To get to the next level, do you:

(a) Openly battle the boss, show no mercy, and defeat the boss as quickly as possible?

(b) Work closely with your boss and expect her to be a mentor and a coach?

(c) Secretly plot to outdo your boss? She's a pain, but you do want to show respect to her face. After all, you'll need her to help you climb the corporate ladder.

If you chose a or b, you are a gamer. If you answered c, you are a boomer. If you ask a boomer to define the term *boss,* he or she will say something like, "A boss is a person who exercises control over others and makes decisions related to hiring and the operation of the business. It is the person who tells you what to do. I don't partially like the boss, but I do show respect. Someday I'll need her to help me climb the corporate ladder." Boomers don't like bosses too much; they would rather be the boss than report to one. But they still respect bosses and typically do not openly battle their boss.

Ask a gamer the same question, and he or she is likely tell you, "A boss is a computer-controlled character at the end of a level that needs to be defeated to move to the next level." Gamers have spent many hours trying to defeat level bosses.

This exercise may seem like semantic trivia; nevertheless, the difference between the gamer's and the boomer's answers is not trivial. It is not that gamers want to literally "kill their boss." They understand the difference between a computer game boss and a boss at work. In fact, gamers would like their real boss to be more like answer b, as I discuss later in the chapter. However, the quiz and its answers do highlight the huge gap between gamers and boomers in their attitude toward authority.

Widening this gap is the fact that gamers have seen the worst in corporate, government, and sports leadership. They have seen a boomer president, on national television, point a finger at them and lie about his relations with a female intern. They witnessed another boomer president mislead the country about reasons for the invasion of a foreign country, and gamers paid the ultimate price.

Gamers have witnessed dozens of cases of conflicts of interest in Congress, not to mention the Enron, Adelphia Communications, Tyco, and WorldCom scandals. Many sports stars they have grown up with have admitted, or almost admitted, or at least not denied taking steroids.

And video games themselves do not do a whole lot to foster respect for authority. In *The Matrix: Path of Neo* game, the first scene involves you, fighting as Neo, defeating progressively more difficult representatives of the law enforcement community from security guards to SWAT team officers. Rock Star Games' controversial *Grand Theft Auto* series deals with stealing cars, committing various other crimes, and running away from police. Even milder

Figure 8.1. Battling the Boss Is Routine for Gamers.

Source: Reprinted with permission of the artist, Kristin Longenecker.

games like *The Fairly Odd Parents! Breaking' Da Rules,* and *Jimmy Neutron Boy Genius* portray the parents, authority figures, as idiots. These two games are taking their lead from the cartoon series that inspired them.

Warning: Gamer with Attitude Ahead

The rock and roll music that young boomers loved also fostered disrespect for authority; however, it was a one-way street. Listeners couldn't interact with or influence the music. It was a passive activity. You simply cranked up the volume and listened to the lyrics and music.

With gamers, it isn't a one-way street. Gamers playing *Grand Theft Auto: Vice City* don't watch the car being stolen. They stop the car, shoot the driver, throw him out the door, and drive off in the stolen car. What players do in the game determines how the game reacts to them. They control the amount of lawlessness and disrespect they have for the authority figures in the game. They don't passively watch; they are an active participant.

In *Jimmy Neutron Boy Genius,* gamers talk to Jimmy's captured parents and learn how clueless they are, especially Hugh, his father. The interactions the player has with the environment and characters in the game are what make games so influential as opposed to the passive act of listening to music.

The Internet has undermined unquestioned authority even more. Now knowledge, facts, and ideas, once the power base for many untouchable professions in society, are all available through a simple Internet search. No longer are a few people the keepers of knowledge; everyone can share knowledge, ideas, and thoughts at any time. Blogs are sharing more information with more people than ever before. In traditional knowledge hierarchies like law and medicine, professionals had to work their way up in the field to obtain even basic knowledge in a specific content area. Now anyone can surf over to WebMd.com and in many cases know more about a specific disease than his or her doctor—although the actual treatment of the disease still requires the training and rigor of medical school and the subtle knowledge and insight that comes from experience. Investors no longer need a high-priced stockbroker to trade stocks. They need four dollars and the right Web address.

Gamers, themselves, feel that they are a type of authority figure and want some recognition for that authority and technical knowledge. They have grown up being in charge of virtual worlds. When they play *Halo 2* as Master Chief, they are in charge. When they run the zoo in *Zoo Tycoon,* they are in charge. When they see a boomer confused by a laptop and know how to troubleshoot the problem, they are the authority. Gamers have a heightened sense of capability and abilities and believe they are experts in many areas. This makes them a little less likely to hand over authority to a boomer or anyone else they see as not being as knowledgeable, especially in the area of technology.

All of these influences, both virtual and in the real world, have shaped gamer attitudes in terms of authority figures, hierarchies, and structured environments. These attitudes are in sharp contrast to boomer attitudes. Boomers respect the corporate ladder; they believe in paying dues and following standard business and academic protocol. Gamers want to circumvent these conventions. They rely on informal structures and unfettered communications access; they don't openly disrespect authority, but they don't blindly follow it either. Gamers look to see if the boomer really does have "street cred" before committing to following the boomer. It also makes gamers seem cocky and overly confident in many situations. The differences in these two attitudes toward authority can cause friction, confusion, and miscommunication in workplace and classroom environments.

The Problem with Being the Boss

To a gamer, the most despised boss is the one who provides explicit, step-by-step instructions, doesn't know how to use technology, and doesn't consider the opinion of subordinates. This boss tells the gamer to wait his or her turn before being promoted or taking on a key project. To top it off, this boss walks around the office at 5:30 P.M. checking to see who is there and who has already left. Telecommuting is not an option: employees need to be seen in the office to be considered productive. "How do I know you are not at home surfing the Internet?" or "What if we need to have an impromptu meeting and you are at home taking a shower?"

The commitment to long hours and paying dues are the very traits that have made boomers so successful in the workplace. Now these boomer bosses believe the same principles and rules apply to this new generation. They don't. Gamers don't respond well to a boss who is dictatorial and doesn't help them achieve their goal. Gamers want flexibility; they can and do want to work from anywhere.

Gamers see most bosses and other authority figures not so much as a threat but as a possible obstacle to achieving their desired goal. They believe they are highly capable. They have achieved great success through many hours of game play and are impatient. They want to advance quickly based on merit and success, not follow some seemingly arbitrary time line until they can move up in the organization.

This expectation goes against most traditional organizational structures where those who have the most experience and have paid their dues are promoted. Yes, boomers were impatient too, but they decided that the fastest road to the top of the ladder was to put in more hours than anyone else because more hours meant they could climb the ladder faster.

Gamers don't want to climb the ladder faster; they want to teleport directly to the top and are not going to wait idly by when a boss or other authority figure appears to be incompetent or unable to perform his or her job. Gamers send an e-mail to their boss's boss with no qualms and wonder why the response is taking so long. They do not have the same patience or respect for protocol or hierarchies as the boomers. In the gamers' world of instant access to information and people, hierarchies don't make a lot of sense.

Gamers do not respond well to a dictatorial, micromanaging boss. They do not want someone to tell them constantly how to do their job. When they play a video game, they are in control and are not given explicit instructions. In most games, there are no real instructions. If you look at any game manual, it does not provide step-by-step instructions for being successful; instead, the manual provides broad parameters or general rules. The gamer wants to determine the methods and procedures necessary to achieve the desired results.

Although gamers don't like step-by-step instructions, they do desire an explicit goal like, "Save the princess." Gamers need flexibility and want to explore options and alternatives rather than travel down a well-worn path. They want to know that the boss is performing effectively and helping to guide them and their company to success.

When a gamer sees someone in a position of authority who is not performing or is struggling with the use of technology, they become frustrated. They expect a high level of performance from themselves and others. They see technology as an answer to many questions when boomers do not. To gamers, the application of technology to a business problem makes perfect sense, and there is no reason not to move forward.

Many boomer bosses have lived through various versions of beta software, spent long hours trying to retrieved lost data, and endured countless computer crashes. Gamers didn't have to deal with the early years of software development and deployment and have little appreciation for or understanding of technological failures. Half of the Gamer 3.0 kids and all of the Gamer 4.0 kids were born after the *Challenger* space shuttle disaster. When the technology cautiousness of the boomers clashes against the technology acumen of the gamers, conflicts are inevitable.

This situation is especially acute in today's fast-paced business environment. The unfettered attitude of the gamers slams into the institutional thinking of the boomers, with a resulting loss of productivity and possibly the loss of talented gamers. A gamer can quickly come to resent a boomer boss for putting too many restraints on his or her ability to work the problem. If this occurs too frequently, the gamer will look for a new position within or outside the current organization.

Gamers are more willing to jump jobs, freelance, and act independently than their boomer or Generation X predecessors. Gamers see jumping from job to job or even career to career as a viable option, even as a sign of success. They believe they are capable in many areas and feel their success is tied to their own skills and abilities, not the company's success.

The Problem with Being the Teacher

Not only are gamers' attitudes toward authority and the traditional methods of relating to a boss changing in the workplace, educational institutions are experiencing a similar phenomenon. The influx of gamers into elementary schools, high schools, and colleges is causing new expectations and requirements of boomer teachers and professors, many of whom are not prepared to make the changes necessary to keep the attention of these students.

The educational tradition of lining students up at desks and lecturing to them is not effective for educating a generation that grew up playing video games and surfing the Internet. As my Gamer 4.0 son has been known to say, "School: the most boring place on earth."

This level of boredom has lead some to believe that the rise in the incidence of attention deficit hyperactivity disorder and the associated problems in school may be partially caused by the unstimulating presentation of material in a classroom setting as compared to the constant interaction of a video game.[1]

The current model of educating students was implemented in the 1800s and does not take into account any of the technological advancement since that time, except for replacing handwritten visual aids with PowerPoint slides. There is no widespread adoption of automated whiteboards, group response systems, or other collaborative educational technology.

Gamers are used to visual and auditory stimulation as they play games on the PC, respond to their ringing (or song-playing) cell phones, and manipulate characters on their portable gizmos. Confining these mobile learners in a classroom with little visual stimulation, passive lectures, and no integrated use of technology is ineffective.

A professor from a college in Kentucky made an interesting observation: in "1913, it took 31 days to build an automobile and 16 weeks to teach Freshman English 101."[2] With advances in technology and process improvements, it now takes only a day and a half to build an automobile, but it still takes sixteen weeks to teach Freshman English 101.

The only time high school students sit in front of a computer is during special computer classes. Even in colleges and universities, many faculty members do not incorporate technology into their classrooms in a meaningful way. Students are confronted with an environment that is devoid of the technology they have in their pockets and use everywhere except in the classroom.

To add to the problem, many boomer teachers and professors are intimidated by students who are savvier about technology than they are. In fact, the Internet has removed some of the instructor's power. No longer is the professor the sole owner of knowledge and ideas to be poured into the minds of ignorant students. (Students are no longer ignorant either; they are much more globally aware than their predecessors.[3])

If a student wants an additional interpretation of the *Communist Manifesto* by Karl Marx, she types those words into Google and retrieves over 384,000 hits in less than half a second. The student doesn't have to take the professor's interpretation as the only one. She has access to many others and can even IM her buddy at another college and see what he thinks.

My eleven-year-old son learned about World War II playing *Metal of Honor* games on the PlayStation 2 and *Rise of Nations.* He knows about the Axis powers, the Allies, and the major battles of the war. He can even describe some of the major strategies of both sides. And he has never picked up a book on World War II or even read an article on the subject.

Contrast this approach with how history is taught in high school. The history teacher comes into the classroom, asks students to turn toward the end of a rather thick textbook, and lectures to them about battles and events. Students are required to memorize specific dates, and on the test, they are asked to recall the facts.

Gamers have an aversion to this technique, which has led many boomers to say that kids don't read. The evidence does not support this position. In fact, the compound growth rate of juvenile hardbound books, as reported by the Association of American Publishers from 2002 to 2005, was 19.6 percent. The growth rate of juvenile paperback books from 2002 to 2005 was 2.8 percent.[4] Gamers can and do read books. The popular Harry Potter series contains some of the thickest books ever written for kids, yet they line up at book stores to buy and read the latest copy.

Of course, it is not about the thickness of the book. The content is important, and kids want entertaining content even in an educational setting. Instructors need to present information to the gamers using multiple forms of delivery. Providing information in only one format, a thick textbook, will not help the gamers learn. Delivery methods need to include computer games, podcasts, blogs, and other forms of presenting information. Schools need to focus on developing learning environments that are interactive and engaging.

One such project was created at Sinclair Community College in Dayton, Ohio. Two professors created an interactive online soap opera, "Young and Litigious," designed to teach consumer law.[5] There is no textbook for the class. Instead, the students are provided with an online soap opera with the same elements found in televised soap operas: a father in a coma, a contested marriage, and legal problems at every turn. Students must search through references, information contained within the instruction, and related Web sites to answer questions and help the young couple through their legal issues. This is an online learning environment that takes advantage of digitized video and Web technologies to deliver instruction right to the student's desktop in an entertaining format.

Online learning environments like these are quickly becoming popular with gamers. They are becoming so popular, they are beginning to threaten the very brick-and-mortar colleges that gave them birth. A study by South Dakota's Board of Regents revealed that 42 percent of the students enrolled in online courses were located on or very near the college campus offering the online course.[6] One in six college students—about 3.2 million—take at least one online course while at college.[7] The director of distance learning at Arizona State, Marc Van Horne, says that students want both high-tech delivery of education and more control over their schedules, attributes offered by online courses and unavailable in face-to-face courses.[8]

Colleges and universities are not the only educational institutions that have begun to make the transition to an online environment. There are now many online high schools, such as Keystone National High School. In fact, Keystone does more than offer online courses to high school students; it has online clubs as well. Students can join a photography, newspaper, or yearbook club. The virtual high school activities allow the students to pursue what they like without the constraints of having to be physically on site with their fellow yearbook staffers.

Every other major institution in the United States and throughout the world has undergone major changes because of technology. Financial institutions now offer services online, hospitals are using radio-frequency identification technology to track patients and medicines, and insurance agencies offer online claim filing.

The only major institution that has remained untouched and virtually unchanged by technology and the incoming gamers are academic institutions. Within the next ten years, the demands of the gamers and the technology they take for granted will radically change educational institutions and cause dramatic shifts in the way gamers access and participate in the education process.

Professors, teachers, and instructors who do not keep up with these changes will be left behind by organizations and individuals who will adapt more quickly. The challenge for teachers of gamers is to reach gamers on their level and work with the gamer ethos to ensure that the necessary knowledge is transferred to the gamer, whether that is in a brick-and-mortar classroom, online, or over a cell phone. The box provides some examples of how K-12 school districts are starting to think about adding gadgets to their curriculum.

Using Gadgets in Schools

The integration of technology-based gadgets within educational environments is slowly starting to alter the instructional techniques that now are used in thousands of classrooms. Recently there have been initiatives to include state-of-the-art technologies within classrooms throughout the United States. Popular gadgets are now tools students are using to receive instructional content, collaborate, and archive materials presented by the instructor.

Student exposure to these technologies within the classroom is starting in the primary grades and being infused throughout their educational career. Second- and third-grade students are being provided with technology gadgets necessary to incorporate learning activities in related subjects through the use of Power-Point, digital cameras, and Web-based resources. These gadgets are slowly transforming classic primary-level projects such as the leaf collection assignment.

In high-tech classrooms, the teacher divides students into teams, equipping each with digital cameras to explore and document the leaves of surrounding trees, creating a digital archive of leaf specimens for their collections. When they return to the classroom, the students match their pictures with specimen types found with online resources, such as netTrekker, that are designed for students of this age level. The project concludes with the creation of a PowerPoint presentation. Each presentation shares the team's discoveries with classmates.

The recent evolution of iPods and TiVo has opened further educational opportunities within school environments. Using these gadgets, a physics instructor can expand instructional lessons beyond the walls of the classroom. After conducting a traditional lesson about rockets, the instructor archives a royalty-free educational video on the topic using a TiVo. She transfers this video to a computer server, which is used to deploy the video segment to each student's video iPod. The student's assignment to watch this supplementary video enhances the educational lesson.

This technique allows the instructor to make strides in continuing the learning process when students return to the classroom having added to their knowledge base through the iPod content. In fact, any class lecture or demonstration can be archived in a video iPod format for the remediation or makeup of any classroom subject area.

Our school has a class that prepares students for careers as federal agents, police officers, soldiers, and emergency personnel. So when I observe a student patrolling the hallways on our school's Segway, it brings a smile to my face, knowing he or she is preparing for a future career and learning to use technology that he or she will encounter on the job.

A Segway is a human transporter that has two wheels, a small engine, and a place for the rider to stand. It self-balances and can reach speeds of up to twelve miles an hour. It works well for officers on patrol in city streets or on academic campuses, and security agencies across the country are embracing the use of the Segway. This is just one way our school is providing gadgets to students in an effort to prepare them for the experiences they will encounter in the future.

As an instructional technologist, I strive to ensure that each course incorporates modern technological innovations such as the Segway to ensure that all of our gamer graduates understand the technology they will face daily.

Technology gadgets that seemed impossible to imagine ten years ago, including text messaging devices and Internet-based video game consoles, now need to become the building blocks for transferring ideas and learning from boomers to gamers. The continual development of new technological gadgets will drive the educational world into the future as an incredibly powerful source of learning.

R. Lynn Hummel Jr. is an instructional technology specialist at a vocational school in Lewistown, Pennsylvania. He is enrolled in the administration and leadership studies doctoral program at Indiana University of Pennsylvania and is a well-respected eBay merchant.

Source: Printed with the permission of R. Lynn Hummel Jr.

Become a Strategy Guide

Instead of being a boss or a teacher to a gamer, it is better to be a coach, guide, or mentor: answer b from the quiz at the beginning of the chapter. In gamer jargon, gamers want the boss to be a strategy guide.[9] A strategy guide is a manual that describes how to play a game. It has tips, techniques, and even spoilers. A spoiler is a hint or tip that gives away a certain element of the game that may spoil the enjoyment for the player. Proper etiquette for listing a spoiler is to indicate that a spoiler is coming and then have the words "end spoiler" in the text when the spoiler information is over. Players look at a spoiler only after they are totally frustrated and unable to play the game anymore.

Gamers use strategy guides sparingly. They enjoy the challenge of the game and do not want to be given step-by-step instructions for successfully completing a level or a game. Nevertheless, when they become stuck and frustrated, they want some advice and counsel—not exact instructions but hints and ideas for proceeding so they can think through what they need to do.

This is the same philosophy and approach that should be undertaken by someone attempting to manage or teach gamers, not an easy task. A boomer boss or teacher needs to be seen by the gamers as a provider of information, that is, a guide to more knowledge rather than a know-it-all dictator.

There are some general techniques that can help boomers teach or manage gamers:

- Make rules, parameters, and goals explicit.
- Allow trial and error.
- Build a support and knowledge community.
- Encourage research.
- Assign multiple tasks to a gamer.
- Make tasks meaningful.

Make Rules, Parameters, and Goals Explicit

Gamers work well within defined boundaries. Most games have rules that cannot be broken and one or two overriding goals that must be accomplished. They provide freedom but also boundaries that cannot be crossed. In *Roller*

Coaster Tycoon, you must work around natural obstacles like trees and water to build the roller coaster. There are clear rules about where you can put a piece of roller coaster track and where you cannot. You can alter the land to make it compatible with the track, but you must follow the rules governing the alterations.

Apply the same concept to managing the gamers. Give gamers clear goals to accomplish, but provide explicit parameters. Then let them work within those parameters to accomplish the desired goals. Periodically remind them of the boundaries, but don't micromanage. Encourage them to come back to you with questions and concerns from time to time. When they do, don't give them explicit instructions; instead, provide them with more rules and parameters that will guide them to the right tasks or conclusions. Gamers need to feel that they have some level of independence and are contributing to the organization or they are in control of their learning experience.

Allow Trial and Error

This can be a tough technique for boomer bosses. It is also difficult for teachers who believe that a response is either right or wrong. Boomers want to get it right the first time and expect everyone else to have the same philosophy. In the gamer world, trial and error is the preferred method of learning.

Gamers are used to making a mistake or failing, but they don't see this as a problem. They call the concept "failing forward," which is gaining incremental knowledge through repeated failure. A death in a video game is not the end; it is just another chance to figure out the problem confronting the gamer. A gamer who makes a big mistake just starts the entire game over again.

With anemic written instructions and few guidelines, the gamer's only choice is to start playing a game and then see what happens. "Should I go to the left or the right?" "Can I open this door, or is it locked?" "How can I jump up to that ledge?" Often the result is that the gamer needs to play a level over again until he or she gets it. Part of the fun of a game is to try out new ideas and directions and observe what happens.

Consequentially, it is important that gamers have an opportunity to try out new ideas and concepts in working and learning environments. They will try various ideas, approaches, and techniques to see what happens. They do not view failure as absolute. They pick themselves up and try again. Provide an environment that allows that type of interaction.

Encouraging trial and error also encourages entrepreneurial activities. Entrepreneurs are willing to take a chance and work with failures until they become successful. Organizations that embrace the gamers' experience in overcoming failure will be successful, in contrast to organizations that punish or frown on failure. Allow the gamers to try things and learn from the results. Encourage trial and error within limits.

Build a Support and Knowledge Community

Gamers need to be connected and like to exchange information and knowledge with each other. They have developed and continue to develop networks of information providers (friends, colleagues, Web sites) who easily and readily share information with each other. Boomers tend to have a mentality of hoarding or not sharing information; for them, information is power.

For the gamers, sharing information is power. If you are a guru at a certain game, you gain fame and recognition by telling others about cheat codes, Easter eggs, and other game secrets. You gain recognition by winning every time, but you also gain recognition by sharing game secrets.

Encourage and support the sharing of knowledge among gamers by working to build communication networks within the organization and between gamers and boomers. The success of online communities is a clear example of how gamers like to be in touch with each other. The Web site www. MySpace.com has over 20 million members who exchange information on everything from favorite rock groups and foods to details about their personal lives. The site is an active community of people from the gamer generation, providing an exchange of information.

In addition, gamers have created thousands, if not millions, of Web sites to discuss games. You can find sites to discuss gaming strategies, recruit members for online guilds, and share cheat codes. These active communities of practice provide places to exchange tips and ideas related to a person's favorite game. If you want to learn about *World of Warcraft* (WOW), go to www.stratics.com

or check out one of the many WOW guild sites such as the Azeroth Guardians (www.azeroth-guardians.net/site/).

Providing a similar community focused on business issues within your organization will give gamers the constant contact and assistance they need to be successful. They will seek out information from others to solve problems and build knowledge within the organization through this process. Gamers need to share information; boomers share information only if they think the other person needs that knowledge. Gamers are moving organizations from the old need-to-know paradigm to one of need to share.

Provide the technology tools necessary to allow constant and instant communications. Gamers value the knowledge of their peers highly and will seek out their advice and ideas before going to a boss or other authority figure. Encourage the creation of an internal support network.

In an academic environment, create an online community where older students can virtually mentor and interact with younger students. Provide a place for the students to talk about school but also about their personal lives and interests. Just as schools have physical clubs and activities, create some virtual clubs and activities. Students don't need to be face-to-face with each other to be connected. Their gadgets and gizmos keep them in constant contact. This constant need for contact should be used for educational purposes.

Encourage Research

Gamers are adept at seeking online information and are curious. When playing a game, they are most successful when they explore the world in which they are placed, finding hidden treasures and secret passages. Gamers research all types of information online, and with broadband, wireless access, they can literally have the computer open anywhere and look up any piece of information any time it is needed. "Google it" is a common gamer phrase.

Use this tendency to your advantage. Encourage gamers to research competitors, new ideas, and innovations on the Web. Gamers are extremely adept at working through the many messages that are thrown at them every day.

Encourage them to seek information to determine industry trends and direction. Give them the leeway to follow leads and discover new information.

Educators should help gamers develop effective methods of searching for Web-based information and cross-checking that information for accuracy. Schools should have courses on information literacy and verifying the veracity of information.

Assign Multiple Tasks to a Gamer

Gamers are used to multitasking. Players must read the health meter, navigate the new level, switch weapons, and work toward several objectives, all at the same time. These game requirements mean that they quickly become bored if they have only one task to perform. Gamers have grown up in a world of information overload. From tickers on the bottom of television screens to multiple windows open on a laptop, they filter through information and can quickly move from one task to another and back again.

Many gamers thrive when given multiple tasks and are able to work more effectively when they have multiple projects. Switching from one task to another gives them a chance to rest their brain in one area while processing the information from the first task in the background.

To take advantage of the gamers' fondness for multitasking, provide guidelines for prioritization, but let them determine how to prioritize the specific tasks. Then ask them how they prioritized the tasks and provide insights and guidance on this.

Make Tasks Meaningful

When playing a game, gamers are the hero, the person in charge. They are doing meaningful work—saving the universe or raising a puppy, for example. When they enter the workforce, they do not want to do low-level busywork. They don't want busywork at school either. Rather, they want the opportunity to excel and perform. They believe in the merit system and want an opportunity to show what they can do by successfully completing tasks that have an impact on the organization. They do not want to patiently perform basic jobs and tasks so they can learn the system.

Provide them with a series of meaningful tasks, each increasingly more difficult. This provides a clear upward path from one level to another while simultaneously challenging them to perform meaningful work.

The same is true in a school setting. Gamers need to know that what they are learning is valuable. They are more than willing to ask, "If I can look up the date on the Internet, why do I have to memorize it?" Provide educational experiences that are engaging and meaningful to the students. Get beyond memorization into problem solving.

Create Self-Directed Teams

"Dad, I want you to know the second clan meeting went better than the first," my Gamer 4.0 son unexpectedly announced one day.

"What's a clan meeting?" was my response. "Clan? What do you mean clan?" I was nervous.

"I formed an online team in Runescape. We call it a clan."

"Oh, of course."

"We have six members but need someone who can cook shark," he stated matter-of-factly.

"Cook shark?"

"We have someone who can catch shark; we need someone who can cook it. In our first meeting, we didn't have any goals or tasks. Nobody knew what to do. It was a waste of time."

"Cook shark?"

"The second meeting was better. We assigned tasks and appointed someone to be third in charge. We picked someone who didn't speak much to bring her into the group. We also assigned someone to create a logo."

Here was my twelve-year-old son in charge of six people he had never met, setting goals, delegating tasks, and assigning roles, as well as posting help-wanted ads for shark cookers. He was running a self-directed work team, virtually.

Defeating the Bad Guy

Imagine it's your first day of work as a project manager. You report to a meeting where you will be given your first assignment. It turns out the assignment is a big one: you are to manage a group of forty people in the completion of a task. Forty sounds like a big number, but you are confident in your ability to manage the team. You then ask, "What's the makeup of the group?" And as a response is given, you start to panic: the group consists of people from China, Australia, India, Malaysia, Puerto Rico, El Salvador, Britain, Canada, and the United States. Each member has a different view of the world, different motivations for being on the team, and different goals at times. They have differing levels of proficiency at speaking English and range in age from fourteen to forty. You will never meet this group in person; the task must be completed synchronously using text chat and voice communication software over the Internet.

As you pull your head up from the bag you are hyperventilating into, you manage to ask one question in between quick, shallow breaths: "What is the task?"

Your supervisor smiles, looks out the window, and replies, "Now this is where it starts to get complicated."

This scenario is completely true, except that none of us were project managers. The task was completed for entertainment. The people in the group were online gamers playing what is known as a massively multiplayer online role-playing game or MMORPG. The game, *World of Warcraft,* is one of the most popular of its type in the world, with over 5 million subscribers.

MMORPGs place users in a three-dimensional environment where they interact with one another, as well as with elements in the game like quests, puzzles, and nonplayer characters. The three-dimensional world they interact with, other than being in a fantasy setting, is not much different from the real world. It has an economy, businesses, professions, and thousands of people to interact with at any time. In *World of Warcraft,* there are nine classes, eight races, sixty levels, and two sides (the Alliance and the Horde), so players can customize their characters with various abilities and traits.

The goals that players must achieve in the game are defined by the players themselves. MMORPGs are successful in part due to the fact that players make their own goals in the game. Our group of forty people shared a similar goal. Our goal was more of a "who" than a "what."

Ragnaros was the name of our goal. Ragnaros is described in *World of Warcraft* lore as the Firelord, a servant of the Old Gods, who was banished to the Elemental Plane. Basically he was the bad guy, and we had to find him and destroy him.

To do this, we had to make our way through a dungeon called Molten Core, a series of lava-filled caves that players must navigate to reach smaller bosses before they reach the main boss, Ragnaros. Moving through a dungeon like this one took a great deal of teamwork and communication. Each person played a different class, which meant they each had a different role to play in defeating Ragnaros. We each had a different job to do.

Although as a team we had a shared goal of killing the Firelord, as individuals we all had our own reasons for wanting to achieve that goal. Some people craved the recognition of being one of the first guilds to kill Ragnaros. Others simply enjoyed the team play and strategizing required to take down a boss. Of course, there was also the "loot," or items that players could procure from the fallen Ragnaros. These items would help players to better themselves in the game. No matter what individual reasons players had for wanting to be there, only the combined efforts of the team would result in success.

For three days every week, for months on end, we all found ourselves standing at the entrance of Molten Core fine-tuning our strategies and teamwork. Communication was difficult at times, not only because there were forty people from around the world on a conference call, but also because the technology we used was unreliable at times.

A great deal of trust among the team members had to be fostered because each player had a significant role in the success of the team. A mistake made by one person could lead to the failure of an entire raid, a critical waste of time for all the team members.

As a group, we relied heavily on the instructions of our raid and guild leaders. Orders about what people should do and suggestions on strategy were always well received and thought out by everyone. A key aspect of our guild's progression and success in the game was our communication. We used an open forum where all members could post ideas or concerns about the guild.

During the online quest to kill Ragnaros, I learned valuable lessons about leadership and teamwork. Virtual worlds and online team work are going to be a big part of the tools we will use in coming years. This experience will serve me well when I am working on a group project for work.

As for Ragnaros, through perseverance, teamwork, and patience, we finally defeated him. There are, of course, bigger and badder monsters to fight, harder strategies to master, and more obstacles to overcome.

It is surprising what forty strangers from around the world can accomplish over the Internet if they use the right tools, strategies, and teamwork. Ten years ago, many people did not expect the Internet to change the way we live today so drastically. We should not make the same mistake with virtual worlds and gaming. The potential they show for increasing the effectiveness of our work is incalculable.

Lucas Blair majored in biology with a minor in anthropology from Bloomsburg University. He recently graduated with a master's degree in instructional technology after interning at Merck.

Source: Printed with the permission of Lucas Blair.

Virtual Teamwork

When you observe how gamers socialize and play together, you notice many of the same traits as a self-directed team. A self-directed team is a group of employees in a company who combine different skills and talents to work together toward a common goal without direct day-to-day managerial supervision. Because a manager or boss does not lead, the team must agree on the rules and deadlines for accomplishing their purpose.

Entire online communities have grown up around games. The video game industry knows gamers form communities and look to work in teams. In fact, they've developed a number of devices to foster the online team experience for gamers. The industry has also enhanced game consoles to allow more players to compete at once. The PlayStation 3 allows up to seven Bluetooth wireless controllers, so seven gamers can play at once. Handheld portable game devices like the Nintendo DS are Web enabled to allow gamers to all enter a virtual game world and play together online.

Gamer teams form around a common goal: winning the game or getting to the next level. The team is typically led by one of the most experienced or knowledgeable players. Each player usually has a specific role to play to help the team win the game. And the team needs to agree internally on the rules and deadlines for accomplishing the task—for example, "Okay, if you die or get to the next level, then it's someone else's turn."

In a MMORPG, the players all work virtually at the same time to accomplish the goal. Team communication is often done through online text chat features. Other games allow gamers to communicate through voice over Internet protocol such as the game *SOCOM 3: U.S. Navy Seals.* Players use a headphone to speak to their teammates as they move around in a virtual battlefield sneaking up on enemies.

When playing a single-player console game in a friend's basement after school or in a dorm room after class, one team member will start with the controller and, based on the task, pass the controller to other team members at the appropriate time. Some team members will have looked up cheat codes. Some will advise the player on the best approaches, and some will reveal tricks he or she found when playing the game previously.

Managers and teachers need to tap into the natural team-forming ability of gamers and use that to help educate and motivate employees and learners. Often boomers want explicit instructions or guidance from management concerning what needs to be done and how it can be accomplished. Gamers, who have explored all kinds of worlds on their own with no instructions and no guidance, would rather just jump in and see what happens.

A number of elements in managing a team of gamers will make the team successful and productive:

- Clear goals

- Defined boundaries

- Flexibility in the process

- Impact

- Accountability

- Exit plan

Clear Goals. Gamers like to have clear goals: free the princess, beat the bad guy, or, in *Lego Star Wars,* collect all the minikits—small groups of virtual Legos. When you collect all the hidden pieces of a minikit, you can build a virtual Lego vehicle, such as the X-34 Landspeeder. Clearly defined goals help gamers focus. The goals and objectives of the team should be clearly understood by the team. Have the team create a mission statement and post it online so they all have access.

Defined Boundaries. Gamers constantly push the boundaries of games and play at the edge of the rules. Let them know at the beginning of a project what general things are acceptable and not acceptable. Do not give step-by-step instructions, but tell them the one or two items that might be off-limits in terms of what they should pursue. While gamers are able to explore in many game worlds, there are clearly places they cannot go. The game tells them when they are "off the battlefield" or warns them they are going in the wrong direction. In a team setting, you need boundaries, rules, and parameters so the gamer knows if he is traveling in the wrong direction or engaging in activities not helpful to the organization.

Teams need to have certain rules and parameters under which they function. These rules and parameters, enforced by all the team members, will help the team function as a cohesive unit. One method is to develop a list of working rules in the early stages of the team formation. The rules can then be posted and referred to when necessary. The rules can include basic process rules such as these:

- Respect each other's opinions.

- Do not speak while another person is speaking.

- Arrive on time for meetings (virtual as well as face-to-face).

- If an idea is controversial, a vote will be taken.

- All votes are final, and an issue may not be addressed again if vetoed.

Flexibility in the Process. Provide gamers the flexibility of trying new approaches because they are comfortable using trial-and-error techniques to achieve a goal. Allow them the flexibility to try new ideas and concepts. The innovative approach to a problem might just be what the organization is looking for. If you try to provide too many rules and regulations, the gamers will become frustrated. They believe they are experts and good at what they do. You need to foster that enthusiasm and confidence by allowing them a long leash.

Impact. Gamers do not want to feel they are being given busywork. They want to be involved on a team that is making a difference and having an impact. In the game world, they determine the fate of the universe. Although they don't expect such grand assignments in the real world, they do expect meaningful assignments. It is a good idea to articulate to the gamers the anticipated results of their actions and how those results will ultimately benefit themselves and the organization.

Accountability. Gamers do not mind being held accountable for their actions. If they fail to do something properly in a game, they are held accountable by having to start over. In MMORPGs, if a player is behaving poorly, his or her peers can inform the game company, and that player is removed from the virtual environment.

Gamers believe that people are rewarded for good work and a job well done, and they expect to be measured on how well they perform. They like to keep score and compare themselves to others. Provide methods of holding the gamers accountable for the outcomes.

Exit Plan. There must be a light at the end of the tunnel. Gamers are multitasking and want to finish a project successfully and move on. Provide a clear time line and exit plan for the gamers as they join the team.

Stay Connected

Gamers are connected, and if you manage gamers, you'd better be also. They are constantly sending messages to each other using AOL Instant Messenger or versions created by Yahoo! or Microsoft. They have created communities where information is shared over wikis and blogs. They create entire online communities so they can remain in touch no matter where they are. Use the tools described in Chapter Six to remain in contact digitally with the gamers.

Even when confined to their rooms, gamers are still in contact with the outside world and each other. A mother of a gamer tells a story of her son who was sick one Saturday and had to stay in bed while his friends went on a field trip to a nature preserve. He was able to participate virtually in the field trip because he was in contact with his friends using his gadgets and gizmos. He looked up the preserve's site online, received text messages from his friends as they walked the grounds, spoke with them when they were at lunch, and received pictures of animals sent to him over a cell phone. It was as if he had gone on the trip himself.

Workplace Implications

Managing gamers is not an easy task for boomers. Managers must position themselves as a facilitator or strategy guide. They must also learn to use and take advantage of the communication tools that are commonplace for gamers. As a manager, you need to learn to use communication tools to provide instant coaching and feedback just as the gamers use them to communicate with each other. Get comfortable with coaching using instant messaging and e-mail.

As Tom Peters says, "You simply can't . . . have a hierarchical organization where people wait for orders."[10] Gamers won't stand for it. They want 24/7 access to everyone in the organization. They do not have the patience to wait for the proper protocol.

Coaching the Boomers

As an executive coach, I work with a diverse group of companies to help improve avenues of communication, refine work flow processes, develop clearly defined leadership roles and responsibilities, and help implement succession plans. Ninety-five percent of my clients are from the boomer generation. Because of this, I have a pretty good understanding of how they work, what their frustrations may be, and where the rubs are with the upcoming gamer generation.

The gamer generation is just starting to penetrate the supervisor and middle management level in organizations, affording me a firsthand look at who they are and how they fit with the boomer generation. There are many challenges. It is important to understand what boomer bosses expect from the next generation and what gamers need to know to be successful employees.

If I were to profile the gamer generation, it would be someone who is chomping at the bit to exercise some, if not all, of his or her zillions of ideas; someone who enjoys sharing ideas, enjoys competition, and doesn't mind using someone else's plan; and someone who sees problems as opportunities for new ideas. Gamers feed on new ways of doing things, form communities, and like to work on teams.

If I were to profile the boomer generation, it would be someone who strives to keep things in check; someone wary of doing things differently, especially if it does not fit into his or her past experience; someone who hoards information to make sure his or her own department or team has what is needed to be deemed successful; and someone who spends a majority of time in reactive mode.

Recently I had a meeting with foremen from a midsize construction company run by the company president and founder. All in attendance were to bring a list of their ideas regarding what areas the company could expand to help the company continue to grow. At the end of the meeting, it was the gamer generation who, with eyes sparkling, said not only would they research the agreed-on idea, but they would come back with detailed information and a business plan, saying, "Don't worry; I will have all you need to move ahead." Their high energy, passion for change, and can-do attitude were clear.

The boomers in attendance spent their time circling around ideas that had been done in the past. I could sense the wariness of some unusual ideas brought up by the gamers at the meeting. One boomer said, "I have only a couple more years," implying that whatever direction the company took, he just had to hang in there for a short while.

Gamers have a heightened sense of capability and ability and believe they are experts in many areas. This, coupled with their need for continued challenge, engaging experiences, and meaningful tasks, can make a boomer's head spin. The boomer sometimes interprets all this as gamers not staying focused because they seemingly move from one thing to another without apparent thought. I had one boomer vice president of engineering who believed he was a good developer of new talent tell me he allows his gamer engineers to pursue their ideas so they would learn what it is like to fail.

So Where's the Rub?

The rub is in perspective. In his book *How to Think Like Einstein,* Scott Thorpe explains that escaping "rule ruts" is key to innovation, and that "what we know is a greater obstacle than what we don't know."* Boomers base most decisions on what they know, their years of experience, which they hold in high regard, and ingrained patterns of thinking supported by those years of experience. Experience and knowledge is good, but this perspective can and does block boomers from working from a different blueprint, truly listening to and entertaining the possibility of other ideas.

I recently worked with a small group of shop floor supervisors in a midsize manufacturing facility. Most were from the gamer generation, and one was closer to the boomer generation. The group was bemoaning the fact that the engineered drawings were so out-of-date that the new shop floor associates were making product wrong, thereby increasing scrap and man-hours, to say nothing of stress and frustration. We decided they would put a presentation together to outline the issue, its impact on the bottom line, and what they wanted to do about it—an action plan. The boomer in the group shook his head, and remarked, "It sounds good, but it won't work. They won't listen, and nothing will change."

To make a long story short, the supervisors gave a presentation, which was attended by the vice president of engineering, the president of the company, and several managers. The action plan outlined in the presentation was accepted. Sounds too good to be true?

Here's the downside of the gamer generation. One of the supervisors e-mailed me soon after the presentation: "It's been a week. I thought having a presentation with the president in attendance and really explaining the importance of our issues would be enough. I don't have time to chase them down and try to convince them improving quality is a good thing. Complacency is so interwoven in this company. It's a shame, but sometimes you even get labeled as an outcast or loose cannon because of your intolerance for status quo."

Remember the first sentence? "It's been a week"! The flip side of all this gamer positive energy and innovative way of approaching problems is keeping them on board and engaged through the process of moving forward. *Patience* is not in their vocabulary! Neither are the words *negotiation* or *persuasion*. And also, where does the boss fit into all this?

Who's the Boss, and What Does That Mean?

Gamers don't think in terms of "boss." To them, the boss is someone who will facilitate needs, offer technical information, share information, give clear direction, and define goals.

The boomer has a very different vision of a boss. To a boomer, the boss is someone to please, to buy loyalty from by impressing, and sometimes to hide information from in order to avoid "interference." In addition, the boomer boss sees himself or herself as a go-to person for information; the one with power to make or break a project, idea, or direction; the one who holds the magic wand, gained through a life of experience, which dictates who, what, and how the departmental goals will be achieved. This level of control is very hard for the boomer boss to relinquish.

Accountability and how to hold others accountable is a conundrum for boomer bosses. For example, I work with a vice president of manufacturing, Ron, who said, "I have more of a hope than a belief," when talking about how to let go and give up some control.

To the boomer, trust is an issue. Ron says he doesn't "trust anybody, especially at work. People don't meet my expectations, which is frustrating. It is also time-consuming because of all the follow-up I have to do to make sure it is done right. I'm at the point where when people walk into my office, I have a difficult time listening to them without first verifying what they are saying as true." He continues, "What happens is these fears that I have trickle down to others, so I manage through fear, but how do I make sure people are doing their jobs?" He ends our session with, "You're right. I am a very strong-willed person, very stubborn, and it's my nature to challenge. So why is that so wrong? Also, I am not ready to give up my stance because I believe there is some substance to my position and way of leading. How else can you hold people accountable?"

Ron was the stereotypical boomer boss. When we did an informal 360-degree feedback, the information confirmed the boomer boss's mantra: he is the go-to person for information; the one with power to make or break a project, idea or direction; the one who holds the magic wand, gained through a life of experience; the one dictating who, what, and how the departmental goals will be achieved; the person who believes his years of experience crown him king of the world and knows what is best and is hard to convince otherwise. I often hear from my boomer clients, "I don't have time to discuss everything." I can just see some of our boomer readers smiling and nodding their heads in agreement.

To boomers, image is very important. They like to see their career path as vertical, with promotion after promotion. That shows success. With that in mind, boomers view work problems as chances to fail, creating negative visibility with their boss and destroying any hope of continuing up the ladder. Boomers see their image as someone who has years of experience making the right decisions and getting the product out the door. How they did it was not as important. I've heard boomer bosses referred to as having "left scorched earth behind," using "steel-tipped boots," and undermining and dismissing others by "doing it their way regardless of what information is brought to the table."

Gamers see bosses as coworkers who are there to facilitate ideas and resources and offer their experience in support of the gamer idea. The gamer sees each problem and issue as an opportunity to try again, bring in others who can help, and gather information from a variety of sources, even if it means going over the boss's head.

To the gamer, being successful means solving problems, working across all boundaries, not seeing boundaries, and helping others succeed. As noted in Chapter One, "The act of obtaining that new skill and the promise of learning a subsequent skill is highly motivating." Gamers in no way see themselves with a vertical career path. Because they are used to processing in a nonlinear way, they build on each success from several sources and look forward to a career that grows and changes from company to company, and even to pursuing an entrepreneurial dream.

Gamers are used to immediate results and gratification, and they have grown up in an era in which the future changes so rapidly that it no longer becomes something to worry about. What boomers label as global uncertainty, gamers see as reality, and they are well equipped to handle this rapid global socioeconomic, technological change environment.

> Alison Stone-Briggs has worked in the field of organizational development and change management for over a decade as the associate director, Corporate Institute, Bloomsburg University. She has built on her master's degree in organizational and industrial psychology by developing and implementing training programs for corporations that address current business trends and issues.

Source: Printed with the permission of Alison Stone-Briggs.

*Thorpe, S. (2000). *How to think like Einstein.* Naperville, IL: Sourcebook, p. 57.

■ ■ ■ ■

SUMMARY

Gamers' view of authority figures is different from the view of many boomers. Gamers are not used to hierarchical command-and-control structures; they want flexibility, freedom, and plenty of real responsibility right out of the gate. This means teaching and supervising them can be difficult. Thinking of yourself as a strategy guide is a good start.

Although gamers might be difficult for boomers to manage, boomers still have to recruit and hire these gamers because soon they will be the majority of the workforce. Tips and techniques for recruiting and retaining gamers are discussed next.

And the Winner Is . . .

IMAGINE STAYING UP LATE to play a video game. You know you have to get up at five o'clock in the morning to go to a tournament that could be worth as much as ten thousand dollars if you win. But you just want to play the video game a few more times. Your mom walks past your room and says, "Go to bed. You have an early day tomorrow, and you need your rest."

"I will, Mom, I am just practicing."

Your mom half-smiles. "Practicing?"

"Yes, Mom, I'm practicing."

"Oh, really. Practicing?" She responds sarcastically.

"Yes, Mom, I am really practicing."

"Isn't it a little late for that? You should already know what you need to do for the tournament."

"I do, but you don't become the world's best *Halo* player without continual practice."

Video game tournaments are serious business. These tournaments are where gamers as young as fourteen years old compete for thousands of dollars in prizes. The Ultimate Video Gamers League has tournaments in California, Tennessee, Georgia, and other states with prizes as high as ten thousand dollars for playing games like *Halo, Halo 2, Madden Football,* and others.[1] The Global Gaming League sponsors competitive online and in-person video game tournaments for games like *Counterstrike* and *Age of Empires,* with total prizes reaching over seventy-five thousand dollars.[2] Some leagues focus on games like *Quake* and *StarCraft,* while others focus on sports games like *FIFA Soccer.* Some tournaments are team based and others single player focused.

One of the first superstar gamers was Dennis "Thresh" Fong, who achieved immortality among hard-core gamers when he won John Carmack's Ferrari at a Microsoft-sponsored tournament for being the best *Quake* player at that time. For the nongamers among you, John Carmack is a famous game developer who has worked on both the *Doom* and *Quake* video games as well as creating popular game engines used in a variety of first-person shooter titles.[3]

A small number of gamer elites support themselves playing video games. Organizations are signing promising young video gamers to management contracts. The goal is to make them stars in the world of video games—cyber-celebrities. Corporate sponsors are investing in the tournaments for a chance to gain visibility in front of their target demographic audience.

Corporations are not just focused on game tournaments. They are also interested in sponsoring a variety of other computer-based competitions, from programming tournaments to competitive events revolving around desktop publishing, digital movies, graphic design, logo design, multimedia, and Web page design.

Programming tournaments are becoming an increasingly popular method of recruiting the world's best programmers for government agencies like the U.S. National Security Agency and companies like Google, Yahoo!, and Microsoft (Figure 9.1). These organizations and others are concerned with how to recruit and retain gamers—new employees who have different ideals, goals, and thinking processes from the currently in-charge boomers.

Figure 9.1. Competing in a Tournament for Fame, Fortune, and a Job.

Source: Reprinted with permission of the artist, Kristin Longenecker.

Recruiting Gamers

Recruitment is a critical issue when it comes to transferring knowledge from the boomers to the gamers. When organizations fail to attract gamers, there will be no one to whom the boomers can transfer their knowledge.

Recruiting gamers is not going to be easy. The traits that make gamers different from preceding generations also make them hard to recruit into boomer-controlled organizations. They want the freedom to be able to work from anywhere, they have little loyalty to any corporation, and they surf the Internet so they know all about your company—good and bad. They are financially savvy, so they are going to request high salaries, and they have high employer expectations in terms of helping them learn and grow personally and professionally.[4] These are just some of the traits that make it difficult for firms to woo gamers.

The predicted labor shortage over the next twenty years doesn't help either. If the statistics are true and there will be a worker shortage of over 10 million workers in 2010 and a shortage of up to 35 million by 2035, companies will need all the gamers they can get.[5] Although many believe that the shortage is overestimated because boomers will work longer, the numbers do not support that theory. Studies indicate that only 19 percent of men ages sixty-five and older are part of today's workforce, a number that is down from 46 percent in the 1950s. People aren't working as long as they did fifty years ago.[6]

Even if the predicted worker shortage is circumvented by increased automation, international labor forces, and new business models, the need for talented individuals will not decrease. In fact, jobs are requiring higher and higher skill levels. The need for talented, skilled individuals is accelerating, especially in the areas of mathematics, science, and programming, and the competition is global.

If firms want to attract the gamers, they need to cater to the needs of this generation when attempting to hire them. One of the first things gamers look for is an organization that provides constant learning opportunities. There is no expectation of life-long employment among gamers. They don't want it, and they don't offer it either. Instead, they look to keep their skills sharp by working for organizations that will give them continuing opportunities for learning and growth.

They want to work with organizations that have ongoing training programs, opportunities to work on multiple projects, and a constantly renewing set of challenges. Gamers know that they can stay sharp only by remaining educated and engaged. A big part of recruiting gamers is selling them on the learning opportunities within the organization.

Gamers have an expectation of instant feedback, which can be difficult for employers during the recruitment process. Gamers have grown up at a time when they didn't really have to wait for anything. No need to wait for Saturday morning to see cartoons; they are on 24/7. No need to wait to go to the library to look up information; it is available instantaneously over the Internet. Gamers see no reason to wait two or three weeks to hear back from an employer. They panic when a single day passes without receiving an e-mail or instant message about their employment status.

When they do get an interview, they want to hear about opportunities. They do not want to work in a job where they sit around paying their dues doing mundane jobs. This has led some critics to call gamers the "entitlement generation."[7] Some claim that gamers feel entitled to the same perks and privileges that ten-, fifteen-, and twenty-year veterans receive. Gamers counter by saying that they do not want to spend their lives working at a boring, meaningless job, only to be thrown out when corporate numbers aren't met.

They want to make a difference, and do it quickly. One gamer, hired to work at a cereal company, showed up on the first day with a recipe for a new cereal.[8] Another gamer left his organization after he was continually told, "Don't make things better; just make things." He was afraid he would lose his "edge and drive."[9] A third gamer wanted to make a major internal sales pitch to his new company after being there only four weeks.[10] Gamers expect to be heard and taken seriously. If they are not, they look for more meaningful employment elsewhere.

Gamers want a balance between work and play. They want a job that allows them to accommodate their personal and family lives. They expect flexibility in terms of work hours and have a high desire for self-fulfillment. They are not constantly chasing ever higher salaries. They will often trade a meaningless job with a high salary for mobility, flexibility, and goal-oriented opportunities. Their job is not their life, as it is for many boomers.

Gamers expect their employer to have a global view of the world. They have traveled more than their parents had at the same age and have been on more airplane flights and trips abroad. They are in touch with people from other cultures through online role-play games and Internet connections.

A growing number are even receiving help with their homework from other parts of the world. Through e-tutoring and voice over Internet protocol, chat boards, digital whiteboards, and other collaborative media, they are receiving instructions, lessons, and insights into their schoolwork. Online tutoring companies in India make as much as $10 million a year from tutoring services.[11] These gamer students are comfortable with international diversity and expect the organizations that recruit them to have a global view as well.

Technological sophistication is also a gamer expectation. Gamers, who have grown up with technology, look to the Internet first when searching for job opportunities. Companies without a strong online job board or online presence find themselves at a disadvantage. Using technology, gamers have access to more information in terms of company history, articles, and corporate positions than any previous generation. Gamers routinely check salary comparison Web sites, have their résumés posted on numerous job boards (even when employed), and quickly learn of a job opening from a friend via instant messaging. They can even respond to the friend by attaching their résumé to an IM.

Once employed, gamers want to know the type of laptop they will receive as part of the employment package and if they will receive any additional gadgets, such as cell phones, personal digital assistants, or iPods. They expect the organizations they join to have the latest technological tools so they can do their job.

Many gamers fully expect to keep a small business on the side even when they are fully employed. In many instances, the freelance work is simply to keep their skills up to date. They don't see freelancing as disloyal; in fact, they would argue that they are staying loyal to their ideas, skills, and interests.

Among the methods that can help with gamer recruiting are tapping into gamers' technological acumen, working through their existing networks, sponsoring tournaments of all sorts, and developing recruiting games. Creating an environment in which gamers want to work is the most important aspect of recruitment.

This new work environment will not be molded after the boomer's command-and-control structure where face time is valued and flexibility is not part of the equation. It will be molded after the gamers, who value flexibility, making an impact, and the freedom of movement made possible by technology.

Take Advantage of Gamers' Technological Acumen

Gamers are heavy users of technology; use that to your advantage. Whenever you have a job opening, make sure that you use the Internet to advertise it. Post job announcements on the major job search Web sites, and place a detailed description of the opening on your corporate Web site as both an HTML document and a PDF. This is the obvious way of using the Web to attract gamers. It also makes sense to take the use of technology a little further when looking to recruit gamers. Follow the lead of consulting firms and create an entire "Careers" section of your Web site complete with specific tools that job searchers can use to learn about your organization and what it has to offer.

Include a frequently asked questions (FAQs) section on the site. This section should answer questions about the recruiting process, time frames for replying to an applicant, questions about submitting a résumé, and any other topics that may be of interest to a gamer considering employment within your organization.

Create a section describing the entire job application process. Let the candidates know what to expect from the application or résumé submission step all the way to an interview. You can even provide postemployment information like the different benefits packages or types of employment options in terms of telecommuting, part-time openings, or even job sharing.

Some firms even have online scenarios or game modules that prospective candidates can interact with to provide a general idea of what it is like to work for that company. The games provide two functions. First, they allow the gamer to better understand the types of work that is done within the organization and what they can expect if they secure a position. Second, if the game is deemed "cool" enough by gamers, you will get a lot of traffic to the site and generate some buzz. The more gamers who visit your site, the higher the chances are of recruiting them. Just be sure to contract with an actual game development company for the conceptualization and creation of the game. You want something that looks and plays like a video game, not a cheap imposter.

In another section of the site, create a searchable database of job openings that allows prospective employees to search for a job by location, title, required skills, or career type. Allow searches to be based on key words from job descriptions or other criteria that make sense within your industry.

Collect information as well. Allow a place for gamers to enter their résumé or complete an online application. Provide specific instructions so gamers can easily complete the required information. Create a message board for posting questions not covered in the FAQ section of the site. Consider creating surveys to poll prospective employees about interests, why they are looking at your company, or even what they are seeking from an employer. This information can be vital as you develop recruitment campaigns.

Create a newsletter to which prospective employees can subscribe. Provide articles about your company, its policies, and other important information. Develop feature articles highlighting gamers who work at your company. Focus on having gamers describe what they do at your organization and why they like working there. Include a section describing your recruitment process and how prospective employees can apply for a position. Provide information about flextime and part-time openings and work-life balance. (You do have work-life balance, right?)

If you do not want to create an entire newsletter, consider creating a really simple syndication (RSS) feed from a blog. Gamers can subscribe to the RSS feed and receive notification when it is updated. Others will just go right to your blog. Your employment blog should contain the same types of information as in the FAQ section and other sections of your "Career" Web site, but in a more informal style that is attractive to many gamers.

Consider having one or more gamers within your organization contribute to the blog on a regular basis, describing what it is like to work for your firm. The blog needs to be perceived as being honest and not too marketing or recruiting focused. If the gamers think someone is trying to trick or fool them, they will never return to the blog.

Taking technology a step further, consider posting job openings as podcasts. They are friendlier and more personal than mere text and can help to create a connection with prospective employees. Each podcast should describe job openings and associated requirements. Include testimonials of current gamer employees and a message from the CEO. It might be appropriate to include a message from customers explaining what they like about your organization. Describe interesting or exciting projects, and provide insight into the social and volunteer aspects of working for your organization.

Do not limit the use of technology to the Internet. In the lobby of your building, create a recruitment kiosk with information about the company, its products and services, FAQs, and other important information. Prospective employees who stop by your location are highly motivated and interested in your organization; provide them a way of learning more information in a quick and easy format.

Consider offering gadgets or gizmos to gamers when they are recruited into your organization. It seems like a gimmick, but actually it is useful in many ways. A large consulting firm is offering new recruits a video iPod when they come on board. The reasoning is that the iPod will contain video messages from the president, a map of the main complex, and podcasts of relevant information. The device is portable, easy to use, and can be updated on a regular basis with new corporate information. Marriott International offers "bit-size 'edutainment' training podcasts so workers can download information to their cell phones, laptops, and iPods."[12]

While gamers are comfortable with technology and electronically networked, they also enjoy a personal touch. Your entire recruitment effort cannot be solely focused on the electronic talents of gamers. Continue campus recruitment, but do it positively and with a high degree of personal involvement with the candidates. The recruiters need to be informed. Gamers do not expect a recruiter to send them to the Web site for additional information; they've already been there. Gamers appreciate timely feedback and are responsive to telephone calls and in-person interviews when given the opportunity. Gamers are both high technology and high touch.

Networked Nation

One of your best recruitment tools should already be in your organization: current gamer employees. A satisfied gamer employee is a great asset in the recruitment process. He or she can relate to peers, provide the message in gamer language, and represent the organization in a way not possible by boomers (or even Gen Xers).

Networked gamers naturally recruit each other into organizations they deem appropriate and that treat them well. Tap into the gamers' existing network, and encourage them to recruit friends and peers. It is not unusual for universities to place one student in an organization and then have that student recruit friends to come to work for that organization.

Sometimes organizations end up with eight, nine, ten, or even more graduates from the same college, all in the same department. As a bonus, they know the inside scoop on work ethic, productivity, and general personality that comes from going to school with someone but is impossible to discover during the traditional interview process. Gamers do the screening process themselves because they don't want to work with someone who doesn't perform.

To encourage this informal recruitment process, provide internal tools and methods to support the gamer's efforts. Create an internal recruitment tool kit so your recruitment message can be presented in a consistent manner. Provide information that can be copied and pasted into e-mails or instant messages and sent to friends. Give gamers the link to the corporate "Careers" Web site. Encourage them to contribute to the corporate blog, and give them opportunities to go back to their colleges to talk to and recruit fellow gamers. Allow them to create a podcast. When recruiting on college campuses, team a gamer with a boomer recruiter so the gamer can speak to the concerns or inquiries of the prospective gamer peer-to-peer. At one company, almost immediately after an application is received, the first person the prospective employee hears from is a fellow gamer. The gamer calls the prospect to answer any questions about the position, the company, and the job.

This process accomplishes a number of goals. It shows the organization is responsive. It connects the gamer peer-to-peer. It eliminates delays that occur when a manager is struggling with day-to-day responsibilities while trying to respond to job inquiries. It provides a sense of responsibility for the currently employed gamers. And if the person is eventually hired, the person with whom he or she made the first contact can serve as a mentor or a friend to the new employee.[13]

Encouraging gamers to network with peers and to help "sell" your organization provides a bonus. The gamers who assist with recruitment feel involved with the organization. They believe they are having an impact and making a difference. This translates into better retention of the gamers once they have been recruited into the organization.

Let the Tournament Begin

Organizations are turning to unique ways to attract talent and gain the attention of gamers. One method is to sponsor game tournaments to get the company's name, logo, and recruitment message in front of prospective employees so they will think about that organization as a viable employment option. Sponsoring a game tournament is a good idea but doesn't necessarily have a direct translation into recruitment success.

Finding the Top Coder. A more direct relationship between recruiting and tournaments, especially for finding top technical talent, is to sponsor a programming tournament. There are now companies that specialize in creating, hosting, and running tournaments specifically to attract top programming talent in the world. The *Wall Street Journal* describes these tournaments as a combination of the performance-under-time-pressure of the *Iron Chef* and the scheming psych-outs of *Survivor*.[14] These tournaments are not for the faint of heart, and that's why companies looking to recruit love them.

The leader and pioneer in the field of creating and promoting these tournaments is TopCoder. The company, located in Glastonbury, Connecticut, creates tournaments in which players from over two hundred countries battle each other for programming supremacy and prizes worth over $150,000.[15] TopCoder is led by Jack Hughes, the founder and chairman of the organization, who created the company because he wanted to "develop a new and different model for recruiting talent."[16] Today the company is known for recruiting programming talent as well as being a top software development firm that taps the talents of the tournament players to create elegant and efficient code.

The most visible and dramatic elements of the company are the tournaments it sponsors. "One of the newest tournament formats revolves around application building," Hughes explains. "We call these tournaments assembly competitions." This is where a group of programmers self-select to work together and then compete against other teams from all over the world to see which team can develop the best application for existing code snippets as well as create new code—virtual team-based programming competitions. Your team member can be across the street or across the globe. Many times the players haven't even met face-to-face."

The best-known tournaments are the ones that pit programmer against programmer. The process works as follows. First, any programmer who wants to compete in a face-to-face tournament becomes a member of the Web site. This allows him or her to compete in a number of online contests and to hone skills in working up through the ranks. The field of contenders is whittled down to a handful of the best through the online phase of the tournament.

The final round is held at a physical location complete with a large gathering of software programmers, fans, and corporate recruiters. The competitors are surrounded by large-display computer screens and cheering fans as they compete for the top prize. In the first round, contestants are given programming problems to solve. The problems are not easy, and the competition is fierce. Each player must solve three problems within a specified period of time. Each problem is assigned a point value. The harder the problem, the higher the points.

In the second round, the contestants can challenge each other's work. They try to present a scenario where the programmed code would fail. If they are successful, the originator of the code loses all his or her points, and the challenger is awarded more points.

Finally, a computer runs the code to determine the ultimate winner of the tournament—at least on the surface. The actual winner is the sponsoring company, which gets first dibs on hiring the best programmers of the day.

Companies like Yahoo!, Microsoft, and Sun have sponsored tournaments and then—when the top competitors have been identified—have used the opportunity to recruit. The situation is ideal because the programmers have a chance to show their skills and the companies have a chance to evaluate the talent from afar.

The contest format is an effective method for reaching programmers who most likely would not have been found with traditional recruiting strategies. No other venue brings together so many programmers willing to endure such a rigorous process. The programmers participate in these tournament because, as Hughes puts it, "the concept cuts across the programmer mind-set; they have a high affinity for competition, contests, and tournaments. They want to stand out because of what they create and how they create it." It is this competitive mind-set that brings these programmers to the competition and provides fertile ground for firms looking to recruit.

Even if a company can't afford to sponsor a tournament outright, it can still benefit from the tournament structure. Because TopCoder has programmers register on its site and tracks performance during the tournament process, they have a vast database of programmers who may never make it to the big game but are still of a high caliber. This database can be mined to find the right person for a particular position.

Sponsoring tournaments and contests can be just as effective for discovering talents other than programming. "We have hosted logo contests and gotten a tremendous response to those types of competitions," Hughes states. "These types of competitions can be used in less technical areas as well. Think of the skills involved with selling. They include having contacts, talent, and product knowledge; you don't need to be with an organization to have those skills. You could have contacts throughout the industry, you could have a good understanding of the industry, and you could have a good understanding of many different products. A company could sponsor a sales tournament for selling a new product and allow the salespeople from all over the world to compete against each other." Hughes predicts that in the near future, "We will hold tournaments that will involve the creation of ideas to build and launch companies. The winners will receive the financial backing to start a company and begin development of the winning idea."

At a much smaller scale than Hughes envisions, many business schools have already created business plan contests pitting one M.B.A. team against another. In some cases, the team that develops the most compelling proposal receives some venture capital to start the business. At Harvard, the award is $10,000; at the University of Iowa, the seed money is $3,000. California State University Fresno has a top prize of $6,500. One of the biggest prizes is offered by Rice University: a $100,000 investment in the company, almost $90,000 in cash, and over $50,000 in prizes.[17]

Answering a Mock Request for Proposal. These types of contests can be held in any field. At Bloomsburg University's Instructional Technology program, designed to teach budding young e-learning developers and designers, a contest is held every semester challenging students to develop the most effective response to an e-learning request for proposal (RFP). The teams complete three interrelated tasks, each evaluated by professionals from the learning and development field.

The first task is to create a forty-page written proposal that must outline the instructional and technical solution to the RFP and contain a project plan and schedule. The proposal is also required to contain a budget and a list of specific deliverables.

The second task is a twenty-minute presentation of the proposal. Each student must present his or her section of the proposal as part of a mock sales team. The team provides an overview of their solution and then answers questions from the attendees for fifteen minutes. The questions can be about the written or oral portion of the students' solution.

The third task is an unveiling of a prototype of the recommended solution. The functionality of the prototype must be demonstrated to the attendees. The job of the students is to explain the prototype, highlighting its features and capabilities.

Once all of the students have presented their solutions, a final winning team is chosen. The learning professionals then have an opportunity to interview all of the students who participated in the event. The advantage to the attendees from the corporations is that they have been able to evaluate, in a real-world situation, the presentation, written communication, and software development skills of the students. In one day, they evaluate over twenty students and choose those that would be the best fit for their organization.

You're in the Army Now (Virtually)

The U.S. Army, always a proponent of simulations and games, was one of the first organizations to see the importance of creating games to attract and recruit the new gamer generation. In the late 1990s, they created a game to take "advantage of young adults' broad use of the Internet for research and communication and their interest in games for entertainment and exploration." On July 4, 2002, the U.S. Army released an online role-play game that "provides civilians with an inside perspective and a virtual role in today's premier land force: the U.S. Army" (Figure 9.2).[18] The game provides the player with a chance to participate in a number of military occupations.

Figure 9.2. The U.S. Army's Online Role-Play Game for Recruitment.

The online game is free to anyone who registers, and millions have—over 7.24 million. The game has been updated and changed several times since its release, but the concept is the same: to recruit, inform, and interest young Americans in a career with the U.S. Army. The game includes everything from a virtual boot camp to learning how to load weapons (as shown in Figure 9.3) to special mission assignments.

The desire is to place soldiering front and center in popular culture. Online players have registered over 94 million hours playing the game. In addition, actual soldiers occasionally go online within the game environment and answer players' questions about being in the military.

The army's efforts seem to be paying off. A growing number of freshmen at West Point have indicated that they've played the game,[19] and a survey by the army showed that 29 percent of all young American adults ages sixteen to twenty-four have had some contact with the game in the previous six months.[20]

In the game, there are "Web links through which players can connect to the Army of One homepage."[21] The game is used to help potential recruits understand the skills and attributes that make a good soldier. The potential

Figure 9.3. Learn Virtually About Firearms Used in the Army.

matching of skills and attributes learned in the game to those actually used in the military reminds some critics of the 1984 movie, *The Last Starfighter.* In the movie, the lead character, Alex Rogan, lives in a trailer and plays an arcade game where the goal is to destroy enemy space ships. The arcade game is actually a simulation of a starfighter. When Alex achieves the highest score, Centauri, an alien, comes to Earth to recruit him to navigate an actual starfighter. Others make the comparison with Orson Scott Card's science-fiction classic, *Ender's Game,* where the main character, Ender Wiggin, competes in a series of military games as he trains to become a great military commander, which he eventually does in a most unexpected way. Critics contend that it might not be so far-fetched for the U.S. military to identify individuals with excellent military leadership skills through the America's Army game.

In spite of the possible similarities with *The Last Starfighter* and *Ender's Game,* the U.S. Army does not identify players and tag them for recruitment. Actual names are not linked to user names or passwords by the army. However, it is possible to request information and reveal your player name to an army recruiter. Only after you have agreed to volunteer that information can the army use your gaming records to facilitate matching career opportunities within the army to the missions in which you have spent a great deal of time. The army uses the statistics about your game play to "provide the best possible match between the attributes and interests of potential Soldiers and the attributes of career fields and training opportunities."[22]

Workplace Implications

The best recruitment tool of all is a work environment gamers enjoy. This doesn't mean gamers are looking for all fun and games (pun intended); they understand the need to work hard to achieve success. In fact, they expect success through hard work. What they want is an environment that is conducive to how they like to work and is not molded in the boomer structure of all work and no play. The hallmark of a gamer-friendly organization will be flexibility. The gamer working environment will have several key aspects:

- Telecommuting and cybercommuting
- Flexible work schedules
- Meaningful assignments
- Mentoring programs
- New score-keeping methods
- Continual personal growth opportunities
- Free agency

Telecommuting and Cybercommuting

Gamers want the ability to work anywhere. These young employees are used to unprecedented freedom to work at odd hours in odd places like coffee shops, bookstores, and airports. Gamers are used to working and learning virtually. Remember, this is a generation that has had online tutors from counties across the world and interacts through online games with friends in countries they've never visited. They are not afraid to work online.

Communications technologies have enabled them to collaborate from anywhere with anyone at any time. Gamers want this flexibility on the job as well. But it can be an issue. Boomers are more in tune with face time than virtual offices. A gamer sends an instant message to the person in the next cubicle, a boomer. In response, the boomer walks over. This explains why telecommuting never took off with the boomer generation.

In contrast, telecommuting or cybercommuting will soar with the gamers. These workers want organizations that provide tools for desk-free work and the policies to support it. Copiers, printers, scanners, and other tools necessary to set up a home office are available at low prices. It won't be long before video phones are a standard part of every office. Gamers want to use those tools to work from home.

In addition, several outside forces are making home offices more and more attractive. The threat of terror and contagious disease and the desire to live in less crowded areas mean that telecommuting is a flexibility gamers want. Companies that provide this option will have success retaining these young employees.

Flexible Work Schedules

Scheduled flexibility attracts gamers to organizations. Gamers want part-time, full-time, and job-share options. They desire to balance, more effectively than the boomers have, their work and their personal life. Companies that understand and accommodate this balance will get dedicated gamers who are highly focused during work hours.

This desire for flexibility is not just within companies; gamers desire to act as independent agents doing work for one company and then another. Many of the earliest gamers in the marketplace have already made the transition several times from being a full-time employee to working as an independent contractor and back to full-time employment. Because they are so networked, they seek to work in virtual organizations with their friends and colleagues whom they know are capable and trustworthy. Once an opportunity is over, they will switch to something else.

Within an organization, it is a good idea to provide a great deal of flexibility and opportunity to work on a variety of different projects. This keeps the gamers engaged and interested in what is happening within the organization.

Meaningful Assignments

Provide gamers with assignments that are meaningful to the organization. They like to know they are contributing to the success of the organization. Give them the opportunity.

This need for meaningful assignments starts early. Jengyee Liang, author of *Hello Real World!* a book that provides advice and insight to both graduates seeking internships and their potential employers, states, "What I mean by meaningful work is an assignment or multiple assignments that has impact on the business, is not tedious, and is well structured but allows some room for the intern to be creative or make decisions. The ideal project also would span across several disciplines or internal departments, which would give the intern opportunities to interact with other individuals at your firm."[23] And that's just at the internship level. Imagine the expectations of a full-blown new employee.

Although it may not be feasible to tie every task directly to the future success of the organization, efforts should be made to let gamers know that their assignment is important and will have an impact somewhere within the organization. If gamers do not find themselves in positions that allow them to make a difference, they often create their own assignments and work to make an impact through skunk works or other nontraditional methods.

If they develop a meaningful improvement or product, give them the opportunity to run with the idea and make it a reality. They need to be guided and provided with instructions and advice, but their energy, enthusiasm, and willingness to keep at a task make them a valuable asset on important work projects.

One of the main reasons gamers leave an organization is that they feel their ideas are not being heard by management. Take the time to let the gamers know that their ideas are being heard. Encourage more ideas if you think the first few are off-base, but don't discourage their desire to make an impact or you will lose them as employees.

These meaningful assignments should also include volunteer activities supported by the company. Gamers are volunteers. They are one of the largest volunteer generations. This proclivity for volunteering is good for organizations and communities and should be supported and encouraged. Not only do gamers themselves like to think they are making a difference, they also want to work for a company that is trying to make a difference. Often these are ways for a company to get in front of even more gamers who will show up at a volunteer event and be exposed to the company.

Mentoring Programs

Mentoring programs can cut both ways in an organization. The traditional program is when a younger employee is teamed with a more seasoned employee who can guide the newer employee and show him or her the ropes. This is a valuable opportunity for a gamer to get to know the boomer employees and become acclimated to the organization. It is also a chance for the boomers to understand a bit more about the gamers.

Taking that concept further is the idea of reverse mentoring, where the goal is not for a veteran employee to teach a new employee but rather for a new employee to teach the veteran. This idea received widespread publicity when Jack Welsh, at the time CEO of General Electric, suggested that the more senior executives within his organization needed to team up with newer employees so they could better understand the Internet. Organizations need to bring in gamers to help managers and other boomers learn about blogs, podcasting, and instant messaging.

Mentoring programs can be valuable for both boomers and gamers if they are structured correctly. Both groups need to learn from each other and share their knowledge and ideas. The strength of an organization is in how well information is shared among its members.

New Score-Keeping Methods

Gamers like to keep score. They want their name on the high score list. It is not enough just to be good; they want others to know it as well. If this obsession with high scores carries over to the workplace, there could be problems. Boomers typically don't talk about salary and money; it is not the proper thing to do, and they are not as financially sophisticated as the gamers have become.

In fact, today's entrants into the workforce are generally savvy when it comes to money and savings. As many as 37 percent expect to start saving for retirement before they become twenty-five years old.[24]

If gamers decide to use salaries to keep score against other gamers and there really is a scarcity of talent as predicted, salaries will be subject to huge increases. In the late 1990s, some of this was seen with signing bonuses, students being hired before they graduated from college or even high school, and employees being wooed away from current positions for twice their salary.

This situation is akin to professional sports players, who demand more money just so they are higher on the list than their peers. When a professional player is paid $42 million, another player insists on $43 million. The extra million dollars is not needed to pay the mortgage or make car payments; it is because he believes he is better than the guy making $42 million and thinks his salary should reflect his skill level. Money is no longer looked at rationally; instead, it is viewed as a way to keep score. Players want to make the high score list in terms of salary, not because they care about the money per se, but because they want to make the "high score."

Gamers will be the same. They want high salaries, not because they value money for money's sake (as discussed before, we know they don't), but because they want to be "better" than their peers, and an objective method of measuring this is salary. Boomers must understand that gamers are going to want to use salaries to keep score.

Salary calculators, job postings, discussion boards, and other technological tools will make it possible for gamers to gauge exactly where they are on the salary scale. If they deem their salaries too low, they may ask for increases so they can make the "high score list." This will not be a favorable position for employers who were caught off guard during the dot-com talent rush. Employers may again find themselves on the wrong side of the supply-demand equation.

To help defend against wage inflation in an environment where everyone wants the highest score, boomer managers are going to need to devise other methods of keeping score and compensating gamers. These might include electronic gadgets as perks, increased days off, shorter workdays, trophies, or other methods of quantitative score keeping. The goal will be to provide low-cost methods of rewarding gamers with items or perks that they can brag about but that do not cost the company too much money.

Continual Personal Growth Opportunities

One saving grace companies may have in terms of salary inflation is the gamers' desire to seek self-fulfillment over pure salary numbers. Gamers indicate on survey after survey that they want to work not just for the money, but for a chance to have an impact and to grow personally and professionally.

When they are looking for jobs, salary-related benefits are often not as critical in the ultimate selection of an employer as are the organization's leadership, the gamers' learning prospects, and a work environment that offers a constant challenge. Gamers also desire the opportunity to work on a variety of projects and receive feedback on how they are doing.

While boomers are accustomed to yearly performance reviews (usually conducted late), gamers want and need feedback more frequently—daily, in fact. Games give instant feedback, and gamers have been programmed to expect instant feedback. The more feedback they receive, the better they perform. This can translate into developing career paths that include more frequent but smaller promotional steps. Gamers don't want to wait five years for a promotion; they want to move quickly. Although it is not always possible, smaller steps can provide a good compromise between the gamer's desire for rapid acceleration and the reality of needing to learn skills and knowledge before truly proceeding up the career ladder.

Free Agency

Top performers of the gamer generation may not want to be an employee with your company even if they do want to perform work for you. Today, if an organization has a problem to solve, it tries to hire the best person with the most appropriate expertise (programming, marketing, operations) to solve the problem. The difficulty arises once the problem is solved; then the company must find something else for that person to do or the investment is wasted. There is a lot of friction involved with the hiring and firing process, so people are typically kept within an organization even if they are not solving an immediate need.

As TopCoder's founder, Hughes, points out, "In the boomer world people would be hired by one company and come to a single physical place to work. Now with the convergence of technologies creating a virtual world, people with high skill levels are looking for multiple outlets for their talents rather than being confined by one organization. The opportunities and the challenges are greater if they act as a free agent instead of an employee of a single company."

Technology is allowing a free agency among top performers who can sell their talents to the highest bidder. While this may seem on the surface to be bad for companies that want to hire and retain the most talented people possible, the process can be beneficial for both the individual and the company that hires a free agent. The most valuable aspect from the corporate perspective is that the traditional costs of hiring and overhead are being driven out of the system by using free agents.

Hughes points out, "As companies get better at figuring out models to work with individual performers, costs will be driven out of the system. The savings from the overall cost reductions within the system will, in part, go to those individuals who are performing at a high level and, in a large part, go to the companies using free agents."

In corporate and academic institutions, the concept of employee needs to be rethought. Companies that offer top performers a chance to work as a free agent may have the best recruitment and retention strategy of all for sustaining a workforce of members of the gamer generation.

■ ■ ■ ■

SUMMARY

Tournaments, games, and interactive Web sites are just some of the tools that can be used to recruit gamers. Once they are recruited, you need to find methods to keep them happy and employed, with flexible work schedules, meaningful assignments, and robust mentoring programs. You also need to throw in an occasional game, simulation, or gadget to hold their attention.

This can be difficult when budgets are tight. Justifying gadgets, games, and gizmos can be a tough sell if upper management and others are not in agreement. The next chapter discusses some ways of introducing the organization to the benefits of these tools.

Please, Please Can I Buy
a Game, Gadget, or Gizmo?

INEVITABLY, AS I AM ABOUT three-quarters of the way through a presentation describing the need to transfer knowledge to gamers through the use of games, gadgets, and gizmos, a hand shoots up in the air.

"This is all well and good, but how do we sell this to our management?" a concerned, somewhat hostile audience member asks.

"Well . . . ," I begin to reply.

Someone else interrupts: "Yes, there is no way I am going to be able to convince my management to pay thousands of dollars for the development of a game or issue iPods to new employees. No way."

"Don't call them games," shouts an audience member trying to help. "Call them simulations or interactive learning experiences."

"That's right. *Game* is a four-letter word," an enthusiastic woman from the back row informs the audience.

I do the math; she's right.

"We'll have to wait until all the boomers retire before we can do this kind of stuff," another audience member contributes.

"Or die," someone shouts.

Tough Sell

Selling the use of gadgets, games, and gizmos to executives and managers is not easy. When digital immigrants hear those terms, images of toys, trinkets, and teddy bears dance in their heads. Many boomers think of these items as frivolous and inappropriate in a business setting. The truth is that today's gadgets, games, and gizmos are tomorrow's business tools. Instant messaging, wikis, podcasts, and games are already working their way into businesses and organizations as serious tools. Innovative companies are using these items to gain a competitive advantage.

Still, boomers have issues. No boomer wants to get caught playing games at work. It would look bad. In fact, a boomer New York mayor fired a city employee when he noticed the employee playing solitaire at work. The employee was given no warning and no severance pay. "The workplace is not an appropriate place for games," the mayor stated as justification.[1] Would the mayor fire someone for reading a newspaper at work, taking too long on coffee break, or reading a magazine? Many boomers don't really believe in this whole "gadget/game thing." They think it is a fad or just an excuse for playing games and not really working (Figure 10.1).

This attitude can make the task of selling gadgets and games difficult but not impossible. Gadgets and games can be brought into organizations in one of four ways. One is for the chief executive officer to somehow "get game" or "get gadgets" and become convinced that games or gadgets are the way to transfer knowledge. This can occur after she has attended a seminar, read an interesting book on the subject, or conversed with a CEO of another organization that has successfully created and deployed game-based or gadget-based learning. This is the ideal situation and makes the use of gadgets or games an easy sell. Unfortunately, this rarely occurs; it is akin to structuring

---

Figure 10.1. It Is Not Always Easy to Sell Management or the Administration on the Use of Gadgets, Games, or Gizmos, But It Can Be Done.

Source: Reprinted with permission of the artist, Kristin Longenecker.

your retirement plan around the fact that you play the lottery every day and at some point expect to hit the jackpot. You need a plan B.

Realistically, there are three methods for selling gadgets and games to an organization. The first is the traditional business case approach and is most appropriate for large-scale initiatives. The second is to dress up the gadgets or games so they look more corporate. The third is to slowly introduce games and gadgets into an organization until one day they are commonplace and no one gives them a second thought.

Regardless of the method chosen, the first step is to understand the culture of your organization. You need to determine how receptive various levels of management and rank-and-file employees may be to the idea of using gadgets and games for transferring knowledge. Understanding how your organization reacts to the introduction of a technological innovation like a game, gadget, or gizmo can help you decide on the best strategy for introducing those items into your organization.

Diffusion of Innovations

The adoption of any innovation is difficult. It becomes even more difficult when that innovation carries with it a stigma of being childish or gimmicky, as is often the case when boomers think of gadgets, games, and gizmos. The problem is how to get the organization to adopt the innovation as part of its operations. Adoption rates can be slow for technological innovations.

Instant messaging was introduced in November 1996, has many advantages over e-mail, is ubiquitous among the gamer generation, and yet is still not widely used for business communications. Yet other innovations like the cell phone have been quickly adopted and are now ubiquitous. These items are diffused into an organization or a culture quickly and almost effortlessly.

Widespread adoption of innovations requires the new technology to have certain traits and attributes that make it attractive to the organization into which the innovation is introduced. One person who has studied the topic extensively is Everett Rogers, the author of *Diffusion of Innovations.* Rogers defines *diffusion* as "the process in which an innovation is communicated through certain channels over time among the members of a social system."[2] He has developed a list of attractiveness criteria required to have an innovation diffused into an organization.

Attractiveness Criteria

These attractiveness criteria should be kept in mind when trying to influence boomer executives and managers to buy into gadgets, games, and gizmos; focusing on them makes the job of selling the games and gadgets easier. Rogers's ideas have been echoed in such works as *The Tipping Point* by Malcolm Gladwell and *Crossing the Chasm* by Geoffrey Moore.[3]

Relative Advantage. This is the degree to which an innovation is perceived as being better than the idea it supersedes.[4] Executives and managers must see the use of games within the organization as having an advantage over the existing training methodologies such as classroom instruction or traditional e-learning. If the new handheld personal digital assistant is not seen as an advantage over a clipboard and a piece of paper, its adoption is delayed. Instant messaging was adopted among the young gamer set because it had an advantage over e-mail: talking to the person instantly with no delay. The younger set saw this as a huge advantage. But for the most part, boomers didn't see the advantage of IM over e-mail. They didn't think an instant response was needed every time a message was sent, and besides, they didn't want everyone else to know whether they were online. So they didn't see the advantage of learning yet another technology.

As one self-identified boomer wrote in a librarian-oriented blog posting, "IM in particular destroys context, there's no easy way to manage attribution, you have to be sitting in front of the PC waiting as the IM comes in. And every IM app I've seen is some gimmicky Flash driven mess, littered with cutesy icons and ads. This sort of thing seems fine for something like a '911' message, or casual chatting, ordering pizza, etc., but for real, literacy-enhancing library work, it appears useless to me."[5] (Yes, our boomer librarian does blog but doesn't like IM.)

Research has shown that the concept of relative advantage is an important predictor of an innovation's rate of adoption.[6] Relative advantage is the idea of a better mouse trap. Executives and managers need to see that gadgets and games are indeed a better mouse trap than traditional methodologies. The higher the perceived value of the innovation, the faster the innovation is adopted throughout the organization. Although boomers may not see these items as having a relative advantage, gamers do.

Therefore, if the training or other departments want to implement gaming as a training methodology, the advantages of using games must be clearly defined and presented. Otherwise the sentiment of our boomer librarian will prevail: "And with no apologies at all, I will say that gaming belongs in Chucky Cheeses and NOT the public library!"

An effective method of showing an advantage is to benchmark with other organizations, providing examples and case studies of how other organizations have implemented gadgets and games in their organization. Let the executives and managers know that neither they nor their organizations are the first to try games as a method of training. Provide the example of the U.S. Army presented in Chapter Nine or the example of Johnson & Johnson from Chapter Two.

Not only executives and managers need to be convinced. Often rank-and-file employees shy away from games or gadgets for fear of being fired or of being seen as not serious about their work. Employees may feel guilty or apprehensive about using games as a form of training.

The training and development team must implement a marketing campaign to articulate to employees the advantages of game-based instruction. Then marketing must show real business reasons for the use of games. Although many of the advantages will be geared toward the entire organization, an effort must be made to personalize the advantages so each individual within the company will realize a personal gain because of the use of games as training. In addition, you may want to indicate that the use of a game as a training tool does not necessarily mean the training will be easy.

Compatibility. This is the degree by which an innovation is perceived by the adopters as being consistent with the current mission of the organization, past experiences of the workforce, current technology, or current needs of the employees. Instant messaging was compatible with the existing network. Using IM was not much different from using e-mail. IM was highly compatible with the e-mail status quo.

The concept of compatibility becomes an issue when working with two different generations. For gamers, the use of games is compatible with their experiences, values, and interests. Gamers use handheld gadgets, wikis, and other new products for sharing information routinely. These technologies are compatible with their Web and game experiences. The same cannot be said for boomers.

To help convince boomers to adopt an innovation, the use of the new technology or technique must not be perceived as an overthrow of all the methods that have come before; a complete overthrow is too radical for most executives, managers, and employees to accept. For example, abandoning all communication systems in favor of nothing but blogs is an overthrow mentality. Overthrow should not be the goal.

All training should not be done as a game, just like all training should not be online or conducted in the traditional way. Not every organizational communication needs to suddenly switch to collaboration using a wiki. A mix of methodologies, approaches, and technologies is important, and gadgets and games need to be presented as just another capability within the tool kit, not as the entire tool kit, as some zealots tend to want.

Compatibility can be achieved by illustrating how the use of games fits with the current training practices of the company. For instance, if employees are now using role-play games to learn how to sell products in a traditional stand-up training class, explain how placing those same role plays online is an advantage in terms of time and opportunities for practice. Show how simple games like hangman and racing games are actually drill and practice in disguise. Provide examples of how the handheld gadget simplifies the paperwork process or how on-demand video is similar to a portable VCR or DVD player.

A critical aspect of compatibility is how well the innovation meets the needs of the current workforce. Surveying the needs of workers and using demographic information to build the case for game-based learning can be effective. The survey may also seek answers about the workforce's thought processes, attitudes, and behaviors. These data can be powerful in helping to convince boomers of the need for games and gadgets. Demonstrate to the executives how the needs of the members of this workforce are compatible with the solutions offered through games and gadgets.

Complexity. One justifiable fear many executives and managers have of online games and these "newfangled gadgets" is that they don't know how to play or use them. Executives and managers know what happens in a training class; they've been in dozens. This is not so with an online game. An intuitive interface for a gamer is complex for many boomers, and working a multifunctional gadget is not something they want to do. Boomers hand it to their kids or grandkids. They can go through a period of deep frustration when they repeatedly fail at mastering a game or using a gadget properly.

As Rogers points out, "The complexity of an innovation, as perceived by members of a social system, is negatively related to its rate of adoption."[7] The higher the perception of complexity, the slower the rate of adoption. Efforts must be made to train boomers on how to use the gadget or play the game in as simple a manner as possible.

One method is to team up a boomer with a gamer and allow the gamer and boomer to learn together how to work a gadget or play a training game. This is the concept of reverse mentoring mentioned in Chapter Nine. The real advantage here is that not only will information be exchanged concerning the game or gadget, but the pair will also transfer other knowledge that can be valuable to the organization.

Another method is to introduce casual games in a classroom environment so that boomers can get a sense of how to play the game. In a classroom, boomers can get help from an instructor if they get stuck or have a problem. The classroom environment can also be used to provide the mental message that it is okay to play. In addition, boomers need to understand that not all game play is fun; sometimes it is frustrating. But frustration is not necessarily a bad thing during game play because it can lead to memorable learning. Tying emotions to learning is a powerful combination.

Providing a basic tutorial on how to play the game is also a good method for making the game more accessible to boomers. The gamers will skip right past the tutorial or "how-to-play" button, but the boomers will take the time to learn how to play the game if the instructions are available.

Trialability. This is the idea of kicking the tires. Later adopters of an innovation are influenced strongly by those who have already adopted the innovation. In some cases, the fact that an innovation has been tried out at another company or even several other companies is enough to persuade people to use games and gadgets within their organizations.

This is where it becomes important to let individuals within the organization know that the use of games as teaching tools and gadgets as business devices is occurring and that the pioneering has already been done. The adoption of these items has begun to occur and will soon reach what Malcolm Gladwell calls the tipping point—the point at which widespread adoption will occur.

The adoption of instant messaging was helped in part by people letting their friends use the software on their computers. In addition, when one person got instant messaging, he or she wanted friends to get it as well so they could communicate: "Hey, this is pretty cool. I'm going to download it onto my computer." Soon most teenagers had instant messaging software.

Create areas on the corporate Web site for games that can be tried out. Encourage groups to play the games in the lunchroom to give everyone a chance to try or observe. Allow the games to be played at home. Have a sign-out system for gadgets so they can be tried out in the privacy of a boomer's home or behind closed doors in an office so no one laughs when the "stupid gadget" won't stop beeping.

Observability. This refers to the ability of a person to observe another person working with the technology. Can the boomer watch fellow boomers use the gadget? Can the boomer watch her colleague in sales successfully complete a level?

An important aspect of observability is that the person being observed is of a similar social status as the person doing the observation. It is important to show boomers that other boomers are playing the games or using the gadgets and to find similar companies that are using games to teach and use them as examples. The closer the observed person or organization is to the potential adopters, the more likely the adoption of the innovation or, in this case, the gadget, game, or gizmo.

Early in the instant messaging adoption cycle, people observed others using instant messaging at the homes of friends. Soon they too started instant messaging. This led to quick adoption by gamers.

With a game, it is a little harder to supply opportunities for observation. This is why introducing the game in the classroom setting is effective. The instructor can play a level or round in the game, and the boomers can observe the game play and then try it themselves. This same technique can be used to help with the adoption of gadgets, which can be handed out in class and worked on together.

The Games and Gadgets Adoption Continuum

Highlight the attributes of the games and gadgets as you sell them throughout the organization. Realize that different boomers within the organization will adopt the innovations at different rates. Certain employees in the company will be attracted to different attributes and accept the use of gadgets or games more quickly than others.

In any organizational system, there are five types of individuals on the adoption continuum. At one end of the continuum are the technology enthusiasts who embrace, almost blindly, any new technology. At the opposite end are skeptics, who reject any use of games or gadgets in a corporate or business setting.[8] In between there are technology visionaries, pragmatists, and conservatives. Each one is more hesitant to adopt games and gadgets as business tools than the previous one. The challenge is to present the use of games and gadgets to the individuals within these different groups appropriately. The difficulty is that the sales pitch used for the technology enthusiasts and visionaries is exactly the opposite of the pitch you should use for the pragmatists, conservatives, and skeptics.

One final piece in the games and gizmos adoption puzzle is a person known as the "knowledge broker," "opinion leader," or, as Malcolm Gladwell has named them, "connectors."[9] These are the people within an organization or group who are connected to everyone and exert a large amount of influence over technology adoption within an organization. The unique characteristics of each group need to be understood to facilitate the adoption of gadgets and games.

Technology Enthusiasts. These are the hard-core gamers of the organization. Techies love technology because it is technology. While many gamers tend toward being techies, not all gamers are techies, and some boomers are techies as well. These technology enthusiasts enjoy and are fundamentally committed to any new technology and are the first to embrace it. They like to fiddle with games and want to be the first ones to know how a new gadget works.

Techies want to know all of the specifications, the system requirements, and any other technical aspect of the game or gadget that can be known.

These are the individuals who bought the three-thousand-dollar bag phones because they wanted to be the first with the new technology. They also bought the twenty-five-hundred-dollar cell phone, the thousand-dollar cell phone, and now the ninety-nine-dollar cell phone. Techies want the latest and greatest at every step. These are the people in your organization who are able to pick out the next big thing. They are not interested in the business advantages of the games or gadgets; they are in to the newness or "wow" factor of these items. They ask, "Is it cool? Does it do neat stuff?" and "What are the specs of this item?"

Visionaries. The visionaries are not interested in technology for technology's sake. Their interest is the business advantage of a gadget or game. They want to know how this new technology is going to position the organization ahead of competitors. How are gadgets and games going to give them a strategic or tactical advantage?

Visionaries typically look for advice and information about new technologies from the techies, with whom they are able to communicate effectively. Visionaries will quiz the techies about the potential business uses and whether other organizations are using these technologies. These individuals are important during the adoption of new technologies because they are able to translate the technological advantages of the gadgets and games into business advantages.

Visionaries are highly interested in gadgets and games because they are new to the business environment and can be used as an advantage over competitors precisely because they are new.

Visionaries ask, "How can I use this new technology to my advantage before the competition gets it?"

Selling to Techies and Visionaries. Together, the techies and the visionaries are the early adopters of gadgets and games within an organization. Both like the idea of a brand-new approach or use for technology even if their reasons are slightly different: techies want to explore the new technology, and visionaries want to exploit it.

Gadgets, games, and gizmos appeal to both groups precisely because they are new and few other organizations are deploying them on a widespread basis. When selling the use of games and gadgets to these two groups, stress the newness of using gadgets and games for business applications.

When selling to techies, let them know the software specifications, the hardware capabilities, and the technology behind them. Stress the newness of the technology and its innovative uses. When selling to visionaries, let them know that it provides an advantage to themselves personally and their organization. Show them how the new technologies will provide a competitive advantage over others. Sell the newness of the idea.

Unfortunately, the newness of games and gadgets is exactly what the pragmatists, conservatives, and skeptics dislike. These individuals, many of them boomers, are not interested in pushing the envelope in either business practices or technological features. They want a solution that is more in line with the status quo.

Pragmatists. This group typically deliberates for some time before adopting an innovation like the corporate use of gadgets or games. This group wants the proof that games are better educational tools than traditional training. They want the white papers, the research basis, and the facts before proceeding. They want to know that the technology is being used by hundreds of others before they will adopt it themselves.

Although they are deliberate and demanding of proof, the pragmatists do not want to be the last group to adopt a new technology. If they see that something is working and seems to make sense, they will move to adopt. They will not take it up as quickly as the techies or the visionaries, but they will adopt gadgets and games after they see a few positive case studies and learn how other organizations are benefiting from the innovation. These are not the pioneers, but they do follow close behind.

The pragmatists ask, "Does this really work?" Once they learn that it does, they embrace the innovation.

Conservatives. Even less eager to embrace innovation are the conservatives. These employees are extremely slow to adopt gadgets and games as business tools and are cautious toward new technologies in general. Whereas the pragmatists wanted to know that games and gadgets are being used by hundreds of others, the conservatives want to know that they are being used by millions of others. This group is hard to please and a bit cynical about new technologies.

Members of this group will not adopt the use of gadgets and games until the techies, visionaries, and pragmatists have all done so. They are unconvinced about the ability of these items to add any value to the organization. Conservatives want assurances that the use of new technologies is more or less like the use of older technologies—just better.

One mistake that is often made when trying to sell the concept of games and gadgets is to spend a great deal of time concentrating efforts on trying to convert the conservatives to becoming enthusiastic about using gadgets and games. The effort is not worth the payoff. It is better to concentrate on the first three groups, and then the conservatives will naturally adopt the use of gadgets and games.

Conservatives ask, "What's the matter with doing this the traditional way? It has worked for years, and I don't understand why we need to change methods."

Skeptics. Skeptics will never think that gadgets and games are appropriate for transferring knowledge. They delight in challenging the hype and claims of the advantages of gadgets and games: "This is childish." "Yes, it might be entertaining, but it doesn't teach." "Where is the evidence that games are better than traditional learning?" "It takes me three times as long to enter information into this handheld gizmo." "The gamers are no different from the boomers."

Skeptics will continually ask apparently innocent questions in an attempt to undermine the implementation of new technologies: "What if I don't have time for this game?" "What if the battery runs out on this handheld?" They will even try to locate stories of failure to support their case.

Skeptics are quick to point out problems and exploit any mistakes or weaknesses in the implementation of gadgets and games. They are the ever-present critics of the new methodology. Fortunately, there are usually only a few skeptics within any particular organization. Unfortunately, they tend to be highly vocal and attempt to persuade the pragmatists and the conservatives to become skeptics (remember our blogging librarian). The point of reference for skeptics is the past.

You can educate the conservatives and pragmatists to avoid having them influenced by the skeptics, but it is impossible to convert a true skeptic. Spending energy and resources attempting to convert skeptics is a waste of time. Let the skeptics vent, but focus energies on the other groups to achieve success.

Skeptics will tell you, "This will never work; it's a fad or gimmick."

Connector. Connectors know people throughout the entire organization. They easily move in and out of the social circles and are widely respected for their knowledge and insights in a variety of areas. Connectors influence the attitudes and even the overt behavior of others informally in a desired way with relative frequency. This informal leadership is "not a function of the individuals' formal position or status within the system. Opinion leadership is earned and maintained by the individual's technical competence, social accessibility, and conformity to the systems norms."[10]

Connectors have a social network that allows them to serve as a social model whose innovative behavior is imitated by other members of the system. Connectors talk with the techies, find out what is cool, translate that coolness to the visionaries, and influence the pragmatists and conservatives with their knowledge, confidence, and enthusiasm about the new technology. Because of their influence, connectors are extremely important in the gadget and game adoption continuum. If they are enthusiastic about the gadgets, games, and gizmos, others in the organization will follow. If they are opposed, others will be as well.

Early in the adoption or sales process, you need to identify the connectors of the organization. This can be done by surveying or interviewing people in the organization to see whose opinion they value and respect. Once you have identified the connectors, provide them with information, resources, and evidence that the innovative use of gadgets, games, and gizmos will be valuable to themselves and to the organization. Send them to conferences, buy them books on the subject, and send them to benchmark against other organizations. Money invested in bringing a connector on board is well spent.

Workplace Implications

Once you know the requirements for making an innovation attractive to your organization and the types of individuals to whom you are going to sell the idea or you are going to recruit to help sell the idea, you need to determine the most appropriate method.

Several methods can hasten the adoption of gadgets, games, or gizmos within your organization. These include the traditional method of creating a business case or more innovative methods like creating a skunk works team to pursue the initiative on the sly until it is ready to be released to the organization or even disguising games so they look more corporate.

Building the Business Case

The best time to create a business case is when large amounts of money are at stake. Of course, what constitutes large depends on your organization and its policies and procedures. You may even need to develop smaller business cases to convince a business line manager of the value of an innovative solution.

The steps to building a business case for the introduction of games, gadgets, or gizmos into an organization is similar to building a business case for other business tools or large-scale purchases. Clearly state your case for the use of a gadget, game, or gizmo over other alternatives and show quantified benefits. Follow these steps for creating a business case:

1. Start with a problem statement.

2. Provide a problem description. Describe the current situation, and indicate the cost of maintaining the status quo.

3. Provide a proposed solution—the rationale for choosing a game or gadget and what you hope to accomplish.

4. State the key objectives and success indicators of the proposed solution.

5. Compare the two solutions by making a financial comparison and analysis of the situation.

6. Make the final recommendation.

You may not need to build a business case for every single initiative or for each purchase of a new gadget; however, certain elements in the business case can be important for selling games and gadgets at any time. For example, the results of collecting demographic information can be helpful in making a case for the use of a single game even if a formal business case is not needed for the particular project.

The focus on the business needs driving the adoption of a game can be helpful even if a complete set of numbers is not required. The business case process does not always have to be formalized to be effective; bits and pieces of the process can be undertaken to provide certain data points throughout the selling cycle.

Problem Statement. Clearly state the problem you are trying to address by proposing the use of a game or gadget. The problem statement needs to be framed as a business problem. You cannot write:

> The purpose of this business case is to propose the creation of a game to teach our sales force how to learn about new product launches without bringing them to headquarters for a training session.

The focus is on the game, not the business need. It would be better to write:

> The purpose of this business case is to create a new method to help our sales force quickly and accurately learn about new product launches so they can sell more product more quickly and thus increase overall corporate profits.

The second approach focuses on the business need driving the use of a gadget or game. Remember that you are not proposing a game or gadget just to have a gadget or game; you are trying to achieve a business result.

Problem Description. The problem description explains the current situation and provides clear evidence of why it is not working. This section should answer the question, "What elements are driving the need for change?" or "Why is the current state not acceptable?" Again, keep the focus on business issues.

One of the best ways to begin the discussion of the current state is to look at the demographics of the organization. How many boomers and how many gamers are employed? Examine the types of people your organization hires and promotes. Look at your current training practices. Gather numbers on the rate at which gamers are entering your organization and boomers are exiting.

Entering and exiting data can be gathered through surveys. Conduct a survey to determine which boomer employees are considering retirement. Be forewarned that the results may scare you. They did for an electric utility company in Fort Collins, Colorado. The company surveyed its employees and was stunned to learn that 40 percent of its workforce of two hundred planned to retire within the next five years.[11] This was a major problem because it takes four years for a technician apprenticeship to be completed.

Use these types of numbers and information as the foundation for your argument to deploy gadgets, games, and gizmos as learning tools. Information and data from Chapter One can be helpful in this section of your business case. Eye-opening or counterintuitive statistics can be highly persuasive when discussing the need to innovate and change existing practices.

Proposed Solution. This section describes your proposed solution and its major features. Here you set out the reasons for the investment and the expected tangible and intangible benefits. Describe the game or gadget you are proposing and its business impact. Contrast the benefits of the solution with the shortcomings of the current situation.

It is a good idea at this point to provide evidence of the effectiveness of your proposed solution. Most senior executives (who are boomers and beyond) will ask, "Do games really teach?" or "Are these electronic gadgets really necessary?" The burden of proof clearly lies with the person recommending the gadget or game. Interestingly, the burden of proof tends to be higher for gadgets and games than for traditional classroom instruction or even e-learning.

Although the use of gadgets and games in corporate settings is relatively new, there are some data points that can be used to help build the business case:

- A leadership simulation called *Virtual Leader* increased the participants' team performance rankings by an average of 22 percent[12] (see the box for more about *Virtual Leader*).

- The racing game *Midtown Madness* is being used by doctors at the Virtual Reality Medical Center in San Diego to treat patients who have a fear of driving after traumatic car accidents.[13]

- The combination dance-video game *Dance Dance Revolution* is helping kids to lose weight and get active. Some kids have shed as much as eighty pounds.[14]

- A corporate trainer found that 88 percent of a group that played a live classroom game based on *Hollywood Squares* passed the final review test on the first try compared to only 54 percent of a group that reviewed the material using traditional methods.[15]

- Research reported in the scientific journal *Nature* indicates that playing action video games can bring marked improvements in the ability to pay attention to objects and changes in the visual environment.[16]

- Surgeons who play a video game three hours a week decrease mistakes by 37 percent in laparoscopic surgery and perform the task 27 percent faster than their counterparts who do not play video games.[17] Laparoscopic surgery uses a tiny camera controlled by a joystick to view the inside of the body.

- The Centers for Disease Control and Prevention is funding a series of computer games to help prepare first responders and health care workers facing bioterrorist attacks, pandemics, and possible nuclear accidents.[18]

- Harrah's Entertainment, owner of casinos in Las Vegas, has put radio-frequency tracking tags on cocktail waitresses in an effort to improve customer service and track areas that may need more waitresses due to high demand.[19] These tags have also been used to track children and Alzheimer's patients to ensure they can always be located.

- Small handheld devices tied to point-of-sale cash registers and reservation systems are allowing hosts and wait and kitchen staffs in restaurants to share data about seating and food requests.[20]

- Advergames are being created by such firms as Coca-Cola to reach gamers who are increasingly turning their attention away from television.[21]

- Canon, the copier company, trained repair technicians with a game in which they had to drag and drop parts into the right spot on a copier. "Workers who played the games showed a 5% to 8% improvement in their training score compared to [those who used] older training techniques such as manuals."[22]

- Cisco Systems, the large Internet hardware supplier, commissioned a study to assess the success of games-based learning and found that games were the best medium for delivering complex information because they created better engagement and retention.[23]

- L'Oreal, the cosmetics giant, introduced online gaming to train its junior brand managers. The company's *e-Strat* game challenges players to build and manage a portfolio of beauty brands. Since the game was introduced, participation in training among junior brand managers has risen from 25 to 88 percent, with 99 percent of eligible employees completing the course.[24]

- Literacy rates at the Chew Magna Primary School in Bristol, United Kingdom, have shot up dramatically since a primary teacher began using the PC game *Myst* as a teaching aid.[25]

Use these data points and other examples from this book to build the case that the use of games and gadgets is not just fun and that games can be used to improve knowledge transfer and provide a competitive advantage.

Independent Research from Corporate and Academic Institutions on the Effectiveness of a Leadership Simulation

Introduction

We developed our *Virtual Leader* product to be an effective, ground-breaking leadership simulation. The goal was to provide a rich, interactive environment in which leaders and potential leaders could hone their skills as they related to power, ideas, and tension—all elements of effective leadership. To that end, we created a three-dimensional office environment where the learner is required to apply leadership skills in a series of meetings culminating with an extremely important meeting held in the board room of the organization. Figure 10.2 shows a character in one of the scenarios.

Figure 10.2. A Character in *Virtual Leader.*

Source: SimuLearn, Inc. Used with permission.

While we initially received extremely positive anecdotal data about the effectiveness of the program, we wanted to challenge ourselves and the learning community by collecting empirical data to determine how effective *Virtual Leader*

was as a leadership simulation. The results from studies conducted by independent third parties demonstrated just how effective a simulation can be for learning new skills.

Case Study One: Executives in Class: From Recalling to Applying New Knowledge

Background

John Dunning, professor of organizational behavior (OB) at Troy University, discovered that despite the popularity and high marks given by students to a required capstone public administration organizational behavior class, when he surveyed multiple classes six months after the courses were over, the knowledge and theories learned were not being applied in the workplace.

Process

Dunning ran two organizational behavior classes. One class studied using the more traditional curriculum, and one class used *Virtual Leader* instead of reading some case studies and writing some papers. The class that used *Virtual Leader* had the following characteristics:

Number of students: 15

Average age of students: 38

Range of ages: 27 to 53

Number of managers: 12

Number of military: 9

Number having previous leadership of management training: 13

Average number of graduate courses taken: 5

Results

Six months after both classes were over, Dunning again polled the students. The differences between the two classes were significant (Figure 10.3). The traditional class using case studies and reports, consistent with the earlier surveys, could recall

Figure 10.3. Comparison of Traditional Classes and Classes Using *Virtual Leader.*

Source: SimuLearn, Inc. Used with permission.

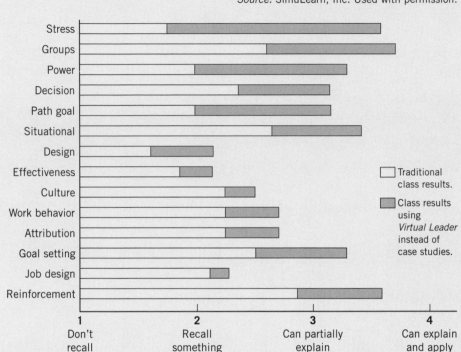

some portion of class material. But the students who went through the class that used SimuLearn's *Virtual Leader* had significantly greater ability to explain the material and, more important, apply it.

Some of the contributors to this can be found in the debriefing at the conclusion of the class. Dunning tallied the following statements:

- Fourteen of fifteen supported the statement that simulations like *Virtual Leader* are the "future of learning."

- Thirteen of fifteen supported the statement that *Virtual Leader* was a valuable tool for learning about theory.

The students and professor supported the observation that the "Three to One" model used in *Virtual Leader* was a more accurate and useful leadership approach than more academic models and that *Virtual Leader* supported much more than just the leadership segments of the OB course.

Summary

Using a simulation significantly increased application, not just memorization of learned content.

Case Study Two: Center for Creative Leadership/North Carolina A&T State University: Cognitive Impact of Learning About Leadership Versus Practicing Leadership Skills

Background

Alice C. Stewart and Jacqueline A. Williams noted that leadership education in most business schools does not match the expected leadership competencies and behaviors outlined for employees at lower levels of the organization. Working out of North Carolina A&T State University and the Center for Creative Leadership, they compared two pedagogical methods, one traditional and one simulation-based and online, and their impact on the participants' understanding of leadership.

Process

Forty-three undergraduate honors students from various university programs were enrolled in a two-day leadership training program sponsored by faculty at the School of Business and Economics North Carolina A&T State University. Four faculty members and two research assistants were engaged in this program. Students who agreed to participate were randomly assigned to either the traditional or experiential condition. They were not told of the other training program. Their behaviors were observed, and pre- and postsurveys were implemented to measure shifts in perceptions of the role of leaders.

Results

The traditional and experiential groups, though taught similar concepts, seemed to incorporate them differently. The challenge of the experiential simulation made participants question their initial perceptions of the ideal leader.

While on an item-by-item basis, there seemed to be more cognitive schematic shift in the traditional group, the magnitude of shift within the experiential group was greater. The conclusion from this research is that the simulation seemed to have a narrower, but stronger, effect on the participants' perceptions regarding leaders. The opposite tends to be the case in the traditional condition.

The research also found that in some areas, students who went through the traditional approach had significantly differing views of leadership (Figure 10.4). Finally, the students that used *Virtual Leader* throughout the sessions exhibited superior collaboration and team skills.

Figure 10.4. Views of Leadership by Class Approach.

Source: SimuLearn, Inc. Used with permission.

Change in mean of item from
pre- to posttraining

	Traditional (Less likely to agree or leaders occasionally or seldom do this)	**Virtual Leader** (More likely to agree or leaders always or often do this)
The Ideal Managerial Leader:		
1. Tries out his or her ideas on the group (creativity)	▽	△
2. Needles the members for greater effort (productive conflict)	▽	△
3. Pushes for increased production (accomplish the right work)	▽	△
4. Is easily recognized as the leader of the group (power and influence)	▽	△

Summary

Traditional pedagogy may create more incremental cognitive change, while pedagogy using the game-based simulation resulted in narrower but deeper cognitive change. Traditional methods are optimized around cognitive needs such as retaining knowledge, while *Virtual Leader* is better for teaching more dynamic skills, including problem solving, social judgment, and collaboration.

Clark Aldrich has been called an "e-learning guru" by *Fortune* magazine, "visionary of the industry" by *Training* magazine, and a member of "training's new guard" by the American Society for Training and Development. He is the author of the books *Simulations and the Future of Learning* (Wiley, 2004) and *Learning by Doing* (Wiley, 2005).

Source: Printed with the permission of Clark Aldrich.

Key Objectives and Success Indicators. In this section, state outcomes you are trying to achieve as well as key indicators of success. Clearly describe measurable objectives and anticipated outcomes from the solution you are suggesting. You may want to indicate anticipated learning outcomes in this section, but only as they relate to business outcomes. The success measures should be easy to obtain and agreed on by others to ensure that the anticipated results are relevant and important.

This can also be the place to list intangible benefits like higher morale, ability to attract and retain the gamer generation, or other benefits of the solution that are hard to quantify but are important to the organization.

Financial Comparison and Analysis. The last element is to compare the cost of creating the game or deploying the gadget with the cost of other solutions or inaction. Show that your proposed solution is cost effective. The method involves adding up all the development and purchase costs as well as the costs of the human resources. This is the cost side of the equation. Table 10.1 shows some average game and simulation costs. Use these as ballpark figures. The actual costs are dependent on a number of factors such as using an existing game engine, number of players involved, level of sophistication of the artificial intelligence, graphical realism, and many variables.

For example, BreakAway Games, Ltd., created a corporate product, *V-Bank,* to train bank auditors for about $500,000.[26] *America's Army,* a MMORPG, cost

Table 10.1. Cost of Creating Games and Simulations.

Level of Realism and Game Play	Low	Medium	High	MMORPG
Highly interactive (third- or first-person perspective)	$100,000–$200,000	$200,000–$500,000	$500,000–$1 million	$1 million–$2.5 million
Medium (branching story, video as main interface)	$15,000–$30,000	$30,000–$50,000	$50,000–$100,000	NA
Low (multiple choice)	$2,000–$5,000	$5,000–$10,000	$10,000–$15,000	N/A

about $2.5 million to develop, and its annual maintenance budget for enhancements, upgrades, and new features is about $2.5 to $3 million.[27] Cisco spends about $30,000 per game to teach the basics of a wireless network to its technicians.[28] The Cisco games are based on a scenario where aliens have landed on earth and will destroy the planet unless they are immediately provided with fast Internet access. Technicians have to set up the network quickly or face the aliens' wrath.

Once all costs are determined, list all the benefits. Assign a dollar value to as many benefits as possible, and then add together the dollar value of all the benefits. It is important to be conservative and to gain buy-in on the numbers from the accounting department so they are in agreement with how you determined the figures. Now compare the costs of the development with the anticipated benefits. The benefits should outweigh the costs.

Final Recommendation. The last step is to make a recommendation based on the facts of the business case. This usually means presenting the case to a group of executives or managers who will need to view the data and make the final decision. If presented well with acceptable numbers, the project is usually funded.

Unfortunately, even if the costs do look good, sometimes the stigma associated with gadgets, games, and gizmos may make the acceptance of the business case difficult. "It's a game; we can't seriously expect to teach our sales force to upsell using a game." "My fifteen-year-old son has a video iPod. We can't give these to customer service representatives; they'll be watching MTV videos all day." This is where some other less straightforward methods may be needed.

Disguising the Game or Gadget

The very word *game* can be enough to block the adoption or even the thought of using any type of game within an organization. It conjures images of *Candy Land, Chutes and Ladders,* and other children's pastimes. These childhood images may impair a boomer's ability to visualize how an online game could be used in a manner appropriate for a corporate setting. To ease in the adoption of the use of games within a corporation, disguise the game with a corporate look and feel. Give it a more professional image.

The Bop the Fox game from Chapter Two looks a little childish; the version shown in Figure 10.5 looks more professional. The game play and instructional elements are exactly the same; the only difference is that the fox

---

Figure 10.5. Corporate Version of Bop the Fox.
Source: Copyright 2006 Institute for Interactive Technologies (IIT). Used with permission.

is converted to a book, and the look is cleaner and more corporate. Changing the skin or look and feel of a game can help to soften the concept of the game for many boomers.

In the corporate version, the learner must identify the elements of the generic instructional design model know as the ADDIE model (analysis, design, develop, implement, and evaluate). Identification is made by clicking (bopping) the book as it pops up, just like bopping the fox when it emerges from its hole.

Another example of making a game more corporate is converting the mountain climbing game from one focused on goats to one focused on the boomer's favorite pastime: climbing the corporate ladder to obtain a corner office (Figure 10.6). The game has the same underlying computer code as the mountain climbing game, just a different presentation.

Figure 10.6. Corporate Version of Goat Climbing Game.

Source: Copyright 2006, Institute for Interactive Technologies (IIT). Used with permission.

The third example shows how a race game can be converted from cartoon animals to corporate executives racing for the finish line (Figure 10.7). Again, the code is the same; just the images are different. This type of corporate aesthetics may help make games a little more acceptable in a corporate environment. These examples show how a casual game can be changed to appeal to boomers.

Figure 10.7. Corporate Version of Race Game.
Source: Copyright 2006, Institute for Interactive Technologies (IIT). Used with permission.

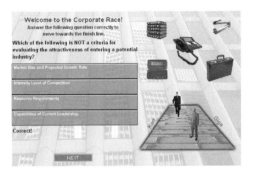

You can do the same thing with gadgets. One consulting firm is deploying video iPods and is having all the iPods branded with its colors and logo. It wants to avoid the traditional back and white versions. The rationale behind the move, besides branding, is for the employees to see right away that these iPods are part of the business and are to be used for business purposes. There are even companies, such as Color-Ware, located in Winona, Minnesota, that specialize in branding items like iPods and laptop computers.

Skunk Works Project

Sometimes it is not possible to sell an organization on the concept of a game, simulation, or gadget even if it looks professional and corporate. The status quo is too ingrained in the organization, and the old paradigms of knowledge transfer are too entrenched.

This is when using a skunk works approach might be appropriate for introducing games or gadgets into an organization. It is less straightforward and more organic than a business plan and may take a little longer. The term *skunk works* was originally used in the aerospace field when a team was working on a black project or a project that was off the radar; no one was to know what the team was working on. Today it is used to describe a team working on a project outside the normal work environment and rules. These projects are usually done when the organization wants to try out a radical new idea or take a new approach to its business but the normal methods of research and development or product creation are too ingrained for the people to break out of the normal processes.

The skunk works approach involves creating games or using gadgets on a less formal basis and allowing them to catch on almost unnoticed. Games or gadgets are simply incorporated into training or daily operations without much fuss. For example, one day the sales manager distributes to the sales force iPods preloaded with sales advice, and podcasting becomes part of the standard process for disseminating sales information. Perhaps a team of gamers is recruited to work on something in their spare time or at home. The energy and enthusiasm of this group usually mean they will be willing to experiment a little to create something that is fun and meaningful. Or find a business line manager interested in being innovative, a visionary. Team with this person to create a project on the sly. These types of individuals can usually find money in the budget allowing the development of a solution involving a gadget, game, or simulation. Look for instances where one of these tools solves a critical business need, and implement the solution under the radar of the rest of the organization. This might fall under the category of, "It's better to beg for forgiveness than to ask for permission." Once the solution is in place and successfully contributing, use the positive results to sell it to others within the organization.

One concern with doing a skunk works project is always cost, and there are times when innovative or visionary managers do not have money in the budget for a large-scale project. Fortunately, there are ways to create low-cost games and simulations.

Low-Cost Development

It is possible to develop basic casual games and even branching story simulations with PowerPoint, an application most people have on their desktop as part of the Microsoft Office suite. Originally designed as presentation software, PowerPoint now contains branching capabilities, ActiveX controls, and some other high-end features that can be exploited to create a fairly robust simulation or game. Dozens of links on a page will enable the creation of *Jeopardy*-type games, as shown in Figure 10.8.

Figure 10.8. *Jeopardy*-Type Game Created in PowerPoint.

Source: Copyright 2006, Institute for Interactive Technologies (IIT). Created by Celina Byers. Used with permission.

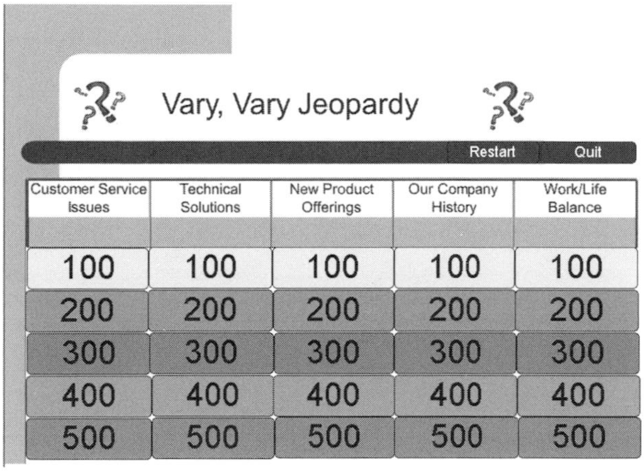

In her book *E-Learning on a Shoestring,* Jane Bozarth describes how links can be used in PowerPoint to create branching stories or action mazes.[29] Begin with a PowerPoint slide explaining the scenario or situation. Then create questions on subsequent slides, and each possible learner response guides the learner to subsequent pages. It must be planned out ahead, since the branching and links can be a little overwhelming, but the result can be a solid first foray into games and simulations for a low cost.

Another low-cost option is to contact a local college or art institute for talented college or community college students who have development skills and might be looking for a project to apply their talents. Contact professors in the instructional technology department, art department, computer department, or other related departments. They will know which students would be best for developing games or simulations. If you are looking for help with gadgets or gizmos, contact the engineering or electrical engineering departments. Community colleges are good resources for students with practical knowledge of handheld technologies. An intern usually works for relatively low wages or even for free while providing your organization with knowledge you may not have. If you want to gain this knowledge internally, ask the intern to create some workshops or classes to share the knowledge with your team.

Look for inexpensive tools on the Web; many places offer free or low-cost game shells such as Hot Potatoes from a company called Half-Baked Software. You need to be careful with licensing and permissions, but for the most part, you will have access to limited but entertaining game shells into which you can add your own content. The games are usually based on well-known games such as *Jeopardy, Who Wants to Be a Millionaire,* hangman, and other familiar game interfaces described in Chapter Two.

Modifying an Existing Game

Another low-cost solution, although not quite as economical as PowerPoint, is to modify an existing game engine for use in your corporate environment. In gamer parlance, this is called *modding*. Modding is simply the act of modifying existing game code to create a new and unique game or, in this case, corporate training program.

A large retail and commercial bank is using the concept of modding to create a game to appeal to new employees (Figure 10.9). The bank has teamed with Bloomsburg University (using low-cost labor) to modify the *Torque* game engine created by the Eugene, Oregon, company GarageGames to create the interactive training piece. GarageGames created *Torque* specifically to allow game developers to modify a basic environment and mold it to any game they want to develop. The hard-core programming is done for the developers through the *Torque* game engine. The game developers add onto the engine or change the engine but do not have to develop it from scratch— a huge time savings.

The university and the bank are developing a game to teach the bank's customer service representatives how to assess client needs and provide the right product to address those needs. The goal is to create a gamelike environment that allows the learner to become immersed in the role of the customer service representative before he or she actually meets a real customer. This provides practice for the new representatives and ensures they understand how they are to interact with customers.

Figure 10.9. Using a Game Engine to Modify a Game for Corporate Use.

Source: Copyright 2006, Institute for Interactive Technologies (IIT). Programmed by Michael Phillips. Artwork by David Cerreta. Used with permission.

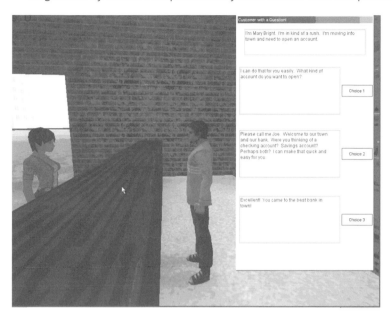

The advantage of modding is that the "physics" of the game have already been created. The engine defines the rules of the environment, which allows the programmer to concentrate on creating the items and people who inhabit the environment without having to program how they interact with each other. The logic behind how objects and people relate is built into the engine of the game. Tools for creating actions such as grabbing an item or bumping into a wall are available to be incorporated into the game. The bank just works on creating realistic customer-representative dialogue and designing a realistic bank office; the engine takes care of most of the background work. This is the same game engine and concept used in the creation of the *3D Language: Spain* simulation discussed in Chapter Three.

SUMMARY

Selling the use of gadgets and games for training in organizations can be difficult but not impossible. There was a time when computers themselves were thought of as toys or novelties; now they are indispensable business tools. Careful consideration of corporate culture and application of the ideas presented in this chapter can help make the process easier.

While selling the idea of buying some gadgets for the team or building a game or simulation is important for knowledge transfer, the real competitive advantage is realized when the entire organization is focused on the knowledge transfer process. The next chapter discusses knowledge requirements planning, a method that can serve as an umbrella under which the ideas from Chapters Two through Eight can be implemented.

11

Getting to the Next Level

IN SPITE OF ALL THE ideas and concepts in this book, the knowledge transfer process will not just happen. Creating one or two games and handing out a few MP3 players will not effectively transfer knowledge. Ideally, the knowledge transfer process from boomers to gamers cascades down from the top of the organization. Although knowledge transfer can occur in isolation within a few departments or divisions, the real impact is when it is conducted at the enterprise level.

Without a systematic plan, knowledge transfer doesn't happen. Knowledge gets lost, misplaced, and forgotten even with the most innovative technologies. When this happens, gamers will be forced to recreate the knowledge of the boomers, a costly process in this fast-paced world economy.

Recreating lost knowledge provides competitors with an opportunity to leap over your organization while they create entirely new knowledge. A good example of this is the new space race. The United States is targeting a return trip to the moon no later than 2020.[1] The reason for the long delay? The National Aeronautics and Space Administration (NASA) has forgotten how to get there. It turns out that "sometime in the late 1990s, NASA lost the knowledge it had developed to send astronauts to the moon. . . . The engineers who designed the huge *Saturn 5* rocket . . . were encouraged to take early retirement. . . . Also lost were the last set of critical blueprints for the Saturn booster."[2] Everything was gone, and they had to start over (Figure 11.1).

Figure 11.1. Where Is That Lost Knowledge?

Source: Reprinted with permission of the artist, Kristin Longenecker.

This is why China, in a new space race, may beat the United States to the moon even though China has never been there before. NASA's current time line to return to the moon predicts a new rocket and crew vehicle ready for a lunar mission later than the current Chinese target (although both dates keep shifting).[3] The United States is recreating lost knowledge while the Chinese are leapfrogging a country that forgot knowledge—knowledge of how to land on the moon.

Organizations (and countries) cannot take a piecemeal approach to transferring knowledge from the boomers to the gamers; there is too much at stake.

What is needed is a systematic strategy for the transfer of knowledge, one that does not allow for forgotten knowledge. One such strategy is known as *knowledge requirements planning* (KRP).

Knowledge Requirements Planning

KRP is based on a macrolevel model of the instructional design process. The process begins with identifying knowledge goals and cascades that information into the rest of the organization so everyone is focused on knowledge transfer and retention. KRP translates strategic knowledge goals into discrete, measurable learning objectives combined with proven feedback methods and performance analysis. Figure 11.2 shows the interrelated elements of the KRP model.

Management

The first element in the KRP model is management. The process of knowledge transfer cannot occur in a haphazard manner. If rules and procedures are not in place, there are no assurances that the proper knowledge will be transferred from the departing boomers to the incoming gamers. Careful management is required.

While much of the knowledge transfer process takes place informally, an infrastructure must be in place to formalize as much of the transfer as possible. Management must position supervisors and others as strategy guides, providing incoming gamers with just the right amount of guidance and information without overwhelming them or giving them step-by-step instructions. Gamers need to be given parameters and goals and then allowed to pursue those goals to the best of their abilities.

For all the other elements in the KRP model to work, the organization must have a strongly managed knowledge transfer process. The management team is responsible for six areas within the process:

- Planning
- Communicating

Figure 11.2. Knowledge Requirements Planning Model.

Source: Author.

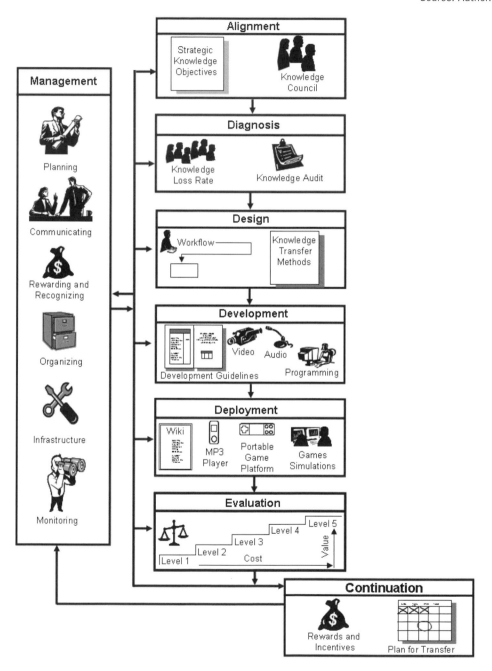

- Rewarding and recognizing

- Organizing

- Infrastructure

- Monitoring

Planning. The management team controls all of the processes and procedures within an organization, as well as the underlying culture. In most organizations, these elements must be aligned to encourage and facilitate knowledge transfer between the boomers and the gamers. A plan needs to be in place to ensure this process occurs. This type of plan includes identifying the people who are connectors, as well as technology enthusiasts, visionaries, pragmatists, conservatives, and skeptics, as mentioned in Chapter Ten, so that information can be presented to them in the appropriate style.

There should be a short-term plan in which boomers can begin to share their knowledge immediately. Identify key knowledge areas and the individuals who have the most knowledge in those key areas. Then determine how to gather and codify their knowledge.

Put into place a comprehensive long-term program that includes regular and systematic methods of capturing, rewarding, recognizing, and disseminating knowledge. The process needs to start with talent recruitment—recruiting people who want to share knowledge—all the way to the exit interview process, which should provide incentives for ensuring that a person's knowledge will be captured before he or she leaves.

Management must realize that a key impediment to knowledge sharing is a perceived lack of time. The message must be sent that time spent sharing knowledge with others in the organization is valuable. Time must be made where boomers and gamers can get together to exchange ideas. Incentives must be created to encourage the sharing of knowledge.

Techniques must be employed to plan for recruitment of new employees who are gamers. The use of tournaments, robust recruitment Web sites, and fellow gamers to aid in the process are important elements for the future of an organization. Companies must always be recruiting gamers if they are not immediately hiring. Otherwise the ramp-up time takes too long.

Finally, management must plan its own knowledge transfer activities. The management team must lead by example, creating mentorship programs in which key leaders mentor up-and-coming talent and up-and-coming talent mentors leaders about technology. When the leadership team models the knowledge transfer process, others within the organization will follow.

Communicating. Knowledge sharing requires trust and reciprocity. Management must communicate trust and value of all employees' knowledge. Boomers may feel that they are giving up their knowledge and not getting anything in return from the gamers. Management must make it clear that both groups have information valuable to the other: boomers and gamers can learn from each other. Conversely, some boomers may feel that what they know is not of value. They may not realize the extent of their own knowledge because it is so ingrained in who they are. Management needs to communicate the value of extracting and sharing that knowledge.

The leaders of the organization must establish clear and effective channels of communication throughout the entire organization that include supervisors of the various business lines, executives, the management team, and employees. These communications must be done with new technologies like instant messaging (IM), blogs, and wikis. Companies must create policies for the use of these tools, as well as encourage everyone within the organization, boomers and gamers alike, to embrace them and use them equally. All members of an organization can benefit from freely exchanging knowledge and ideas through blogs, wikis, and IM.

Rewarding and Recognizing. Recognition and rewards should be part of any management strategy designed to encourage knowledge sharing. This is especially true if the organization does not have a history of recognizing and rewarding the sharing of knowledge.

Often in boomer-oriented environments, there are disincentives for sharing knowledge. Power and position typically come from knowing information, processes, or procedures that others in the organization do not know. A boomer who is a go-to person for information is a valued member of the organization. It is difficult to give up that power and feeling of importance.

A number of models can be followed for providing incentives and rewards. They range from simply sending out a message in the company newsletter about a knowledge-sharing incident to a complex pay-for-knowledge system. Pay and reward systems need to be examined to make sure gamers are properly rewarded but not overly paid. Since gamers like to keep score, new score-keeping methods (other than salary) will need to be explored and developed by organizations, as described in Chapter Nine.

In terms of knowledge sharing, some companies have adopted the academic model, with knowledge recognized as published articles, white papers, or presentations at conferences. Other companies have used that model but kept it focused internally. Someone who shares some knowledge over a brown-bag lunch session or through internal company documents is rewarded.

Some organizations provide incentives to act as a mentor to new employees. Many organizations have knowledge sharing as part of their performance reviews. Still others establish internal rating systems for an expert's blog, where employees rate the usefulness of postings and the employee with the highest rating is rewarded or recognized for his or her effort.

Regardless of the method, some type of program needs to be put into place. Knowledge is shared only when that sharing is rewarded. Management must make sure that any disincentives for knowledge sharing, like rewarding the hoarding of knowledge, are eliminated.

Organizing. To encourage the sharing of knowledge, management may need to reorganize the structure of the company. It may be that lines of reporting, methods of sharing, and information dissemination practices are ineffective at fostering a sharing environment. Take a hard look at the organizational structure to see if it fosters or inhibits knowledge transfer. If it inhibits transfer, consider reorganizing to place each employee on two or more teams. This helps with the cross-pollination of information from one area of a company to another. Require different departments to interact with each other. Create opportunities for informal exchanges of information at company social events or even throughout the workday.

Create communities around similar business issues, and encourage groups to organize around areas of interest. Use collaborative online technologies such as a wiki to develop internal dialogues about topics of interest. Create online repositories of information that can be freely exchanged among groups or divisions.

Provide funding for projects that bring together boomers and gamers but might not have an immediate payoff. Create a skunk works project for the development of a casual game. Organize mentoring programs, internal conferences, knowledge newsletters, and other processes to facilitate the transfer of knowledge at all levels within the organization.

Infrastructure. Technology is necessary but not sufficient for large-scale knowledge transfer initiatives. Technology alone will not deliver just the right knowledge at just the right time to just the right person. It is only a catalyst. Without having the other management elements in place, infrastructure initiatives alone fail.

Knowledge transfer can occur without technology, but with geographically dispersed workforces, the need for technology is real. The advances in Web-based tools such as wikis, blogs, and IM make it imperative that management teams put into place the procedures, policies, and tools to enable the transfer of knowledge.

Management is responsible for allocating funds for an enterprisewide system, ensuring consistency of applications, and requiring employees to share knowledge at all levels of the organization. Organizations need to invest in a technology infrastructure that supports collaboration. The preservation of boomer knowledge cannot be easily accomplished without automated methods of codifying what they know. They are leaving too fast, and information is growing too quickly. A well-supported, well-funded infrastructure program goes a long way toward enabling the knowledge transfer process.

Think about how the organization can replace education with automation. What processes can be automated to avoid costly training programs? Can you find a method of enhancing the work flow of an employee by having a computerized system ask the right question or perform a certain task?

Monitoring. A knowledge transfer process cannot be put into place and then ignored. If an initiative does not continually receive attention from the management team, it will eventually fade away. Monitoring the results of the transfer process can be beneficial by indicating whether the process is working and when to change elements to achieve the desired results.

The team could monitor the use of wikis, blogs, and other internal knowledge transfer technologies and review the performance evaluations or conduct interviews to see if the process is working at the individual level. A systematic monitoring process ensures that resources dedicated to the knowledge sharing process are appropriately used. It also ensures the continuation of the process and keeps the knowledge transfer initiative from being a brief management fad.

Alignment

The next element in the KRP model, alignment, focuses on the alignment of corporate and knowledge transfer goals. "Knowledge assets, like money or equipment, exist and are worth cultivating only in the context of strategy. You cannot define and manage intellectual assets unless you know what you are trying to do with them."[4] Trying to transfer everything every boomer knows to every gamer is untenable. The organization must be strategic about what knowledge actually needs to be transferred. In this process, ask the following questions:

- What kind of knowledge exists in our organization?

- What knowledge is important to keep?

- What knowledge gives us a strategic advantage or makes us different from our competitors?

For the knowledge transfer process to be valuable, it must be closely aligned with the strategic goals and objectives of the organization. The process needs to support the organization in accomplishing its operational goals.

The alignment step of KRP begins with identifying what types of knowledge need to be transferred. Not all knowledge is equal in an organization; some knowledge can be outsourced to specialization companies, for example, logistics. A manufacturer may want to outsource its logistics and focus on production. Or a small computer software development firm may want to outsource its accounting and payroll functions. These are areas that do not require knowledge transfer.

Firms should focus on the knowledge that makes them competitive: processes, methods, customer databases, or other knowledge assets. A manufacturing firm might have knowledge of a certain production process that is invaluable to its long-term survival. A consulting firm may have problem-solving knowledge and methodologies that are critical to servings its clients.

In the alignment step of KRP, the organization must operationally define these knowledge areas as strategic knowledge objectives (SKOs)—for example:

- Maintain and expand on our knowledge of our proprietary circuit board assembly process.

- Create innovative methods to solve our clients' information technology problems through the intelligent application of our problem-solving methodology.

- Create engaging and exciting educational simulations based on our ability to bring together a talented group of individuals and focus them on a common instructional goal.

- Have each mechanical employee attend a training program that supports consistent work practices and standards regardless of regional location.

The SKOs serve as the foundation of the knowledge transfer process. They are the key knowledge areas that need to be preserved and transferred to incoming employees.

Organizations rarely have just one SKO; often there are three or four critical knowledge areas. The SKOs are the brains of an organization, the intangible competitive advantage that is gained through knowledge.

Organizations should look at key areas and determine what knowledge is competitive and what knowledge is common or baseline. For example, there is a certain degree of manufacturing knowledge that is basic, such as the process for counting inventory or the basic elements of Six Sigma, but other processes, such as a proprietary method of producing product, are not generic. In that case, the knowledge of the individuals doing those processes needs to be captured. The areas to search for specific knowledge advantages are shown in Table 11.1.

Identifying these areas and their associated SKOs is the task of a group called the knowledge council, comprising stakeholders from the lines of business, the organization's learning professionals, and executive leadership. The council works to continually align the knowledge transfer goals within the

Table 11.1. Areas to Search for Strategic Knowledge Objectives.

Proprietary production processes	Specialized technical knowledge
Unique design capabilities	Innovative sales methods
Specialized research and development processes	Special formulas, algorithms, or techniques

organization to the operational goals. Its mission is to ensure that knowledge transfer is at the forefront of policy and strategy decisions. If a new line of business is created based on existing knowledge, the council helps to ensure that a knowledge transfer process is in place. If a large number of boomers are retiring at the next retirement window because of a new contract, the council puts specific knowledge transfer processes into place.

The council needs to have as members boomers, Generation Xers, and gamers to bring each unique perspective to the table. Educate the council on the thinking process of each group so they understand each other's perspectives. Provide an open environment, both face-to-face and virtually, to promote the exchange of ideas among this group. The members of the council should be comfortable with all types of technologies, and if they are not, they need to learn from one another and then think about how these technologies can be distributed throughout the organization. Include techies, visionaries, and connectors on this team, and even a skeptic or two to keep the council grounded.

To help guide the council, some organizations have created the position of chief knowledge officer, who is responsible for managing the processes, procedures, and policies related to organizational knowledge. This person works closely with the council to ensure the goals of the organization, in terms of knowledge transfer, are being met.

Diagnosis

Once the strategic knowledge objectives are defined, the next step is to determine how much tangible knowledge exists to support each strategic knowledge objective. This can be done through a knowledge audit, a comprehensive review process in which an organization reviews all of its knowledge assets and associated systems. This includes an examination of who knows what, as well as a look at what documentation exists to assist people with doing their current jobs. Are standard operating procedures available? Is there a training curriculum for the information? Does the software vendor have classes on this production management system? Can the textual information be placed into a searchable format?

The knowledge audit should not be focused on the entire organization. Center it around the strategic knowledge objectives identified during the alignment process. One problem that organizations encounter with knowledge audits is that they attempt to look at everything. Results are more tangible and operational when the audit is focused. The knowledge audit consists of four actions:

1. Identify knowledge types.

2. Review existing knowledge transfer processes.

3. Determine knowledge loss rate.

4. Quantify the results of the audit.

Identify Knowledge Types. The first step is to identify the various types of knowledge that exist throughout your organization as it is tied to the strategic knowledge objectives. Organizational knowledge can be divided into two main areas: explicit knowledge and tacit knowledge.

The knowledge audit should look first at tangible knowledge, or what is known in knowledge management circles as *explicit knowledge*. This is the written-down or codified information that can be easily accessed by incoming gamers. These are the existing databases, employee manuals, standard operating procedures, and other information that can be seen, discussed, edited, or changed. It is the information that is readily available. To identify explicit knowledge, ask questions like these:

- What current knowledge is codified?

- Where is the codified knowledge? In what software applications (MS Word, Excel, databases)?

- Is it easily accessible?

- Is the codified knowledge searchable?

- Is this knowledge regularly updated?

- Are training materials available internally or from a vendor?

The second area that should be examined is the area of *tacit knowledge,* or intangible knowledge. This is the information boomers have in their heads, their know-how. It is not written or codified in any manner. These are the traditions, special techniques, and individual methods that are invaluable to the organization's success in certain areas. This is the knowledge you really want to transfer to the gamers. To identify tacit knowledge, ask questions like these:

- Who knows what?

- Who has critical knowledge?

- What knowledge is in people's heads that needs to be codified?

- Are there any obstacles to sharing tacit knowledge?

- Do we conduct exit interviews?

- What person would we miss the most if he or she retired today? Why?

Review Existing Knowledge Transfer Processes. Next, examine the knowledge transfer processes already in place. Do you have a mentorship or a reverse mentorship program in place? Are there internal databases where information is stored and accessed by a number of people? Is knowledge traded in meetings? Do you have any videotaped exit interviews? Are some employees already using IM, wikis, or blogs to share knowledge? These questions are critical to seeing if it is possible to tap into already existing knowledge transfer processes. Ask questions like these:

- How does knowledge currently flow within the organization?

- Is any knowledge currently being transferred? If so, in what manner, how, and by whom?

- Do we have existing databases that store knowledge?

- Do we have technologies in place to support the sharing of knowledge?

- Are there informal knowledge exchanges that we could capture?

Determine Knowledge Loss Rate. The next item to examine during the diagnosis step is the knowledge leak or knowledge loss rate. You want to find out how quickly the organization is losing boomer knowledge. Look to Chapter One to see if your organization is in one of the industries that is ready for a large-scale retirement. At a recent college graduation at Bloomsburg University in Bloomsburg, Pennsylvania, faculty and staff who were retiring were honored. The number of years they had collectively served was remarkable, as shown in Table 11.2. Ironically, on the same day that hundreds of eager gamers entered the workforce, the very university that prepared them for the future lost 250 years of combined experience.

Table 11.2. Number of Bloomsburg University Faculty Retiring in Spring 2006.

Department	Years Served
Accounting	Sixteen years
Nursing	Twenty-six years
Educational studies and secondary education	Fourteen years
Psychology	Thirty-three years
Sociology, social work, and criminal justice	Twenty-eight years
Economics	Thirty years
Biology and allied health sciences	Twenty-one years
Exercise science and athletics	Thirty-eight years
Communications studies and theater arts	Forty years

Different organizations have different rates in which employees and their knowledge are leaving. In the utility and health care industries, the rate of retirement is typically faster than it is in the software development industry, because the first two industries are older and have traditionally had high levels of job security.

The overall rate of turnover in the software industry may be higher because people change jobs frequently. The knowledge loss rate will show if the churn is in key knowledge areas or in basic knowledge areas. Less experienced programmers may be leaving software companies with some degree of frequency, while the more experienced programmers may not be leaving. The important point is to check to see the rate and degree of loss. You don't want to panic unduly, but you don't want to be caught by surprise either. Ask questions like these:

- What is the average tenure of employment at the organization?
- Is there a contract retirement window that may encourage people with years of knowledge to leave?
- Has there been an increase in retirements lately?
- Is the turnover rate increasing or decreasing within our organization or within the industry?
- When did most people start their career in this field?
- How old is this field?

Because some of these questions can be sensitive, especially around the age issue—and litigation is always a concern—you may want to conduct an anonymous survey to see how many employees anticipate retiring in the next two, five, or ten years.

Quantify the Results of the Audit. When you are done with the knowledge audit, you will have an inventory of existing knowledge sources, a list of what is known in the organization but not codified, a list of formal and informal knowledge transfer processes, and a general idea of how quickly the boomers are exiting your organization.

Comparing the results of the knowledge audit with the strategic knowledge objectives will show a clear picture of what processes, procedures, and policies need to be put into place to capture and subsequently transfer critical organizational knowledge from those who currently possess the knowledge to those who need the knowledge.

In many knowledge audits, a surprising finding is that some of the knowledge the newer employees think is only in the heads of the more experienced employees is in fact available in a codified form. It has just been forgotten or ignored.

The next step in the knowledge requirements planning is to design methods that allow the newer employees, the gamers, to obtain the knowledge that is already codified in the organization. It also includes designing methods for capturing the tacit knowledge of the boomers and finding ways to transfer that knowledge to the gamers.

Design

The design of the knowledge transfer process or processes will most likely take place using a number of systems, such as an electronic performance support system, gadgets like iPods, or systems like a specially designed wiki or even boomer-designed games. The process requires determining the best methods of transferring knowledge from the boomers to the gamers in terms of sequence, presentation format, availability, and distribution.

While it is good to provide system guidelines and goals from a central location, the transfer of knowledge needs to occur on a local basis. Executive leadership needs to design general systems and provide tools and then encourage the employees to use those tools as effectively as possible.

Consider the creation of corporate cheat sheets to distribute information. Design casual games that teach basic concepts and can be developed inexpensively. Distribute gadgets with podcasts or vidcasts of boomers presenting their war stories to gamers who can learn from these insights. Consider giving gamers in the field tools for communicating with boomers in the home office.

When designing an effective knowledge transfer process, there are critical issues that must be kept in mind:

- When possible, make the knowledge transfer process part of the normal work flow.

- Don't mistake information availability with knowledge transfer.

- Don't forget the motivational or attitudinal impact of the knowledge transfer process.

- Design knowledge transfer processes with gamers in mind.

Normal Work Flow. The knowledge transfer process needs to become ingrained into the overall work flow process. Designing a system in which the employee needs to interrupt work to learn or obtain new knowledge is not productive. The system needs to be designed around the everyday flow of information throughout the organization.

The biggest opportunity for passing knowledge from boomers to gamers is to embed the transfer into the everyday work flow. Boomers must be taught how to take advantage of teachable moments to provide guidance and training. Teachable moments occur in a number of ways:

- Conversations in the hallway with a subordinate

- Debriefing after a client meeting

- Discussions while repairing an engine

- Instructions provided in an e-mail

- Coaching through instant messaging

- Mentoring during a project

However, there are typically not enough teachable moments to transfer all the boomer knowledge to the gamers. There need to be automated systems to help facilitate this process. Electronic support systems mentioned in Chapter Seven are useful, as are appropriately constructed online help systems and job aids, visually based or written.

When systems or processes are being designed or redefined within an organization, a portion of the project plan should be dedicated to determining the best methods for embedding education and training information into the process itself.

When new software applications are being considered, think about how easy they are to use, how effectively help or instructions can be added to the software, and how much knowledge can be embedded into the software itself.

Information Availability Is Not Knowledge Transfer. Information is not learning, training, or knowledge. Too often organizations seem to believe that the mere availability of standard operating procedures, manuals, guidebooks, and other written instructions is enough to transfer knowledge. If you hear the statement, "We don't need a knowledge transfer process; new employees will just read the manual," it means no knowledge transfer process is in place.

Information has to be appropriately designed to change employee behavior. There are specific design strategies that help employees retain and apply knowledge. These strategies must be employed to ensure that learning and transfer have occurred. For example, teaching problem-solving skills requires a completely different instructional strategy from teaching facts or concepts. The different levels of knowledge and methods for teaching that knowledge as games or simulations are contained in Chapters Two and Three.

Motivational Aspects of Knowledge Transfer. Most employees will not voluntarily embark on a knowledge transfer quest. Typically the employees with the most valuable knowledge are the ones in most demand. Organizations are loathe to take the most productive salesperson or a highly skilled technician "off-line" for something as fuzzy as knowledge transfer. These individuals are typically not provided incentives for sharing their knowledge either.

Organizations need to motivate boomers to share knowledge with the gamers and motivate gamers to seek knowledge. This cultural aspect of knowledge sharing needs to be fostered through examples. If upper management has a positive attitude toward sharing knowledge and leads by example, employees will follow. If upper management has a poor attitude toward knowledge sharing, employees will follow as well.

The attitude toward knowledge sharing also has to be evident in the actions of management. Waiting until a boomer is about to walk out the door with valuable knowledge and then trying frantically to capture that knowledge is one or two years too late. Organizations must identify key individuals and assign one or two or three gamers to that person and have them learn from them before it is too late. The argument is always that "they are too valuable to be teaching others; we need them producing." This short-term rationalization leads to long-term knowledge problems and signals to employees that management is not serious about knowledge transfer.

Design Transfer Processes with Gamers in Mind. Most of the individuals responsible for learning and development activities within organizations are not gamers. They are boomers or Gen Xers, and they tend to want to provide knowledge transfer activities using familiar methods. These methods such as classroom instruction and thick manuals will not cut it for the gamers, however.

One of the initial steps of the design process should be to involve gamers with the design of the knowledge transfer processes. Ask gamers within your organization how they would like to learn the information that is required for them to be successful. This can include surveys and interviews, but it must also involve appointing gamers to the design team for direct input regardless of their tenure with the company.

Organizations need to seriously consider developing learning events around the tools of the gamers: games, simulations, handheld gadgets, wikis, blogs, and instant messaging. Even if the current workforce is not heavily vested in the tools of the gamers, the upcoming employees are going to expect the availability of those types of knowledge transfer tools. The learning styles of the gamers need to be accommodated for the process to be successful.

Development

The development of materials or solutions to support the design will include a number of efforts, ranging from the creation of simple Web pages to outsourcing the creation of a full-blown simulation or the programming of a series of casual games to teach jargon. Some of these efforts will be done by learning professionals and others by internal experts contributing to something like a wiki for the research and development department.

The key to the development process is not to let the technological aspects of the knowledge transfer process overwhelm the business needs of the organization. Development of knowledge transfer tools needs to focus on the knowledge. In some cases, an elaborate solution may be proposed when a simpler solution would be just as effective.

A full-blown simulation to teach product knowledge might not be as cost-effective as providing a weekly blog on the features of new products. At other times, such as training customer service representatives on how to handle difficult customer problems, a full-blown simulation will be exactly what is needed because the information is relatively timeless and doesn't change with every new product release.

The development process should include guidelines for the uses of different types of knowledge transfer methods. Provide guidelines for contributions to wikis. Establish a committee or a person to periodically review content to determine if it should be placed in another format, updated, or deleted. Create rules for the use of blogs. Which knowledge experts in your organization will be able to publish blogs? What type of content will be on the blog? What is acceptable, and what is not?

Create policies for the use of Instant Messenger software. Many software vendors are working on enterprise versions of IM that will be safer to use in a corporate setting than some of the current consumer versions. If IM sessions are going to be saved for future reference, you need to let all the employees know the policy so there are no misunderstandings.

When developing more formal knowledge transfer products, such as online learning modules, create templates so that the development process can be accomplished quickly. Do not reinvent the wheel every time. Look for ways of reusing game engines for different content but the same game play. This will minimize development times and maximize learning. Be cognizant of times when new interfaces need to be designed from scratch. Templates and reusable content are realities in many organizations, but there also needs to be room for originality and uniqueness. Keep in mind when developing knowledge transfer processes that gamers like constant stimulation and novelty.

Don't be afraid to embark on small research and development expeditions to determine the most appropriate development method. It might be that a video iPod is the appropriate platform for delivering knowledge to gamers in the field, or perhaps a small mobile computer like the Microsoft Origami is appropriate. Take time and invest dollars in small pilot projects to determine the best methods of transferring knowledge before investing hundreds of thousands of dollars in a full-scale rollout.

Deployment

Once the knowledge transfer tools are properly designed, prepared for delivery, and aligned with corporate strategic knowledge objectives, the next step of the KRP process is deployment, which can be particularly tricky. "If you build it, they will come" works only in the movies. To ensure that knowledge transfer takes place, efforts must be made to engage employees in the transfer process.

Often some sort of change management plan or marketing campaign is required to bring the desired focus on knowledge transfer to the employees. Employees need to understand the importance of knowledge transfer and why the transfer is being introduced, and they need to continually transfer knowledge from one person in the organization to another.

Several methods have been found effective for helping to deploy knowledge transfer processes throughout an organization:

- Endorsement by credible role models
- Awareness of the likelihood of success
- Display of confidence and enthusiasm by those in charge
- Active participation in the knowledge transfer process

Credible Role Models. One method used frequently by advertising agencies is a celebrity endorsement. People are influenced by credible role models. Involving a person with a high level of credibility in your organization will help with the knowledge transfer process regardless of the method you are using.

Many organizations have hired individuals who are well known in the field of learning or knowledge management to serve as consultants to the team. Hiring an individual of high caliber, an author of several books, the president of a professional society, or a well-known adult learning guru adds credibility to the knowledge transfer process. It also sends a message to the employees that the company is not alone in the struggle to develop effective knowledge transfer processes. It projects a positive message that the organization is seriously approaching the knowledge transfer process and is seeking advice and counsel from some of the best minds available.

Another version of this concept is to use well-respected people within the organization and ask them to endorse knowledge transfer and be a champion of the process. Seek out the connectors and ask their help in your knowledge requirements planning. Ask these individuals to convey the message that this is a positive event for the organization. Internal champions contribute greatly to building a positive attitude. They also carry a great deal of credibility and make the knowledge transfer process easier and more successful.

Awareness of the Likelihood of Success. Let employees know that successfully transferring large amounts of knowledge from the boomers to the gamers is not an impossible goal. In the 1950s, some psychologists thought that no human could break the four-minute mile. But on May 6, 1954, Roger Bannister broke the four-minute mile barrier, stunning the world. He proved that a seemingly impossible task was in fact possible. And in the next year, thirty-seven runners broke the four-minute mile barrier. Bannister provided proof that the four-minute mile could be broken. Once other runners' attitudes changed from believing that breaking the barrier was impossible to knowing it was possible, they too broke the barrier.

This same technique is effective for knowledge transfer efforts. When employees know that success is possible, they will work toward that success, knowing it can happen in their organization. Provide case studies from other organizations, have speakers come to the company to discuss successes in the field, or send key managers to conferences and events that explain how effective knowledge transfer can be.

Display of Confidence and Enthusiasm. People constantly look to authority figures for cues on how to act and behave. Putting knowledge transfer processes into place will not be easy. There may be resentment by the boomers, indifference from the gamers, and a general lack of enthusiasm by the rank-and-file employees who have too much on their plates already. Managers may not be that interested in the process either, especially if they see their retirement on the horizon. The knowledge transfer team needs to remain positive and enthusiastic during the process. If the team is upbeat and positive, the organization will reflect that attitude. Do not let setbacks deter the team from the ultimate goal. Avoiding problems is not an option. How they are dealt with and addressed is where positive attitude and having a vision of the future helps the team.

Active Participation in the Knowledge Transfer Process. Encourage as much participation in the deployment of the knowledge transfer process as possible. Research studies indicate that if a person can be encouraged to perform an important act counter to his or her own private attitude, a change in attitude can occur.[5]

Involving employees in different phases of the knowledge transfer process can be accomplished in a number of ways. If someone doesn't believe in knowledge transfer, give that person the responsibility of running a blog or contributing to a wiki. Monitor it, and see how he or she is doing. Team boomers with gamers in mentorship programs. Place employees on a team to identify the knowledge that needs to be transferred. Ask employees for new and original ideas for transferring that knowledge. Ask them to write down their thoughts and ideas when it comes to certain knowledge areas. The important thing is to get them active in the process and let them know that their knowledge and ideas are valuable.

Evaluation

For a knowledge transfer process to be acceptable and taken seriously within the organization, it must be held accountable for results. Manufacturing processes, sales processes, fundraising processes, and other organizational processes are held accountable for results and productivity, and knowledge transfer needs to stand up to the same close scrutiny.

The KRP process has five levels of evaluation. This evaluation methodology is based on the work of both Jack Phillips and Donald Kirkpatrick.[6] The classification serves as a framework for evaluating knowledge transfer efforts. Each of the five levels requires the creation of knowledge analytics to measure, track, and monitor the knowledge transfer processes within the organization.

Level 1 evaluations are conducted by questionnaires at the end of the knowledge transfer events. For example, there could be a questionnaire at the end of a blog or a wiki and an online evaluation after a simulation. Level 1 answers questions like these: Is the knowledge that is available applicable to your job? Do you see any obstacles to implementing what is written in this blog? Do you understand where to get the resources you need to complete your task? Was the information in the wiki written in a manner you could understand? Did you have to search too much to find what you were seeking? At this level of evaluation, ease of use and employee perception are being measured. Does the employee believe he or she can use the knowledge presented on the job? Does the learning seem applicable to the employee? Level 1 evaluations measure the face validity of the knowledge transfer event.

A level 2 evaluation tests participant knowledge retention and recall. The idea is to see if the learner can pass a test, multiple choice or a performance assessment, covering the knowledge that was supposed to be transferred. The evaluation includes measurable feedback indicating what knowledge was learned and what was not. This information is then used to help provide remediation and determine areas in which the knowledge transfer process needs to be strengthened.

Level 3 evaluation checks to see if the knowledge provided is being used on the job. This level evaluates the transfer of knowledge from the knowledge source to the job and can be used to determine the effectiveness of current knowledge management techniques. Level 3 answers questions like these: Did the mentor program change the behaviors of the gamers being mentored? Did the game alter the players' behaviors on the job? Did access to the video of the boomer change the way the repair took place? Are the employees behaving differently as a result of the knowledge transfer process? At this level, the knowledge transfer process really makes an impact. This is the place to observe whether the gamers are getting the knowledge they need from the boomers.

Level 4 evaluation looks at the organizational impact of the knowledge transfer process regardless of the cost. It answers questions like these: Is the business improving because of the knowledge transfer processes? Is the knowledge transfer process producing tangible results? Do the employees now act proactively to have an impact on the business based on their new knowledge? Are the knowledge transfer efforts tied to business objectives?

The goal is to measure the organizational impact of the knowledge transfer process by looking at performance measures and predefined metrics such as on-the-job performance, production levels, error reduction, or even measurements like cost of goods sold or cost of research and development efforts.

Level 5 evaluation attempts to measure the bottom-line result of the knowledge transfer process. It includes "dollarizing" both the costs and results of knowledge transfer efforts and making a comparison between the two. Level 5 answers questions like these: Do the knowledge transfer techniques we use have a positive impact on the organization with minimal costs? What is the relationship between knowledge transfer and the investment in creating the tools required for an effective transfer? This level of evaluation is difficult to obtain, but it must be measured to ensure that the organization is not wasting its knowledge transfer dollars.

These five levels of evaluation ensure that the KRP process is effective and yielding the desired results. Evaluation is the cornerstone of transferring knowledge from the boomers to the gamers.

Continuation

Knowledge transfer is not a process done once. It requires continual feeding, maintenance, and monitoring. Someone must be responsible for managing, scheduling, and coordinating the KRP process within the organization.

As boomers begin leaving the organization and new gamers enter, the need to continually transfer knowledge will not subside. There will be a constant need for policies, procedures, and a corporate culture that encourages knowledge transfer.

One method of assuring a continual focus on knowledge transfer is to appoint a chief knowledge officer (CKO) whose job is to monitor internal knowledge transfer practices and position internal learning events and technology to support the knowledge transfer process. This person must also participate in planning the knowledge transfer from the boomers to the gamers, focus executives on knowledge transfer initiatives, and champion organizational knowledge-gathering and distribution efforts to help maintain the organization's knowledge resources. The chief knowledge officer must also help to establish incentives and plan for the influx of gamers.

The organization must continually work to make the knowledge transfer process part of the organization's culture and ensure that the knowledge of the boomers is transferred over the next ten years to the gamers within the organization.

Workplace Implications

Following the KRP is not like following the other suggestions in this book. Most of the previous suggestions can be done in isolation within a small portion of the organization. The implications of KRP are huge: it involves the entire organization and a focus on knowledge transfer that is unprecedented in most organizations.

This process cannot be led from the bottom up. It needs to start at the top and work its way through the organization. In the absence of KRP, organizations will build islands of knowledge. At best these islands will be loosely connected with ineffective methods of sharing. At worst, there will be no sharing, and gamers will end up recreating all the knowledge that was once known by the departing boomers.

KRP Case Study

A large retail banking institution wanted to determine what knowledge it needed to capture to remain competitive and what it needed to do to attract and retain gamers. It undertook knowledge requirements planning to ensure success. A brief review of what it did and what it accomplished follows.

Management

The first step for the management team was to develop a plan for implementing KRP. They put together a short-term plan to address immediate knowledge transfer needs and created a long-range vision to help secure the future of the bank.

One of their first steps was to determine areas with potential for a number of retirements. Surveys and a review of hiring records provided them with an overall sense of the level of tenure of critical bank employees in important areas. The review showed that the average length of service for the critical employees was over twenty years, with some as high as thirty. And the team learned as well that some key retirements would cause problems.

The team next examined the bank's current hiring and training structure to see how conducive it was to hiring gamers. It wasn't. It had a lecture-rich program with little technology-based training initiatives and nothing aimed at recruiting or retaining gamers.

The team also learned that the bank culture rewarded the hoarding and accumulating of knowledge and punished those who would share. No formal processes existed for sharing knowledge other than memos and regularly scheduled meetings. Important information was expected to trickle down to those who needed to know.

Alignment

The next step was to define strategic knowledge objectives. The bank hit on three main objectives. The first was to provide the sales teams with the knowledge needed to cross-sell products to customers. Cross-selling takes place when a customer comes to the bank to purchase one product and the teller or bank associate identifies additional needs of the customer and can offer them related products. The idea is to increase the sale of products while meeting the customer's needs.

The second objective was to maintain and expand the extensive network of regional business leaders that had been fostered by the senior leadership of the bank. The third was to leverage the knowledge of key marketing people to continue to create innovative and exciting product offerings by combining existing products and introducing new ones.

To help the organization focus on these goals, the bank formed a knowledge council with boomer, gamer, and Gen X members. This council's charge was oversight of the methods that would be put into place to support the three strategic knowledge objectives.

Diagnosis

Based on the preliminary work of identifying retirement issues in terms of the knowledge loss rate, the management team decided to expand the initial study into a full knowledge audit. The audit took about three months and consisted of cataloguing the paper and electronic knowledge assets of the bank, reviewing processes for transferring knowledge such as weekly meetings, and then reporting the results.

Development

The next step was to develop interventions that would help to transfer knowledge. Perhaps the most visible and immediate solution was the development of a computer game that taught new employees how to cross-sell products. A three-dimensional game based on the Torque Game Engine created by GarageGames was written in the first-person perspective and allowed new employees to earn points by working with virtual customers and trying to sell them as many products as possible. The game was developed with input from boomers who described the cross-selling process. It was presented to new gamer employees and was used as a recruitment tool. It also served as a spark for revamping the entire new employee training program at the bank. Lecture-based stand-up instruction was not totally abandoned, but many aspects of it were made more interactive through team-based exercises, group work, and online collaboration tools.

Another major change was the implementation of a mentoring program. Senior bank executives were given an assistant who was to shadow them when they met with regional business leaders. The idea was for the assistants to get to know the members of the network of the senior bank executive and then eventually become a member of the network on their own.

The mentoring was instituted in the new product development area, but without the same level of success. In that area, it was determined that teams would be formed with a conscious effort to evenly distribute boomers, gamers, and Generation Xers onto each team. So while direct one-on-one mentoring was not occurring, the members of each team could learn from each other. Also, a policy was enacted that required each marketer to keep a notebook tracking his or her thoughts during the new product development phase. Each week the team got together and shared information from their notebooks.

Deployment

This phase of KRP met with some resistance. At first, senior executives felt that having assistants shadowing them at every meeting with a client would be cumbersome, and a number of executives attended key meetings without their assistants. When the CEO found out, he called everyone to task and set an example: his assistant followed him to every meeting, internal and external. This helped to get the message across that assistants were valuable and needed to be mentored.

The game encountered some problems since it was so graphically intensive, it could not be downloaded on the corporate intranet. It had to be copied onto a CD-ROM and distributed through the mail to branch offices. This proved to be more expensive than anticipated.

Finally, the initial attempt at establishing mentors in the marketing department did not work. However, the balanced team approach worked extremely well. After about five months, the marketing department was functioning at a higher level than before the team-based approach.

An effort was made to share knowledge at all times. Knowledge sharing was rewarded at company meetings, during executive retreats, and on a weekly basis through the issuing of a "sharing award" to the employee who shared the most knowledge that week.

Evaluation

To hold individuals and departments accountable for the KRP, the performance appraisal system was revamped to include knowledge sharing, recording, and mentoring as key factors for success. The mentoring program and the cross-selling games were evaluated at levels 1 and 2. Evaluations are being put into place to examine the impact of those two items at levels 3, 4, and 5.

Also, surveys are being conducted more frequently, and the human resources department is responsible for conducting focus groups to determine which knowledge sharing methods are successful and which are in need of refocus.

Continuation

The bank has made a commitment to the KRP process by continually examining what it has accomplished and hiring people who are willing to share knowledge. Although the transition was difficult for senior management, they knew they were confronted with a major problem that would only get worse if they failed to take action.

By approaching the problem seriously, the team was able to reconfigure basic processes like hiring, training development, and resource allocations to focus on the act of transferring knowledge. Perhaps the watershed moment was when the CEO called in the senior managers who were not working with their assistants and "strongly suggested" they follow his example—or else. His willingness to lead others by example in the area of knowledge sharing helped as well.

Now that systems have been put into place that institutionalized the knowledge sharing process, the challenge of the bank is to maintain vigilance in the area of knowledge transfer and new employee recruitment.

■   ■   ■   ■

SUMMARY

Failure to embark on a systematic knowledge transfer process may doom many organizations to ultimate failure as competitors learn how to transfer knowledge and achieve advantages based on the speed at which their gamer employees gain knowledge. The processes described in this chapter can be used to avoid failure and position organizations for future success. The same concepts are equally applicable in academic, nonprofit, and for-profit organizations.

In the next chapter, we discuss how boomers can learn to better understand gamers. A list of ideas and concepts to be tried—either together or in isolation—is presented for consideration by boomers. But gamers do not get off without their own list. The chapter also focuses on how gamers can better understand boomers. A vision of the future in which gamers literally rule the world is presented.

It's Not "Just a Game"

TRAVELING TO CALYPSO is similar to traveling to any foreign country. You exchange your currency for the currency of Calypso, and when you return home, you can exchange left-over Calypso currency back to your currency. The only difference? Calypso is not a physical place. It is a virtual world—a *metaverse* (short for "metaphysical universe" or "online world").

In the Calypso metaverse, you exchange real money for virtual money and then exchange it back. Calypso has its own virtual economy, which works almost seamlessly with physical economies. The game, called *Project Entropia,* is free to download and has no monthly fees, unlike most massively multiplayer online role-play games (MMORPG). Instead, the universe works on a cash basis. You are required to have cash to purchase items like a laser rifle, a house, or a vehicle. The Project Entropia Dollar (PED) has a fixed exchange rate linked to the U.S. dollar. Currently ten PEDs equal one U.S. dollar (USD).[1]

Once inside the game, you create items to barter with other players, get a job, and find hidden treasures throughout the virtual world. You can mine items of value like gold or ore, manufacture goods, set up a store, or trade on the virtual stock exchange. You constantly exchange PEDs for goods and services and then, if you want, exchange the PEDs back for real dollars.

Recently a gamer purchased a virtual space resort. The purchase allowed the gamer to rent out apartments built on the resort, rent out space in the resort's shopping mall, and collect hunting and mining taxes. The owner can even rent out advertising space on the resort's billboards. The price for purchasing this piece of virtual real estate? A mere $100,000 USD. That's right: someone purchased a virtual space resort for $100,000.[2] No real land, no real minerals, no real mall, just a virtual rendering of an asteroid-based space resort. Not only that, it is expected that the gamer will actually make money on the resort because of its revenue generation potential.

Of course, the introduction of real money into a virtual game can cause problems. A man was arrested in Japan on suspicion of carrying out a mugging spree—a virtual mugging spree. He was using bots (an artificial intelligence found masquerading as a human user, also know as agents) to beat up online players and steal their virtual possessions in the game *Lineage II*.[3] He then sold the stolen items for actual cash. These agents (like Agent Smith from *The Matrix*) are capable of carrying out repetitive or tedious tasks within a game environment without being directly controlled by a player. A bot is programmed and set loose to complete a task. Bots and agents are also sometimes called nonplayer characters.

It's a Virtual Black Market

There is an entire black market for virtual characters and game items.[4] In the popular MMORPG *Star Wars Galaxies,* a Jedi character sold for two thousand dollars on eBay.[5] If you want to play *World of Warcraft* but don't want to spend hours and hours trying to get to the highest level, you can simply pay for an already created character. It is against the rules of the game and frowned on by many, but go to eBay or Web sites specifically created for this purpose and you can find virtual characters, gold, and other items all for sale for real money.

Clever (and unscrupulous) players can profit from the law of supply and demand within these games. In one infamous *World of Warcraft* (WoW) scam,

> two players took it upon themselves to corner the Ironforge Auction House market by purchasing every single item of trade goods available one day. In the ensuing panic, Auction House visitors found themselves without rations of basic items such as Powerful Mojo, Blasting Powder, Devilsaw Leather, and Black Vitriol. Waiting at the side-lines to save the day were the two cunning WoW traders [who originally bought up all the goods]—selling off their items at a much higher price than their original cost. An impressive and lucrative scheme, The Great Ironforge Auction House Buyout illustrates just how easily inhabitants of epic online kingdoms can formulate a simple scam and turn it into a highly profitable plan.[6]

Farming and selling online assets is becoming big business. Analysts estimate the marketplace for virtual assets in metaverses is approaching $900 million. Some experts believe that within the next five years, the market for virtual assets will reach over $7 billion.[7]

Making an Honest "Online" Living

Anshe Chung, a character in the metaverse of *Second Life,* makes over $150,000 a year in real cash. Actually, it is Anshe Chung's human alter ego who pockets the money. Chung makes a living buying undeveloped virtual land, enhancing the land with virtual landscaping and buildings, and then selling or renting the developed land to other second lifers who pay real money to inhabit her developed acreage. She is a virtual land developer.[8]

Second Life is "an immensely popular 3-D online world in which users, known as 'residents,' build and own their own content online."[9] To date, the world has over 1.3 million inhabitants.[10] Second Life is a metaverse where you create your own character, land, and accoutrements using drag-and-drop commands and a simple scripting language. The kicker is that you also own your own content, which means you can sell virtual land, shirts, and other items in the *Second Life* world. Once you create your character, you can roam the metaverse doing whatever you want. The figures you create are completely customizable. My own alter ego, Abbott Bundy, is shown in Figure 12.1. The alter ego was created in *Second Life* using the development tools available to any *Second Life* resident.

Figure 12.1. Author's *Second-Life* Alter Ego, Abbott Bundy.

Source: Author.

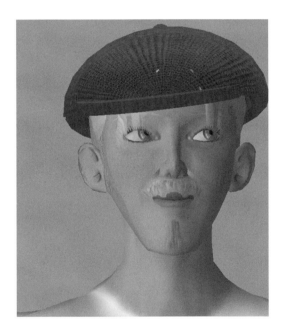

The development tools within the game can be used for far more than the creation of clothes or facial hair. You can create your own games within the world. One especially popular creation is *Tringo,* a cross between the game *Tetris* and bingo.[11] You can play music in *Second Life.* In fact, rock groups are debuting songs and having virtual listening parties in a New York City lofts existing only in *Second Life.*[12] As you are probably guessing by now, *Second*

Life is not just an online world; it is a "social environment, a chat room on steroids—a platform for an alternative life."[13]

Corporations are starting to latch on to the *Second Life* platform and have begun to hold meetings within the environment. One such spot is the "Island of Chatsubo."[14] On the island, team members log on for discussions that display reports and documents created by others in midair for review by all in attendance.

The advertising agency, Leo Burnet, has created a *Second Life* space called the "Ideas Hub," where its 24 hundred creative staffers meet with each other and clients.[15] An international hotel company has created a virtual rendition of a hotel it plans to build to test concepts and ideas.[16]

Companies like Wal-Mart, American Express, IBM, and Intel are experimenting with ways to foster more collaboration and learning within the *Second Life* environment through virtual lectures and other techniques.[17] The news agency, Reuters, has set up a full-time reporter to cover the events in the *Second Life* universe.[18]

Academic institutions are developing a *Second Life* presence as well. More than sixty schools are exploring ways in which the three-dimensional virtual world can be used to create a feeling of community for their online education programs.[19] A Harvard Law School professor, Rebecca Nesson, holds classes and office hours at a virtual campus in *Second Life*. She states, "students interact with each other, and there's a regular sense of classroom interaction. It feels like a [physical] college campus," only it's in *Second Life*.[20]

If all this seems like a little too much for you to jump right in, you can always rent a player and see if you like it. Several Web sites such as www.gamepal.com allow you to try out a game by renting an already established account. That way you can see what you are getting into before you make the long-term commitment to a particular MMORPG world.

Enter the Matrix

The line between games and reality becomes more blurred every day. It is not that gamers can't see the difference between games and reality. As my older son once said to his younger brother who was struggling with a difficult game,

"Nick, you are not *really* a superspy trying to save the universe. You are just playing a game." No, it is just that gamers are equally as comfortable in either world—real or virtual. They bring a technology comfort level unachievable by generations that have not grown up with video games, gadgets, or the Internet. As Steve Keifer, a school superintendent in rural Pennsylvania, says, "kids today are wired differently. They learn differently. Technology for today's kids is second nature."[21] Gamers can trade in either virtual or physical economies and don't see the lines between games and reality as clearly as boomers do.

In Silicon Valley and other centers of technological acumen, video games are morphing into the corporate equivalent of golf. Corporate leaders, venture capitalists, and software entrepreneurs have "discovered the bottom-line benefits of encouraging their employees to play at work. What better way to boost morale while keeping twitchy employees glued to their screens? When it comes to team building, nothing could be more interactive. And, studies show, video games trigger the release of dopamine in the brain, a natural buzz that relives stress."[22] Deals, meetings, and even job offers are being conducted in online worlds. If you pay $100,000 for a virtual asteroid, you want visitors and online activity.

Games and gadgets have simultaneously become ubiquitous and serious. Large sums of money are at stake, and the dynamics of game playing and electronic gadgets are constantly changing. Nissan, the large automobile manufacturer, has teamed with Microsoft to create an automobile design that has the first fully integrated gaming system within a vehicle. The concept car, named the URGE, has a built-in Xbox that allows the driver, when the car is in park, to play a racing game.[23] While playing the game, you press the car's gas pedal to go faster, tap the brake to slow down, and turn the steering wheel to maneuver around virtual cars. In essence, the car becomes one giant game platform. Think driver's ed.

An even more critical application for a virtual driving simulation is in the area of truck driving. A simulator built into a truck or bus could help to prepare and test individuals for a commercial driver's license. Providing a safe learning environment for people preparing for their commercial driver's licenses is important.

The need for drivers is acute. *USA Today* reported that consulting firm Global Insight estimated that in 2005, the trucking industry was short 20,000 drivers and forecasts a gap that could reach 111,000 in 2014 based on demographics and demand for transporting goods.[24]

Driver's education is not the only area affected. Budding young attorneys can pick up the Nintendo DS and play a game called *Phoenix Write: Ace Attorney.* As a defense attorney, it's your responsibility to pick apart the arguments of opposing counsel. The goal is to get a "not guilty" verdict for your client.[25]

Boomers are not being completely left out of the video game arena. Nintendo has created what it calls *Brain Age.* In the game, the challenge is to reduce your brain age by completing a series of puzzles. The puzzles have audio components where you must recite information quickly and accurately and game elements where you solve simple arithmetic problems or create drawings. The developer of the game Ryuta Kawashima, a professor of neuroscience at Tohoku University, believes that spending a few moments a day with the game will help keep the brain young and the person sharp.[26]

Games and gadgets, once the sole purview of basement-dwelling teenagers and techno-geeks, are becoming mainstream, whether boomers like it or not, in much the same way that rock and roll, the rebellious, antiestablishment anthem of boomers, has become mainstream. Witness the use of songs like Janice Joplin's anticonsumerism rift "Mercedes Benz" used by DaimlerChrysler to sell the ultimate symbol of consumerism, a Mercedes Benz (or the Rolling Stones' song "Start Me Up" to sell Microsoft Windows or Paul McCartney's songs to sell retirement plans). Over time, the fringe becomes the middle. Video games are no different.

As the technology of television shaped the lives of the boomers, changing everything from the creation of TV dinners to cultural points of reference like *Saturday Night Live,* games are changing this new generation. Just as television did not replace radio or movies and the Internet did not replace traditional shopping avenues or books, games will not replace traditional media or training methods.

However, television did have an impact on radio, and the Internet does have an impact on brick-and-mortar retailers. Radio no longer broadcasts dramas when television can show the visual aspects of what the radio actors were trying to convey. Retail stores now have to compete on customer experience rather than price. The ability to purchase and watch movies at home did not destroy movie theaters, as many had predicted. Instead, it changed the nature of distribution and the business model of many film studios.

Games, simulations, gadgets, and gizmos will not cause a wholesale replacement of traditional knowledge transfer methods, but they will recast those methods into specific and much more limited niches. Face-to-face class-room training will always have a role, but it will be much more limited than in the past. Gamers will begin to demand games as methods of instruction for science, math, and history lessons.

Learning History Through *Age of Empires II*

Maybe it's my generation and the influence of video games, but I like to use every sense possible when learning. For example, a lecture on American and Japanese foreign politics won't hold my attention for more than fifteen minutes, but lace that information into a storyline in a *Metal Gear* game, and you've got my atten-tion for hours.

It's all about delivery. How much do you learn when someone tells you about a great sandwich she had for lunch? You learn what her interpretation of the sand-wich is and have to use your imagination to fill in the rest.

Now think about how much the experience changes when you go to that same restaurant and eat that same sandwich for yourself. You can see it, feel it, smell it, and taste it. You get to experience it firsthand. The experience and enjoyment are well beyond any explanation given to you because now you are part of it.

Learning about history creates a similar situation. Sitting in a classroom and hearing lectures about the Byzantines, the Turks, or the Vikings can be a little dry for almost anyone. It's like someone telling you how good that sandwich was that she ate. You can get a feel for it, but you would surely have a better experience if you could dig your own teeth into it.

So why not add in a few hours of playing *Age of Empires II* (Figure 12.2)? This way, you can read, see, hear, learn, and experience success and failure right in the middle of history. You can become a part of it.

Figure 12.2. Rich Historical References in *Age of Empires II*.

Source: Microsoft's *Age of Empires II* box shot
reprinted with permission from Microsoft Corporation.

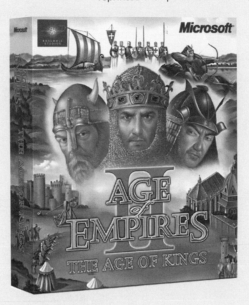

In *Age of Empires II,* you command a great civilization from the past through battle and conquests by using each civilization's historical strengths to strategize the best courses of action. Each civilization is based on historical reality, so you must be conscious of each civilization as it crosses your path and what it may have in store for you and, conversely, how best to defeat it. You can read about it in the history books, or you can dive right in and try to conquer it yourself. Surely if you get slaughtered in the game by a certain group, you will remember what their strength is in quite a different way than if someone just told you the group's strength.

Once in the game, you can take yourself out of the lecture about each civilization's past strengths and weaknesses and learn about them even further by using them in the game as a strategy. For example, the Byzantines had a great military defensive. To showcase this in the game, you can buy defensive units to help your army. Another case is the Turks, who had some great scientific achievements.

In the game, the Turks can research things like gunpowder technologies at a lower cost than any other civilization. The Vikings were remarkable craftsmen, sailors, explorers, and traders. In the game, the Vikings perform exceptionally well in locations on the water but show signs of weakness when they are on land. Immersing yourself in these civilizations' strengths and weaknesses is a way to get you closer to experiencing what each group went through in the past, whether controlling the seas with great skill or being able to stop almost any threat.

Age of Empires II comes equipped with campaign modes, including stories surrounding interesting historical figures such as William Wallace (the Scottish patriot), Joan of Arc, Attila the Hun, and Genghis Khan. The more you can immerse yourself in a subject and the more senses you use, the higher your retention of the information will be. If you want me to learn about a new subject and there's a choice of immersing myself in an interactive environment, I'll jump at the chance every time. And if you wonder if this type of game would sell or appeal to the masses, consider the fact that this franchise has sold over 15 million copies.

> Chris Carro is a lifetime video game enthusiast and a Gamer 2.0, from playing *Pong* at his grandfather's house to soccer on Atari with his father to today playing *Halo* online against his hometown friends in New York. After reviewing games for his college newspaper, *The Voice,* he went on to a public relations career at a top video game publishing company in Manhattan for five years. Currently he is finishing graduate work in instructional technology at Bloomsburg University.

Source: Printed with the permission of Chris Carro.

Crossing the Bridge

The tools and ideas outlined in this book are primarily aimed at the enterprise level. Using the concepts in the previous chapters to mold and shape your organization will help to make the knowledge transfer process between boomers and gamers much more efficient and effective. To summarize the methods:

- Conduct meetings and discussions within the organization to make everyone aware of the gap between boomers and gamers and some actions that can be taken to bridge the gap.

- Identify the key knowledge areas within your organization that need to be preserved and passed on for continued success.

- Create casual games to teach facts and concepts.

- Create simulations of procedures, principles, and problem solving.

- Develop an organizational structure around true self-directed teams. Gamers are used to working with peers both face-to-face and in metaverses.

- Use the portability and power of gadgets to provide instant access to knowledge and information.

- Create organizational cheat codes to lead gamers to sanctioned shortcuts and let them know when rules can be bent or broken and when they cannot.

- Develop techniques to make information and knowledge searchable and easy to access. Think in terms of small chunks of information instead of courses, lessons, or manuals.

- Whenever possible, replace the need to educate employees or students with automation. Think of the cash register that calculates change. Incorporate those types of operations into your organization.

- Set up the organizational structure to reflect the concept of the boss as a strategy guide. Let the gamers have some freedom to learn what they need to learn, but provide guidance and encouragement along the way.

- Use tournaments, Web tools, and other gamers to recruit gamers into your organization or academic program. Recruiting gamers is going to be different from recruiting boomers or Generation Xers. Focus on their needs and natural inclination toward communities and technology.

- Consider the best method of selling the need for gadgets, games, and gizmos within your organization. Academic institutions and corporate organizations that begin to apply the concepts outlined in this book will have a jump on the competition.

- Develop a knowledge requirements plan to pull all of these concepts together within the organization.

While the enterprise can certainly create an environment in which the knowledge transfer process can occur easily, more is needed. To make the process truly successful at the enterprise level, actions must be taken on an individual level. It is the daily interactions between boomers and gamers that make the knowledge transfer possible. Boomers have learned to deal with change and technology. They have been retooling all their lives as new technologies have been showered on them. It is time for them to retool again—retool to transfer the years of knowledge and business acumen to the new generation.

Spanning the generations will not be easy, but it is necessary. Boomers have a lot to learn about gamers, and gamers have a lot to learn from boomers. Each side needs to make efforts and concessions to ensure they understand and are understood.

What the Boomers Can Do

One of the first things boomers can do is try to understand and use the tools of the gamers. Clark Aldrich, author of *Learning by Doing,* a book about games and simulations, states, "I don't understand any manager in a corporation today who doesn't have a working comfort level with computer games." It is time to develop a working knowledge of these items to see how they might help your organization. The challenge is to figure out how to transfer knowledge to a generation more familiar with Adam Sessler and Morgan Webb than with Walter Cronkite.[27] Consider doing several of the following:

- Open an IM account.

- Play *Roller Coaster Tycoon.*

- Play *The Sims.*

- Join a massively multiplayer online role-play game (MMORPG).

- Purchase a personal digital assistant.

- Use the text message feature on your cell phone.

- Purchase an MP3 player, and download a song.

- Buy something on eBay.

- Google your name.

- Buy "black market" gold for your MMORPG.

- Challenge a gamer to a game using cheat codes.

- Comment on a blog, such as http://karlkapp.blogspot.com/.

- Contribute to a wiki.

- Commission a game for your next training requirement.

- Pick three educational processes in your organization that can be replaced with automation.

- Travel to an unknown location using a global positioning system device.

- Rent a MMORPG player for a few days.

- Learn to fly a plane in a software flight simulator.

- Purchase a handheld game platform.

- Create cheat codes for your department.

- Buy iPods for every person in your department.

- Conduct a weekly podcast on departmental issues.

- Create reverse mentoring in your department.

- Hire interns from the local college's game development program.

- Attend a game tournament, and consider entering it.

- Read a video game review.

- Watch X-Play, a show that reviews and rates video games.

- Go to a kid-oriented Web site like Nickelodeon or Disney and play some of the games.
- Buy a video game targeted to adult players.
- Subscribe to a really simple syndication feed from CNN or MSNBC. Set up an aggregator via My.Yahoo.com or another such service.
- Buy a copy of *You Don't Know Jack,* and play it at a party with some friends.
- Look up your favorite artist at www.livemusicplasma.com.
- Go to the *America's Army* Web site, and sign up.
- Buy a video gaming magazine, and read it.
- Rethink your organization's online recruiting efforts.
- Create an alter ego in *Second Life.*

What Gamers Can Do

Gamers need to work to understand the boomer generation. The boomers have built one of the most technologically advanced societies ever. In fact, most of the video games that gamers play are based on technology created by boomers. The boomers have a lot to teach the gamers. Gamers can learn a lot by doing several of the following:

- Seek out a boomer to serve as a mentor.
- Mentor a boomer.
- Learn the hierarchical structure in your organization, and respect it.
- Learn the history of the boomer generation.
- Create cheat sheets for yourself, and verify with a boomer.
- Be patient.
- Ask open-ended questions to glean knowledge from your boomer coworkers.
- Offer to IM with a boomer.

- Set up a wiki and give lessons (in a classroom) on how to update.

- Buy a boomer a copy of *The Sims* and then the expansion pack, *The Sims: Open for Business.*

- Create games on your off-time that are related to work, bring them into the office, and incorporate them into training.

- Show a boomer how to work a gadget.

- Create a podcast, and show boomers how to download and listen.

- Take some time to read corporate policies and procedures. They can be interesting.

- Think of ways to interact with boomers to help them understand your thinking, and work to understand their thinking.

- Take a different boomer to lunch every day, and as you talk about what he or she knows, take notes.

- Get up and visit a boomer. Don't just send an e-mail or IM.

- Volunteer to digitally record production operations, and chunk them for quick viewing.

- Provide feedback to the human resource department about the recruiting process.

- Request permission to contact prospective gamers who might be interested in working at your company.

- Provide input into the training department concerning e-learning, games, simulations, and gadgets.

- Listen. You will learn a lot by keeping your mouth shut and your ears open, especially in the lunchroom area.

- Buy a video game targeted to adult players, and check it out.

- Realize not all training issues can be covered by a game, simulation, or gadget.

- Use the help system supplied by the software vendor. Sometimes it is actually helpful.

- Interview boomers, and record key knowledge insights.

- Tell your manager how you like to learn and what degree of oversight you anticipate as you work on your project.

- Ask "stupid" questions. Sometimes boomers know so much they won't mention the simple things because they've been internalized.

- Don't expect every online learning experience to be a game or simulation.

- Respect the fact that a lot can be learned in a face-to-face classroom environment.

- Understand that the adoption of games, gadgets, and gizmos may occur at a slower rate than you find comfortable.

- Try not to sprinkle your language with too much game jargon.

- Save text messaging and IM shortcuts for casual instant messages. Use standard spellings for business-related messages.

- Understand that trial and error is not the best method for learning everything, especially when safety issues are at hand.

- Use your strengths and abilities to complement those of the boomers.

- Show a boomer how to create an alter ego in *Second Life.*

The Future

The Gamer 4.0 group doesn't begin to hit the workforce until 2010, and a few decades later, these gamers will enter the boardrooms of organizations, become provosts of universities, and gain political power (Figure 12.3). These uber-gamers will have an impact far beyond the slight bump that organizations are currently experiencing with the Gamer 1.0, 2.0, and 3.0 generations.

The world they shape will be a mix between the virtual world and the real world, with seamless movement between the two environments. Meetings will

Figure 12.3. Gamers Will Soon Be Entering Boardrooms and Running
Organizations.

Source: Reprinted with permission of the artist, Kristin Longenecker.

be held in virtual conference rooms, machines will teach operators, gadgets
will provide instructions, and games will become an acceptable way to learn.

Simulated environments (golf courses, asteroids, remote islands) will be
commonplace for holding meetings, training classes, and academic lectures.
High-level executive meetings will occur online, with executives entering the
world from various locations and conversing in a language that the others will
understand through the use of voice translators. Entire universities will have
online campuses with avatars representing students and faculty. The great
imperative of universities to create physical structures (buildings) will wane
as more and more gamers become comfortable going to a college located in
a metaverse. Shopping malls will be online, where avatars with the same measurements, skin tone, and hair color as their physical real-world counterparts
will meet with other avatars and try on clothes and chat and spend time together. When a purchase is desired, the person will enter a credit card number
or click a virtual card, and a few days later the delivery truck will arrive with
the product. The driver will have been trained in a virtual delivery truck.

Simulations, gadgets, and games will allow gamers to acquire knowledge in just a few years instead of a few decades—like the twenty-one-year-old poker players who quickly caught up to the grand masters through their repetitive playing of online poker.

We need to implement these techniques and strategies now. Boomers are shifting priorities and leaving the workforce at this very moment. Gamers at all levels are entering schools and the workforce on a daily basis. As organizations consider strategies, competitive position, and their very future, they must keep in mind gadgets, games, and gizmos.

Epilogue

ALL OF THIS TECHNOLOGY and talk about the use of gadgets, games, and gizmos as business tools may make you and your organization a little afraid of the future.

Boomers may say, "We don't have these items in place, we don't really think they will work, and we aren't comfortable with this concept. This is just a normal generational thing." Gamers may say, "I want the new methods of getting knowledge. I'm afraid I can't learn with the old methods, but the boomers are still in control. There is nothing I can do." Boomers and gamers may both be a little unclear about where all this is leading.

But remember that I didn't write this book on gadgets, games, and gizmos to tell you how this boomer-gamer knowledge transfer process is going to end. I wrote it to tell you how this is going to begin.

I wanted to show boomers a world they may not always want to see: a gamers' world and one seemingly without boundaries, rules, or a respect for the past. I wanted to show the gamers a world they are not familiar with but one in which they must survive: the boomers' world, one seemingly of corporate ladders and face-to-face meetings. But the reality is that both worlds need each other, and there are infinite knowledge transfer possibilities.

Now that you have information about the two worlds, where organizations go from here is a choice I leave to you.[1]

Please continue this discussion by visiting www.gadgetsgamesandgizmos. com, where you can post comments, update a wiki, and contribute to the dynamic community that is attempting to bridge the boomer-gamer knowledge gap.

Notes

CHAPTER ONE

1. Pasha, P. (2005). Corporations woo baby boomers. *CNNMoney.* Retrieved October 4, 2005, from http://money.cnn.com.

2. Story, T. (2005). The big bang electronic version. *OCLC Newsletter.* Retrieved October 4, 2005, from http://www.oclc.org/news/ publications/newsletters/oclc/2005/267/thebigbang.htm.

3. DeLong, D. W. (2004). *Lost knowledge: Confronting the threat of an aging workforce.* New York: Oxford University Press, p. 3.

4. DeLong. (2004).

5. This information comes from two sources: Pasha (2005) and Story (2005).

6. Sivy, M., Kalwarski, T., & Gandel, S. (2005). Will the boomers bring down the market? *Money Magazine.* Retrieved October 4, 2005, from http://money.cnn.com.

7. DeLong. (2004), p. 3.

8. Gandel, S., Sivy, M., & Kalwarski, T. (2005). Work the brain drain. *Money Magazine.* Retrieved October 4, 2005, from http://money.cnn.com.

9. Gandel, Sivy, & Kalwarski. (2005).

10. Block, S., & Armour, S. (2006, July 10). Many Americans retire years before they want to. *USA Today,* 1A-2A.

11. Updegrave, W. (2005). Get real about working in retirement. *Money Magazine.* Retrieved October 4, 2005, from http://money.cnn.com.

12. Block & Armour. (2006).

13. Fielding, R. (2006). Early retirement will fuel skills shortage. *Accountancy Age.* Retrieved July 11, 2006, from http://www.computing.co.uk/accountancyage/news/2144885/early-retirement-fuel-skills.

14. Bick, J. (2006, May 14). Golfing and gardening (and working) in retirement. *New York Times.* Retrieved July 11, 2006, from http://www.nytimes.com/2006/05/14/business/yourmoney/14retire.html?ex=1305259200&en=cbac9fb9176faf61&ei=5088&partner=rssnyt&emc=rss.

15. DeLong. (2004).

16. King, M. (2005). Manufacturers: Baby boomer retirement to cost big bucks. *APICS e-News, 5*(19). Retrieved October 4, 2005.

17. Kelly, D. (2006). The shortage. *APICS Extra, 1*(5). Received June 28, 2006.

18. King. (2005).

19. Pasha. (2005).

20. Greene, K. (2005). Bye-bye boomers? Companies may face exodus as workers hit retiring age: Some bosses are afraid to ask. *Wall Street Journal,* B1. Retrieved October 5, 2005, from ProQuest database. Butting heads over retirement plans. (2006, July). *Training,* 8.

21. Harris, P. (2006, January). Beware of the boomer brain drain. *TD,* no. 1, 32.

22. Theil, S. (2006, January 30). The new old age. *Newsweek International.* Retrieved March 1, 2006, from http://www.msnbc.msn.com/ id/10967825/site/newsweek/.

23. Engardio, P., & Matlack, C. (2005, January). Global aging. *BusinessWeek.* Retrieved March 1, 2006, from http://www.businessweek.com/ magazine/content/05_05/b3918011.htm.

24. Theil. (2006).

25. Engardio & Matlack. (2005).

26. Story. (2005).

27. All statistics describing the desire for personalization come from Horovitz, B. (2005). You want it your way. *USAToday.* Retrieved October 5, 2005, from http://www.usatoday.com.

28. Masci, D. (2004, May 7). Future of marriage. *CQ Researcher Online, 14,* 397–420. Retrieved October 5, 2005, from http://library.cqpress. com/cqresearcher/cqresrre2004050700. Document ID: cqresrre 2004050700.

29. Candy Lightner. Retrieved June 25, 2006, from Wikipedia at http:// en.wikipedia.org/wiki/Candy_Lightner.

30. About Us. American Beverage Institute. Retrieved June 25, 2006, from http://www.abionline.org/aboutUs.cfm.

31. Courtesy of Sprint Nextel, used with permission. Graf, G. (Executive Creative Director). (2006, January 29). The man sticks it to . . . himself. *CBS Super Bowl Broadcast.* Television commercial. Danville, PA: CBS. Howard, T. (2006, January). Sprint crafts Super Bowl ads. *USA Today.* Retrieved March 1, 2006, from http://www.usatoday.com/ money/advertising/adtrack/2006–01–08-sprint-track_x.htm.

32. Peters, T. (2003). *Re-imagine! Business excellence in a disruptive age.* London: Dorling Kindersley Limited, p. 47.

33. Prensky, M. (2001). *Digital game-based learning.* New York: McGraw-Hill. Kitchen, P. (2005). Members of video-game generation transfer skills to workplace. *Knight Ridder Tribune Business News.* Retrieved October 5, 2005, from ProQuest database.

34. Kitchen. (2005).

35. Story. (2005).

36. The history of the *Legend of Zelda.* (2003, November 23). G4TV.com. Retrieved March 1, 2006, from http://www.g4tv.com/techtvvault/features/24842/The_History_of_The_Legend_of_Zelda.html.

37. Demaria, R., & Wilson, J. L. (2002). *High score: The illustrated history of electronic games.* New York: McGraw-Hill, p. 240.

38. Demaria & Wilson. (2002).

39. About *Myst.* Retrieved June 25, 2006, from http://www.cyan.com/.

40. GDC 2005: Iwata keynote transcript. (2005). Retrieved June 25, 2006, from http://cube.ign.com/articles/595/595089p2.html.

41. Fox, S. (2005). Digital divisions. Report by the Pew/Internet: Pew Internet & American Life. Retrieved October 6, 2005, from www.pewinternet.org/pdfs/PIP_Digital_Divisions_Oct_5_2005.pdf.

42. U.S. Department of Commerce. (2002, February 5). *Evans: Census data show America is online: Internet usage promising for economic vitality.* Retrieved from http://www.commerce.gov/opa/press/Secretary_Evans/2002_Releases/Feb_05_Evans_Census_Online.html.

43. This information is from a press release on January 3, 2005, by the Stanford Institute for the Quantitative Study of Society for their study, *Ten Years After the Birth of the Internet, How Do Americans Use the Internet in Their Daily Lives?* It is a study of over four thousand respondents concerning their behavior on the Internet. Retrieved October 4, 2005, from http://www.stanford.edu/group/siqss/Press_Release/press_detail.html.

44. Leaders: Breeding evil; Defending video games. (2005, August 6). *Economist.* Retrieved October 5, 2005, from ProQuest database.

45. Oser, K. (2005). Game enthusiasm rises up from the basement. *Advertising Age.* Retrieved October 5, 2005, from ProQuest database.

46. Walsh, D., Gentile, D., Walsh, E., Bennett, N., Robideau, B., Walsh, M., Strickland, S., & McFaddin, D. (2005, November 29). *Tenth annual MediaWise video and computer game report card.* Retrieved March 18, 2006, from http://www.mediafamily.org/research/2005_VGRC.pdf.

47. Kitchen. (2005).

48. Wakefield, J. (2006, October). All women gamers, please stand up. *BBC News.* Retrieved November 5, 2006, from http://news.bbc.co.uk/2/hi/technology/5407490.stm. Douglas, N. (2006, April). The future of games does not include women. *grrlgamer.com featured article.* Retrieved November 11, 2006, from http://www.grrlgamer.com/article.php?t=futureofgames.

49. Waters, D. (2006, August). Games industry is "failing women." *BBC News.* Retrieved November 5, 2006, from http://news.bbc.co.uk/1/hi/technology/5271852.stm.

50. Wakefield. (2006).

51. Oser. (2005).

52. Brightman, J. (2005). Puppy love puts Nintendogs on top. *GameDaily.* Retrieved June 25, 2006, from http://biz.gamedaily.com/industry/toppers/?id=10566.

53. Shank, R. (1997). *Virtual learning: A revolutionary approach to building a highly skilled workforce.* New York: McGraw-Hill, p. 16.

54. This information is consolidated from Bates, B. (2001). *Game design: The art and business of creating games.* Roseville, CA: Prima Publishing. Rollings, A., & Adams, E. (2003). *Andrew Rollings and Ernest Adams on game design.* Indianapolis, IN: New Riders Publishing. Salen, K., &

Zimmerman, E. (2004). *Rules of play: Game design fundamentals.* Cambridge, MA: MIT Press. Celina Byers from Bloomsburg University's Instructional Technology Program first provided me with this information.

55. This information is consolidated from Csikszentmihalyi, M. (1991). *Flow: The psychology of optimal experience.* New York: HarperCollins. Squire, K. (2003). Video games in education. *International Journal of Intelligent Simulations and Gaming, 2*(1), 49–62.

56. Begley, S. (2003, May 29). The kid flunked, but he sure pays attention. *Wall Street Journal,* B1. Retrieved October 10, 2005, from ProQuest database.

57. Dye, M.W.G., & Bavelier, D. (2004). Playing video games enhances visual attention in children. *Journal of Vision, 4*(11), 40a. Retrieved from http://journalofvision.org/4/11/40/, doi:10.1167/4.11.40. Roach, J. (2003, May 28). Video games boost visual skills study finds. *National Geographic News.* Retrieved March 18, 2006, from http://news.nationalgeographic.com/news/2003/05/0528_030528_video games.html.

58. Begley. (2003).

59. Begley. (2003).

60. Squire. (2003).

61. Csikszentmihalyi. (1991).

62. Bates. (2001).

63. Rollings & Adams (2003), p. 13.

64. Bates. (2001).

65. Rouse, R. III (2001). *Game design: Theory and practice.* Plano, TX: Wordware Publishing.

66. This article makes a good case about why the video game industry is not bigger than Hollywood, as many claim. Gilbert, R. (2004). It's

that time of year again. *Grumpy Gamer.* Retrieved June 25, 2006, from http://grumpygamer.com/5378171.

67. Kerr, A., & Flynn, R. (2002). Revisiting globalization through the movie and digital games industries. *Massachusetts Institute of Technology Web Page.* Retrieved November 19, 2006, from http://web.mit.edu/cms/Events/mit2/Abstracts/KerrFlynn.pdf.

68. *DW-World* staff. (2005). Video gaming in Germany lags behind. *DW-World. DE Deutsche Welle.* Retrieved November 19, 2006, from http://www.dw-world.de/dw/article/0,2144,1684952,00.html.

69. BBC staff. (2006). French to set budget in web game. *BBC.* Retrieved November 19, 2006, from http://news.bbc.co.uk/2/hi/europe/4946496.stm.

70. CBC staff. (2006). Video game creators join France's Order of Arts and Letters. *CBC.CA.* Retrieved November 19, 2006, from http://www.cbc.ca/arts/story/2006/03/13/france-order.html.

71. Caldwell, P. (2006). Report: Korean game market to surpass $2 billion in 2007. *GameSpot.com News.* Retrieved November 19, 2006, from http://www.gamespot.com/news/6153903.html.

72. Brightman, J. (2006). Report: China's video game market to reach $2.1 billion in 2010. *GameDailyBiz.com.* Retrieved November 19, 2006, from http://biz.gamedaily.com/industry/feature/?id=12513.

73. Brightman. (2005).

74. PR-Zoom Newswire staff. (2006). DTK computer targets Middle East's booming PC gaming market. PR-Zoom Newswire. Retrieved November 19, 2006, from http://www.przoom.com/news/7253.

75. Information retrieved from the Electronic Arts Web site on November 5, 2006, in the "Company Information" section, http://info.ea.com.

76. Hyman, P. (2004). "Casual" video games are serious business. *Hollywood Reporter.* Retrieved June 15, 2006, from http://www.thehollywoodreporter.com/hr/columnis/tech-reporter_display.jsp?vnu_content.

77. The statistics about non-PC devices and online Internet game market are from Deloitte Touche & Tohmatsu, Technology, Media and Telecommunications Practice. (2004). *Moore's law and electronic games: How technology advances will take electronic games everywhere.* Retrieved October 5, 2005, from http://industries.bnet.com/ whitepaper.aspx?cid=261&docid=100191.

78. Kolodny, L. (2006). Video games set for global explosion. *Hollywood Reporter.com.* Retrieved June 25, 2006, from http://www.hollywood reporter.com/thr/video_games/article_display.jsp?vnu_content_id= 1002691152.

79. The origin of the information for this list came from Beck, J. C., & Wade, M. (2004). *Got game: How the gamer generation is reshaping business forever.* Boston: Harvard Business School Press. But it was actually based on a list created by Story (2005) and information from Prensky (2001).

80. Gouskos, C., with Gerstmann, J. (2004). The greatest Easter Eggs in gaming. Retrieved October 9, 2005, from http://www.gamespot.com/ features/6131572/.

81. Computer-related Easter eggs. Retrieved October 9, 2005, from http://en.wikipedia.org/wiki/Easter_eggs_%28virtual%29.

82. Beck & Wade. (2004), p. 107.

83. Beck & Wade. (2004), p. 89.

84. Beck & Wade. (2004), p. 88.

85. Beck & Wade. (2004), p. 81.

86. Beck & Wade. (2004), p. 144.

87. Wile E. Coyote was created in 1949 by Chuck Jones and Michael Maltese. He first appeared in a cartoon titled *Fast and Furry-ous.*

88. Beck & Wade. (2004), p. 94.

89. Kitchen. (2005), Prensky. (2001).

90. Beck & Wade. (2004), p. 112.

91. Flash mob. Retrieved October 11, 2005, from http://en.wikipedia. org/wiki/Flash_mob.

92. Maney, K. (2004). Halo 2 reveals new generation gap: Boomers vs gamers. *USA Today,* B3. Retrieved October 5, 2005, from ProQuest database.

93. Gates, B. (2005). Bill Gates' "America's high schools are obsolete." Speech to the National Governors Association. Retrieved June 25, 2006, from http://blogoehlert.typepad.com/eclippings/2005/05/ bill_gates_amer.html.

94. Beck & Wade. (2004).

CHAPTER TWO

1. *Halo 2* is the sequel to the highly successful *Halo.* In *Halo 2,* a character named Master Chief—a genetically enhanced supersoldier—is the only thing standing between a relentless evil empire and the destruction of all humankind. You play the hero in the game and save the universe or die trying.

2. Reimer, J. (2005). Cross-platform game development and the next generation of consoles: The runaway cost of game development. *Arcs Technica.* Retrieved January 1, 2006, from http://arstechnica.com/ articles/paedia/hardware/crossplatform.ars/2.

3. Keighley, G. (2005, September 1). Massively multinational player. *Business 2.0 Magazine.* Retrieved March 15, 2006, from http://money. cnn.com/magazines/business2/business2_archive/2005/09/01/835652 1/index.htm.

4. Reimer. (2005).

5. Absolut search. Retrieved July 24, 2006, from http://www.absolut.com.

6. Hyman, P. (2004). "Casual" video games are serious business. *Hollywood Reporter.* Retrieved June 15, 2006, from http://www.thehollywood reporter.com/thr/columnis/tech-reporter_display.jsp?vnu_content.

7. Gagné, R. M. (1985). *The conditions of learning and theory of instruction* (4th ed.). New York: Holt.

8. Personal interview with Mark Oehlert, June 30, 2006.

9. The Johnson & Johnson Campaign for Nursing's Future Raises Funds for Tennessee Nursing Shortage. (2006, March 10). Retrieved March 15, 2006, from http://www.jnj.com/news/jnj_news/20060310_142227.htm.

10. Samurai Challenge. (2006). *Samurai Challenge Game.* Created by GameTrain. Retrieved July 24, 2006, from http://www.gametrain.net/samurai_game/main.html.

CHAPTER THREE

1. Introduction. (n.d.). *World of Warcraft* Web site. Retrieved March 20, 2006, from http://www.worldofwarcraft.com/info/basics/guide.html; jsessionid=FB7655F71C3BC98490B5979B0C2A0204.08_app02.

2. Gagné, R. M., & Glaser, R. (1987). Foundations in learning research. In R. M. Gagné (Eds.), *Instructional technology foundations.* Mahwah, NJ: Erlbaum, p. 71.

3. Gagné & Glaser. (1987), p. 71.

4. Shank, R. (1997). *Virtual learning.* New York: McGraw-Hill, p. 39.

5. Personal interview with Richard Mesch, June 14, 2006.

6. Leshin, C. B., Pollock, J., & Reigeluth, C. M. (1992). *Instructional design strategies and tactics.* Upper Saddle River, NJ: Educational Technology Publications.

7. Aldrich, C. (2005). *Learning by doing.* San Francisco: Pfeiffer/Jossey-Bass.

8. Mandel, S. (2005, October 17). Scorecard: Joe cool. *Sports Illustrated, 103*(15), 22.

9. Clark, R. C. (1999). *Developing technical training: A structured approach for developing classroom and computer-based instructional*

material (2nd ed.). Silver Spring, MD: International Society for Performance Improvement.

10. Klabbers, J.H.G. (2000, September). Learning as acquisition and learning as interaction. *Simulation and Gaming, 31*(3), 380.

11. Kriz, C. W. (2003, December). Creating effective learning environments and learning organizations through gaming simulation design. *Simulation and Gaming, 34*(4).

12. Kriz, C. W. (2003), p. 501.

13. Personal interview with Mark Oehlert, June 30, 2006.

14. Koster, R. (2005). *A theory of fun.* Scottsdale, AZ: Paraglyph Press, p. 34.

CHAPTER FOUR

1. This information is gleaned from two articles. Ackman, D. (2003). Playing with FAO Swartz Electronics Edition. *CNN Money.* Retrieved October 14, 2005, from http://www.forbes.com/2003/12/11/cx_da_1211topnews.html. Bhatnagar, P. (2004). Bankruptcy in store. *CNN Money.* Retrieved October 14, 2005, from http://money.cnn.com/2004/01/14/news/companies/retail_bankruptcies/index.htm.

2. Tech-toys are tops this holiday season. (2005). *CNN Money.* Retrieved October 14, 2005, from http://money.cnn.com/2005/10/06/news/funny/tech_toys.reut/index.htm.

3. Deloitte Touche & Tohmatsu. Technology, Media and Telecommunications Practice. (2004). *Moore's law and electronic games: How technology advances will take electronic games everywhere.* Retrieved October 5, 2005, from http://industries.bnet.com/whitepaper.aspx?cid=261&docid=100191.

4. Information retrieved from the Nintendo Web site, "In the News" section. The article was titled "Nintendo and Wayport Join Forces to Bring Free U.S. Wi-Fi Access to Nintendo DS Users" and retrieved October 24, 2005, from http://www.nintendo.com/newsarticle?articleid=ZRzLtQZgFZiOvHfsAvXKUDxYUloypXJv.

5. GDC 2005: Iwata keynote transcript. (2005). Retrieved June 25, 2006, from http://cube.ign.com/articles/595/595089p2.html.

6. Lenhart, A., Madden, M., & Hitlin, P. (2005, July 27). *Teens and technology: Youth are leading the transition to a fully wired and mobile nation.* Retrieved March 17, 2006, from http://www.pewinternet.org/pdfs/PIP_Teens_Tech_July2005web.pdf.

7. Pickoff-White, L. (2005). *Consumer electronic companies target teens.* United Press International. Retrieved October 24, 2005, from http://medialit.med.sc.edu/consumer_electronic_companies_target_teens.htm.

8. Levitan, B. (2005, October). Communications technology pipeline. *Commercial Services Symposium, 6*(44). Retrieved October 20, 2005, from ProQuest database.

9. Gruman, G. (2005). Wireless broadband: The long and winding road. *InfoWorld,* p. 32. Retrieved October 20, 2005, from ProQuest database.

10. Personal interview with Michael T. Qaissaunee on July 10, 2006.

11. Wireless Philadelphia Executive Committee Mission Statement. Retrieved October 25, 2005, from http://www.phila.gov/wireless/.

12. Baldwin, H. (2002). Keeping track of digital assets Electronic Edition. *Thinkpad.* Retrieved October 24, 2005, from http://techupdate.zdnet.com/techupdate/stories/main/0,14179,2875220,00.html.

13. What boomer wants to sit down for ten hours either? No one, regardless of the generation, wants to sit and absorb ten or more hours of video.

14. DeLong, D. W. (2004). *Lost knowledge: Confronting the threat of an aging workforce.* New York: Oxford University Press.

15. Excerpted from an IBM white paper titled *MARVEL: Multimedia analysis and retrieval system.* Intelligent Information Management Department. Retrieved October 14, 2005, from http://www.research.ibm.com/marvel/Marvel%20Whitepaper.pdf. Kanellos, M. (2004). IBM's "Marvel" to scour net for video, audio. *CNET.* Retrieved October 24, 2005, from http://news.zdnet.com/2100–9596_22–5388718.html.

16. Baldwin. (2002).

17. Virage Products. Virage product overview. Retrieved June 21, 2006, from http://www.virage.com/content/products/#vs_videologger.

18. Terdiman, D. (2005). Folksonomies tap people power. Retrieved July 12, 2006, from http://www.wired.com/news/technology/0,1282,66456,00.html.

19. Terdiman. (2005).

20. According to Wikipedia, an online encyclopedia, "Moore's Law is the empirical observation that at our rate of technological development, the complexity of an integrated circuit, with respect to minimum component cost, will double in about 24 months. It is attributed to Gordon E. Moore, a co-founder of Intel."

21. Hall, E. C. (1996). Journey to the Moon: The history of the Apollo Guidance Computer. Retrieved October 24, 2005, from http://scholar.google.com/scholar?hl=en&lr=&c2coff=1&q=cache:bf615GzyBfEJ:www.iee.org/OnComms/pn/History/HistoryWk_Apollo_CSM.pdf+author:%22Williamson%22+intitle:%22THE+APOLLO+COMMAND+AND+SERVICE+MODULE-FIRST+AND+ONLY+MOONSHIP%22.

22. Flash mob. Retrieved October 11, 2005, from http://en.wikipedia.org/wiki/Flash_mob.

23. See http://www.batmanbeyond.com for more information.

24. Personal interview with Erik Poole, June 6, 2006.

25. Gorman, C. (2006, January 18). Updating the stethoscope with an iPod. *Time*.

26. Nike and Apple team up to launch Nike + iPod. (2006). Retrieved July 12, 2006, from http://www.nike.com/nikebiz/news/pressrelease.jhtml?year=2006&month=05&letter=k.

27. Personal interview with Andy Howe, May 18, 2006.

28. Company: Our RFID tags. (n.d). Retrieved March 23, 2006, from http://www.verichipcorp.com/content/company/verichip#implantable.

29. See www.orbitz.com for more information on the Alert Care feature.

30. Kapp, K. (2005). An interview with Cisco's Tom Kelly and Nader Nanjiani. e-learningguru. Retrieved March 1, 2006, from http://www.e-learningguru.com/interviews/interview_tomKelly.htm.

CHAPTER FIVE

1. Courtesy of Paramount Pictures. Copyright STAR TREK II THE WRATH OF KHAN © by Paramount Pictures. All Rights Reserved.

2. My Gamer 4.0 son gave me these cheat codes. I didn't know them until he enlightened me.

3. Morris, C. (2005, July 21). Did "Grand Theft Auto" get off too easily. Retrieved March 22, 2006, from http://money.cnn.com/2005/07/21/commentary/game_over/column_gaming/index.htm.

4. Block, R. (2005). Brute-forcing unreleased GTA San Andreas cheat codes. Engadget Web log. Retrieved October 25, 2005, from http://gaming.engadget.com/entry/1234000000027945/.

5. Robinson, A. G., & Schroeder, D. M. (2004). *Ideas are free.* San Francisco: Berrett-Koehler.

6. Robinson & Schroeder. (2004), p. 97.

7. The For Dummies success story. (n.d.). Retrieved March 15, 2006, from http://www.dummies.com/WileyCDA/Section/id-100052.html.

8. Banner on PunkBuster Web site. Retrieved June 15, 2006, from http://www.punkbuster.com.

CHAPTER SIX

1. Battelle, J. (2005). *The search: How Google and its rivals rewrote the rules of business and transformed our culture.* New York: Portfolio.

2. Deloitte Touche & Tohmatsu, Technology, Media and Telecommunications Trends. (n.d.). *Predications, 2006.* Retrieved March 24, 2006, from http://www.deloitte.com/dtt/cda/doc/content/us_tmt_tech predictions2006_020206%281%29.pdf.

3. 2002 words of the year. (2003, January 13). Retrieved March 16, 2006, from http://www.americandialect.org/index.php/amerdial/ 2003/01/.

4. Prensky, M. (2001, October). Digital native, digital immigrants. *On the Horizon, 9*(5). Retrieved March 16, 2006, from http://www.twitch speed.com/site/Prensky%20-%20Digital%20Natives,%20Digital% 20Immigrants%20-%20Part1.htm.

5. Murry, B. (n.d.). *What makes students stay.* Retrieved March 16, 2006, from http://www.elearnmag.org/subpage.cfm?section=articles&article= 22–1.

6. Schooley, C. (2004). *Maximizing your human capital investment through knowledge, communications and continuous performance metrics.* Forrester Research, Inc., EduNeering Annual Client Meeting. Painter, D. (2006). Missed steps in Intelligence Column. *TD Magazine, 60*(7), 10.

7. Kapp, K. (2005). An interview with Cisco's Tom Kelly and Nader Nanjiani. *e-learningguru.* Retrieved March 1, 2006, from http:// www.e-learningguru.com/interviews/interview_tomKelly.htm.

8. Charny, B. (2005, November 10). *Is e-mail becoming the new snail mail?* Retrieved January 21, 2006, from http://www.eweek.com/ article2/0,1759,1885289,00.asp.

9. Lenhart, A., Madden, M., & Hitlin, P. (2005, July 27). *Teens and technology: Youth are leading the transition to a fully wired and mobile nation,* (p. i). Retrieved January 21, 2006, from http://www.pew internet.org/pdfs/PIP_Teens_Tech_July2005web.pdf.

10. Lenhart, Madden, & Hitlin. (2005).

11. List of terms courtesy of Nathan Kapp, Gamer 4.0.

12. Kerner, S. M. (2004, October 15). *Enterprising the instant message.* Retrieved January 25, 2006, from http://www.internetnews.com/ bus-news/article.php/3422361.

13. The Cooler. (n.d.). *AOL News Blog.* Retrieved March 16, 2006, from http://journals.aol.com/thecoolerblog/AOLNewsCooler/.

14. Lenhart, Madden, & Hitlin. (2005).

15. About Technorati. (n.d.). *Technorati.* Retrieved July 14, 2006, from http://www.technorati.com/about.

16. Armstrong, H. (n.d.). *About this site.* Retrieved March 16, 2006, from http://www.dooce.com/about.html.

17. Simonetti, E. (n.d.). *Diary of a fired flight attendant.* Retrieved March 16, 2006, from http://queenofsky.journalspace.com/.

18. Crawford, K. (2005, February, 15). *Have a blog, lose your job?* Retrieved January 28, 2006, from http://money.cnn.com/2005/02/ 14/news/economy/blogging/index.htm.

19. McGregor, J. (2005, April). It's a blog world after all. *FastCompany,* no. 81. Retrieved January 29, 2006, from http://pf.fastcompany.com/ magazine/81/blog.html.

20. McGregor. (2005).

21. Eldelman and Intelliseek Corporations. (2005). *Talking from the inside out: The rise of employee bloggers.* Retrieved March 16, 2006, from http://www.edelman.com/image/insights/content/ Edelman-Intelliseek%20Employee%20Blogging%20White%20 Paper.pdf.

22. Wiki. (n.d.). *Wikipedia.org: The free encyclopedia.* Retrieved March 17, 2006, from http://en.wikipedia.org/wiki/Wiki.

23. Taylor, P. (2003). *Correspondence on the etymology of wiki.* Retrieved July 14, 2006, from http://c2.com/doc/etymology.html

24. Wiki. (n.d.).

25. Wiki. (n.d.).

26. Giles, J. (2005, December 14). Internet encyclopedias go head to head. *Nature.* doi:10.1038/438900a. Retrieved March 17, 2006, from http://www.nature.com/news/2005/051212/full/438900a.html.

27. Wikipedia survives research test. (2005, December 15). *BBC News.* Retrieved January 17, 2006, from http://news.bbc.co.uk/1/hi/technology/4530930.stm. Giles, J. (2005).

28. Personal interview with Marty Siederer, June 13, 2006.

29. Personal interview with Gordon Synder Jr., July 13, 2006.

30. Fastest text message. (2004). *Guinness World Records.* Retrieved March 17, 2006, from http://www.guinnessworldrecords.com/content_pages/record.asp?recordid=57979. Bellett, B. (2006, January 23). *Text messaging world record smashed.* Retrieved March 17, 2006, from http://www.mobileburn.com/news.jsp?Id=1959&source=HOME.

31. Text message record smashed again. (2005, January 21). *BBC News.* Retrieved March 17, 2006, from http://news.bbc.co.uk/1/hi/technology/4194191.stm.

32. Maier, M. (2006, January 19). Extra, extra! Gannett gets the (text) message. *Business2.0.* Retrieved March 17, 2006, from http://money.cnn.com/2006/01/18/technology/thirdscreen/.

33. Battelle. (2005), p. 2.

34. del.icio.us/about/info. (n.d.). The Site. The Company. *del.icio.us.* Retrieved June 23, 2006, from http://del.icio.us/about/info.

35. del.icio.us/about/info. (n.d.).

36. About Technorati. (n.d.). *Technorati.* Retrieved July 14, 2006, from http://www.technorati.com/about.

37. Battelle. (2005), p. 6.

38. Learning-John Cone. (1998). *FastCompany.* Retrieved March 17, 2006, from http://www.fastcompany.com/magazine/20/cone.html.

39. Maisie, E. (2006). Nano-learning: Miniaturization of design. *Chief Learning Officer Magazine.* Retrieved July 15, 2006, from http://www.clomedia.com/content/templates/clo_article.asp?articleid=1221.

40. Talanca, J. (n.d.). Let's get small. *e-learningguru.com.* Retrieved on March 17, 2006, from http://www.e-learningguru.com/articles/art_misc_1.htm.

41. Kapp. (2005).

42. Battelle. (2005).

CHAPTER SEVEN

1. Little, C. (1997, September/October). The Intelligent Vehicle Initiative: Advancing "human-centered" smart vehicles. *Public Roads Magazine, 61*(2). Retrieved March 17, 2006, from http://www.tfhrc.gov/pubrds/pr97-10/p18.htm. Woodyard, C. (2005, November 10). Cars soon may "talk" to roads, each other. *USA Today,* 1B–2B.

2. Vance, A. (2004, January 20). How HP invented the market for iPod resellers. *Register.* Retrieved March 12, 2006, from http://www.theregister.co.uk/2004/01/19/how_hp_invetnted_the_market_/print.html.

3. Uncanny Valley. Retrieved March 29, 2006, from http://en.wikipedia.org/wiki/Uncanny_valley.

4. McCloud, S. (1994). *Understanding comics.* New York: HarperCollins.

5. All information about *You Don't Know Jack* and Jellyvision was used with permission from Jellyvision, Inc., and The Jellyvision Lab, Inc. All rights reserved.

6. Gery, G. J. (1991). *Electronic performance support system: How and why to remake the workplace through the strategic application of technology.* Boston: Weingarten Publications, p. 34.

7. Gery. (1991).

CHAPTER EIGHT

1. Jones, S. D. (2006). Professor of Special Education, Department of Exceptionality Programs, Bloomsburg University, personal correspondence, January 12, 2006.

2. Be here (or there) now with holoprojection. (2006, January). *Green Tree Gazette,* p. 130.

3. Survey: Millennials seek balance, continuing education. (2006, May). *Chief Learning Officer.*

4. Industry Statistics, Table S-1 estimated book publishing net sales February 2, 2005. Association of American Publishers. Retrieved July 17, 2006, from http://www.publishers.org/industry/index.cfm.

5. Two professors turn consumer law into a soap opera. (2006, January). *Green Tree Gazette.*

6. Students prefer online courses. (2006, January 13). *Education with student news.* Retrieved January 13, 2006, from http://www.cnn.com/2006/EDUCATION/01/13/oncampus.online.ap/index.html.

7. Report: Number of students taking online courses rises. (2006, November). *Education with student news.* Retrieved November 11, 2006, from http://www.cnn.com/2006/EDUCATION/11/09/colleges.online.ap/index.html.

8. Students prefer online courses. (2006).

9. Kapp, K. (2005). Interview with John Beck. e-learningguru. Retrieved March 1, 2006, from http://www.e-learningguru.com/interviews/interview_beck.htm.

10. Peters, T. (2003). *Re-imagine! Business excellence in a disruptive age.* London: Dorling Kindersley Limited, p. 63.

CHAPTER NINE

1. Ultimate Video Gamers League. (n.d.). Retrieved March 17, 2006, from http://www.gamerstournaments.com/.

2. DigitalLife 2005 teams up with Global Gaming League to produce national gaming tournament. (2005, April 5). Ziff Davis Media. Retrieved March 17, 2006, from http://www.ziffdavis.com/press/releases/050405.0.html.

3. Dennis Fong. Retrieved March 17, 2006, from Wikipedia at http://en.wikipedia.org/wiki/Dennis_Fong.

4. Armour, S. (2005, November 8). Generation Y: They've arrived at work with new attitude. *USA Today.* Retrieved March 13, 2006, from http://www.usatoday.com/money/workplace/2005–11–06-gen-y_x.htm. Sacks, D. (2006, January). Scenes from the culture clash. *Fast-Company,* no. 102.

5. Lefkow, D. (2005, August 23). The future labor shortage: Alarmist myth or frightening reality? *Electronic Recruiting Exchange.* Retrieved March 17, 2006, from http://www.erexchange.com/ARTICLES/DEFAULT.ASP?CID=%7B328A6F88–8180–4CDD-A809–862FFEF5D565%7D.

6. Ohlemacher, S. (2006, March 9). Older Americans are not working as late in life. *Danville News.*

7. Irvine, M. (2006). The young labeled "Entitlement Generation." *ABC News, Associated Press.* Retrieved March 13, 2006, from http://abcnews.go.com/Business/print?id=883733.

8. Armour. (2005).

9. Foss, A., & Prensky, M. (2005, January 16). Members of video-game generation transfer skills to workplace. *Knight Ridder/Tribune Business News.* Retrieved October 10, 2005, from ProQuest database.

10. Sacks. (2006).

11. American high schoolers receive help from India. *CNN.com.* Retrieved November 3, 2005, from http://www.growingstars.com/news/CNN_com%20-%20American%20high%20schoolers%20receive%20help%20from%20India%20-%20Oct%2026,%202005.htm.

12. Sacks. (2006).

13. Three ways to find generation Y. (2003, September). *Workforce Management.* Retrieved March 13, 2006, from http://www.workforce.com/section/06/article/23/51/81_printer.html.

14. Gomes, L. (2006, February 8). Programming contest pits world's top geeks in battles over coding. *Wall Street Journal Online.* Retrieved March 14, 2006, from http://webreprints.djrerints.com/1404341094425.html.

15. Baker, S. (2006, January 23). The NSA: Security in number. *BusinessWeek online.* Retrieved February 5, 2006, from http://www.businessweek.com/magazine/content/06_04/b3968007.htm. Hahl, D. (2006, January). Put a hacker to work. *INC. Magazine,* 39–42. Available at www.topcoder.com.

16. Personal interview with Jack Hughes, July 7, 2006.

17. Press release, University of Iowa, May 12, 2006. Retrieved July 17, 2006, from http://itsnt166.iowa.uiowa.edu/uns-archives/2006-copy-5–12/may/051206volding_award.html. Harvard Business School Business Plan Contest Web site FAQ. Retrieved July 17, 2006, from http://www.hbs.edu/entrepreneurship/bplan/faqs.html. California State University Fresno Web site. Retrieved July 17, 2006, from http://www.lylescenter.com/10k_student_business_plan_competition.php. Rice University Business Plan Competition Web site. Retrieved from http://www.alliance.rice.edu/alliance/RBPC.asp.

18. FAQ. (n.d.). Retrieved March 17, 2006, from http://www.americasarmy.com.

19. Gwinn, E. (2003, November 7). Army targets youth with video game. *Chicago Tribune.* Retrieved February 4, 2006, from http://www.notinourname.net/resources_links/video-game-7nov03.htm.

20. Downing, J. (2004, December 7). Army to potential recruits: Wanna play? *Seattle Times.* Retrieved February 4, 2006, from http://seattletimes.nwsource.com/html/localnews/2002111412_wargames07e.html.

21. FAQ. (n.d.).

22. FAQ. (n.d.).

23. Liang, J. (2006). *Hello real world! A student's approach to great internships, co-ops and entry level positions.* Charleston, SC: BookSurge Publishing.

24. Armour. (2005).

CHAPTER TEN

1. NYC mayor fires man for playing solitaire. (2006, February 9). Retrieved March 18, 2006, from http://www.msnbc.msn.com/id/11261224/.

2. Rogers, E. M. (2003). *Diffusion of Innovations* (5th ed.). New York: Free Press.

3. Gladwell, M. (2002). *The tipping point: How little things can make a big difference* (2nd ed.). New York: Back Bay Books. Moore, G. A. (1991). *Crossing the Chasm.* New York: HarperBusiness.

4. Rogers. (2003).

5. Turner, A. (2005). *Response to post millennial librarians training the boomer librarians.* Retrieved July 17, 2006, from http://tametheweb.com/2005/06/millennial_librarians_training.html.

6. Rogers. (2003).

7. Rogers. (2003).

8. Moore, G. A. (1995). *Inside the tornado.* New York: HarperBusiness. Rogers. (2003).

9. Gladwell. (2002).

10. Rogers. (2003).

11. Greene, K. (2005). Bye-bye boomers? Companies may face exodus as workers hit retiring age: Some bosses are afraid to ask. *Wall Street Journal,* B1. Retrieved October 5, 2005, from ProQuest database.

12. Aldrich, C. (2005). *Learning by doing.* San Francisco: Pfeiffer/Jossey-Bass.

13. Greenleaf, W., Fitter, J., & Rosser, J. (2005, February 21). Playing games for health. *Knight Ridder/Tribune Business News.* Retrieved October 5, 2005, from ProQuest database.

14. Video game fans dance off extra pounds. (2004, May 5). *USA Today.* Retrieved March 18, 2006, from http://www.usatoday.com/tech/news/2004–05–23-video-health_x.htm.

15. Totty, M. (2005, April 25). Technology (a special report): Business solutions. *Wall Street Journal.* Retrieved October 5, 2005, from ProQuest database.

16. Begley, S. (2003, May 29). The kid flunked, but he sure pays attention. *Wall Street Journal.* Retrieved October 10, 2005, from ProQuest database.

17. Dobnik, V. (2004, April 7). Surgeons may error less by playing video games. *Associated Press.* Retrieved March 18, 2006, from http://www.msnbc.msn.com/id/4685909/.

18. Christopher, A. (2005, January 13). Games tackle disaster training. *Wired.* Retrieved January 1, 2006, from http://wired.com/news/technology/0,1282,69580,00.html?tw=wn_tophead_2.

19. Miller, B. (2006, January 10). Rio's use of radio tags on servers causes concern. *Las Vegas Business Press.* Retrieved January 11, 2006, from http://lvbusinesspress.com/articles/2006/01/10/news/news01.txt.

20. Gayeski, D. M., & Petrillose, M. J. (2005). No strings attached: How the gaming and hospitality industry uses mobile devices to engineer performance. *Performance Improvement Journal, 44*(2). Retrieved January 9, 2005, from ProQuest database.

21. And now a game from our sponsor. (2005, June 11). *Economist, 375*(8430), p. 4. Retrieved October 5, 2005, from ProQuest database.

22. Jana, R. (2001, March 27). On-the-job video gaming. *BusinessWeek* online. Retrieved March 28, 2006, from http://www.businessweek.com/print/magazine/content/06_13/b3977062.htm?chan=gl.

23. Flood, S. (2006, March 23). All play and more work. *vnu.net*. Retrieved March 28, 2006, from http://www.vnunet.com/computing/analysis/2152597/play-work.

24. Flood. (2006).

25. Guttridge, L. (2005). *Myst* aids teaching at UK school. Ferrago, Ltd. Intelligent Gaming Opinion. Retrieved July 18, 2006, from http://www.ferrago.com/story/6407.

26. Peck, M. (2004, December). "America's Army" fan base expanding. Retrieved March 28, 2006, from http://www.nationaldefense magazine.org/issues/2004/Dec/AmericasArmyFan.htm.

27. Jana. (2001).

28. Flood. (2006).

29. Bozarth, J. (2005). *e-learning on a shoestring: Help for the chronically underfunded trainer.* San Francisco: Jossey-Bass.

CHAPTER ELEVEN

1. President's Commission on Implementation of United States Space Exploration Policy. (2004). *Report of the President's Commission on Implementation of United States Space Exploration Policy: A journey to inspire, innovate and discover.* Retrieved July 18, 2006, from http://www.nasa.gov/pdf/60736main_M2M_report_small.pdf.

2. DeLong, D. W. (2004). *Lost knowledge: Confronting the threat of an aging workforce.* New York: Oxford University Press, p. 11.

3. Wheeler, L. (2006). U.S. losing unofficial space race, congressman says. *Florida Today.* Retrieved July 18, 2006, from http://www.space.com/news/ft_060331_nasa_china_congress.html. China's space quest gathers speed. (2006). Retrieved July 18, 2006, from http://www.cnn.com/2006/TECH/space/03/12/china.space/index.html.

4. Stewart, T. A. (1997). *Intellectual capital: The new wealth of organizations.* New York: Doubleday, p. 70.

5. Smith, P. L., & Ragan, T. J. (1999). *Instructional design* (2nd ed.). Upper Saddle River, NJ: Merrill.

6. Phillips, J. (1997). *Return on investment in training and performance improvement programs.* Houston: Gulf Publishing Company. Kirkpatrick, D. (1998). *Another look at evaluating training programs.* Alexandria, VA: American Society for Training and Development.

CHAPTER TWELVE

1. Home page. http://www.project-entropia.com. Retrieved March 26, 2006, from http://www.project-entropia.com.

2. Sanders, T. (2005, October 26). *Gamer shells out $100,000 for virtual property.* Retrieved March 14, 2006, from http://www.vnunet.com/articles/print/2144707.

3. Knight, W. (2005, August 18). Computer characters mugged in virtual crime spree. Retrieved March 24, 2006, from http://www.newscientist.com/article.ns?id=dn7865.

4. Siegel, R. (2005, November 30). Paying real money to win online games. *National Public Radio: All Things Considered.* Retrieved March 24, 2006, from http://www.npr.org/templates/story/story.php?storyId=5032947.

5. Krotoski, D. (2005, June 16). Virtual trade gets real. *Guardian Unlimited.* Retrieved March 24, 2006, from http://technology.guardian.co.uk/online/story/0,3605,1506928,00.html.

6. Farshi, O. (2005, July 29). Making moolah in MMORPGs. Retrieved March 25, 2006, from http://www.twitchguru.com/2005/07/29/making_moolah_in_mmorpgs/page6.html.

7. www.ige.com. (n.d.). *Our business.* Retrieved March 25, 2006, from http://www.ige.com/about.

8. Sloan, P. (2005). The Virtual Rockefeller Electronic Version. *Business 2.0 Magazine.* Retrieved July 21, 2006, from http://money.cnn.com/

magazines/business2/business2_archive/2005/12/01/8364581/index. htm.

9. Sire records plans to launch virtual world for Regina Spektor in popular online world *Second Life*. (2006). *Yahoo!Finance*. Retrieved June 6, 2006, from http://biz.yahoo.com/iw/060522/0130654.html?pinter=1.

10. Kirkpatrick, K. (2006, November 10). No, *Second Life* is not overhyped. *Fortune*. Retrieved November 18, 2006, from http://money. cnn.com/2006/11/09/technology/fastforward_secondlife.fortune/ index.htm?section=money_technology_personaltech.

11. Thompson, C. (2006). The game within the game. *Wired*. Retrieved June 30, 2006, from http://www.wired.com/news/columns/ 0,70945–0.html?tw=rss.index.

12. Sire records plans to launch virtual world for Regina Spektor in popular online world *Second Life*. (2006).

13. Thompson. (2006).

14. Stewart, C. (2006). Corporations learn from online games. *TimesLeader.com*. Retrieved July 24, 2006, from http://www.times leader.com/mld/timesleader/business/14521822.htm.

15. Steel, E. (2006, November 13). Avatars at the office. *Wall Street Journal*. Retrieved November 18, 2006, from http://online.wsj.com/ article_email/SB116338308666421252-lMyQjAxMDE2NjEzMz MxODMzWj.html.

16. Kirkpatrick. (2006).

17. Hof, R. (2006). My virtual life. *BusinessWeek Online*. Retrieved July 24, 2006, from http://www.businessweek.com/magazine/content/06_18/ b3982001.htm.

18. Kirkpatrick. (2006).

19. Wong, G. (2006, November 14). Educators explore "Second Life" online. *CNN.com*. Retrieved November 18, 2006, from http://www. cnn.com/2006/TECH/11/13/second.life.university/index.html.

20. Wong. (2006).

21. Gessel, D. (2006, September 21). Staying ahead of the curve. *The Danville News,* p. 1.

22. Guynn, J. (2006). Making gaming pay off. *San Francisco Chronicle.* Retrieved July 31, 2006, from http://www.sfgate.com/cgi-bin/article.cgi?file=/c/a/2006/07/23/BUGJ1K36NI1.DTL&type=printable.

23. Xbox 360 powers all-new Nissan URGE concept car. (n.d.). Microsoft press release. Retrieved March 25, 2006, from http://www.microsoft.com/presspass/press/205/dec05/12–27URGE360PR.mspx?pf=true.

24. Hagenbaugh, B. (2006). Think convoys are a beautiful sight? Have they got a job for you. *USA Today.* Retrieved July 25, 2006, from http://www.usatoday.com/money/economy/employment/2006–04–24-trucking-usat_x.htm?POE=click-refer.

25. www.nintendo.com. (n.d.). Web site. Phoenix Write. Retrieved March 26, 2006, from http://www.nintendo.com/gamemini?gameid=b8576b18-bd0d-4f17–8bfc-dfd2e90113e4&.

26. Brain workouts with computer gamers a hit with baby boomers. (n.d.). *People's Daily Online.* Retrieved March 25, 2006, from http://English.people.com.cn/200603/08/print20060308_248827.html.

27. For the gamers, Walter Cronkite was the *CBS Evening News* anchor from 1962 to 1981. For the boomers, Adam Sessler and Morgan Webb are the hosts of the show *X-Play,* which reviews and rates video games.

EPILOGUE

1. With apologizes to Larry and Andy Wachowski for the loose parody of Neo's speech at the end of *The Matrix.*

Index

About the Author

KARL M. KAPP, Ed.D., CFPIM, CIRM, is a consultant, scholar, speaker, and expert on the convergence of learning, technology, and business operations. He is the assistant director of the Institute for Interactive Technologies at Bloomsburg University in Bloomsburg, Pennsylvania. In that position, he has overseen the creation of hundreds of games, simulations, and e-learning development projects for use in corporate, academic, and nonprofit settings. His background teaching e-learning classes, knowledge of adult learning theory, and experience training CEOs and frontline staff provides him with a unique perspective on organizational learning.

Kapp is a noted technologist with a vision toward the future of technology, learning, and business operations. He is the software editor for a manufacturing trade journal and an external evaluator for two Advanced Technology Education grants funded by the National Science Foundation. He sits on the boards of several learning technology companies and advises Fortune 500 companies on the use of technology for transferring knowledge to their employees.

He is committed to helping organizations develop a strategic, enterprisewide approach to organizational learning through his writing, keynote addresses, and consulting, as well as his work as a professor of instructional technology at Bloomsburg University. He is the father of two gamers, which keeps him busy. He believes that the effective convergence of learning and technology is the key to increased productivity and profitability, and he helps organizations achieve those goals. Visit his Web site at www.karlkapp.com, his blog at http://karlkapp.blogspot.com/ and this book's Web site at www.gadgets gamesandgizmos.com.

Pfeiffer Publications Guide

This guide is designed to familiarize you with the various types of Pfeiffer publications. The formats section describes the various types of products that we publish; the methodologies section describes the many different ways that content might be provided within a product. We also provide a list of the topic areas in which we publish.

FORMATS

In addition to its extensive book-publishing program, Pfeiffer offers content in an array of formats, from fieldbooks for the practitioner to complete, ready-to-use training packages that support group learning.

FIELDBOOK Designed to provide information and guidance to practitioners in the midst of action. Most fieldbooks are companions to another, sometimes earlier, work, from which its ideas are derived; the fieldbook makes practical what was theoretical in the original text. Fieldbooks can certainly be read from cover to cover. More likely, though, you'll find yourself bouncing around following a particular theme, or dipping in as the mood, and the situation, dictate.

HANDBOOK A contributed volume of work on a single topic, comprising an eclectic mix of ideas, case studies, and best practices sourced by practitioners and experts in the field.

An editor or team of editors usually is appointed to seek out contributors and to evaluate content for relevance to the topic. Think of a handbook not as a ready-to-eat meal, but as a cookbook of ingredients that enables you to create the most fitting experience for the occasion.

RESOURCE Materials designed to support group learning. They come in many forms: a complete, ready-to-use exercise (such as a game); a comprehensive resource on one topic (such as conflict management) containing a variety of methods and approaches; or a collection of like-minded activities (such as icebreakers) on multiple subjects and situations.

TRAINING PACKAGE An entire, ready-to-use learning program that focuses on a particular topic or skill. All packages comprise a guide for the facilitator/trainer and a workbook for the participants. Some packages are supported with additional media—such as video—or learning aids, instruments, or other devices to help participants understand concepts or practice and develop skills.

- *Facilitator/trainer's guide* Contains an introduction to the program, advice on how to organize and facilitate the learning event, and step-by-step instructor notes. The guide also contains copies of presentation materials—handouts, presentations, and overhead designs, for example—used in the program.

- *Participant's workbook* Contains exercises and reading materials that support the learning goal and serves as a valuable reference and support guide for participants in the weeks and months that follow the learning event. Typically, each participant will require his or her own workbook.

ELECTRONIC CD-ROMs and Web-based products transform static Pfeiffer content into dynamic, interactive experiences. Designed to take advantage of the searchability, automation, and ease-of-use that technology provides, our e-products bring convenience and immediate accessibility to your workspace.

METHODOLOGIES

CASE STUDY A presentation, in narrative form, of an actual event that has occurred inside an organization. Case studies are not prescriptive, nor are they used to prove a point; they are designed to develop critical analysis and decision-making skills. A case study has a specific time frame, specifies a sequence of events, is narrative in structure, and contains a plot structure—an issue (what should be/have been done?). Use case studies when the goal is to enable participants to apply previously learned theories to the circumstances in the case, decide what is pertinent, identify the real issues, decide what should have been done, and develop a plan of action.

ENERGIZER A short activity that develops readiness for the next session or learning event. Energizers are most commonly used after a break or lunch to stimulate or refocus the group. Many involve some form of physical activity, so they are a useful way to counter post-lunch lethargy. Other uses include transitioning from one topic to another, where "mental" distancing is important.

EXPERIENTIAL LEARNING ACTIVITY (ELA) A facilitator-led intervention that moves participants through the learning cycle from experience to application (also known as a Structured Experience). ELAs are carefully thought-out designs in which there is a definite learning purpose and intended outcome. Each step—everything that participants do during the activity—facilitates the accomplishment of the stated goal. Each ELA includes complete instructions for facilitating the intervention and a clear statement of goals, suggested group size and timing, materials required, an explanation of the process, and, where appropriate, possible variations to the activity. (For more detail on Experiential Learning Activities, see the Introduction to the *Reference Guide to Handbooks and Annuals*, 1999 edition, Pfeiffer, San Francisco.)

GAME A group activity that has the purpose of fostering team spirit and togetherness in addition to the achievement of a pre-stated goal. Usually contrived—undertaking a desert expedition, for example—this type of learning method offers an engaging means for participants to demonstrate and practice business and interpersonal skills. Games are effective for team building and personal development mainly because the goal is subordinate to the process—the means through which participants reach decisions, collaborate, communicate, and generate trust and understanding. Games often engage teams in "friendly" competition.

ICEBREAKER A (usually) short activity designed to help participants overcome initial anxiety in a training session and/or to acquaint the participants with one another. An icebreaker can be a fun activity or can be tied to specific topics or training goals. While a useful tool in itself, the icebreaker comes into its own in situations where tension or resistance exists within a group.

INSTRUMENT A device used to assess, appraise, evaluate, describe, classify, and summarize various aspects of human behavior. The term used to describe an instrument depends primarily on its format and purpose. These terms include survey, questionnaire, inventory, diagnostic, survey, and poll. Some uses of instruments include providing instrumental feedback to group members, studying here-and-now processes or functioning within a group, manipulating group composition, and evaluating outcomes of training and other interventions.

Instruments are popular in the training and HR field because, in general, more growth can occur if an individual is provided with a method for focusing specifically on his or her own behavior. Instruments also are used to obtain information that will serve as a basis for change and to assist in workforce planning efforts.

Paper-and-pencil tests still dominate the instrument landscape with a typical package comprising a facilitator's guide, which offers advice on administering the instrument and interpreting the collected data, and an initial set of instruments. Additional instruments are available separately. Pfeiffer, though, is investing heavily in e-instruments. Electronic instrumentation provides effortless distribution and, for larger groups particularly, offers advantages over paper-and-pencil tests in the time it takes to analyze data and provide feedback.

LECTURETTE A short talk that provides an explanation of a principle, model, or process that is pertinent to the participants' current learning needs. A lecturette is intended to establish a common language bond between the trainer and the participants by providing a mutual frame of reference. Use a lecturette as an introduction to a group activity or event, as an interjection during an event, or as a handout.

MODEL A graphic depiction of a system or process and the relationship among its elements. Models provide a frame of reference and something more tangible, and more easily remembered, than a verbal explanation. They also give participants something to "go on," enabling them to track their own progress as they experience the dynamics, processes, and relationships being depicted in the model.

ROLE PLAY A technique in which people assume a role in a situation/scenario: a customer service rep in an angry-customer exchange, for example. The way in which the role is approached is then discussed and feedback is offered. The role play is often repeated using a different approach and/or incorporating changes made based on feedback received. In other words, role playing is a spontaneous interaction involving realistic behavior under artificial (and safe) conditions.

SIMULATION A methodology for understanding the interrelationships among components of a system or process. Simulations differ from games in that they test or use a model that depicts or mirrors some aspect of reality in form, if not necessarily in content. Learning occurs by studying the effects of change on one or more factors of the model. Simulations are commonly used to test hypotheses about what happens in a system—often referred to as "what if?" analysis—or to examine best-case/worst-case scenarios.

THEORY A presentation of an idea from a conjectural perspective. Theories are useful because they encourage us to examine behavior and phenomena through a different lens.

TOPICS

The twin goals of providing effective and practical solutions for workforce training and organization development and meeting the educational needs of training and human resource professionals shape Pfeiffer's publishing program. Core topics include the following:

Leadership & Management

Communication & Presentation

Coaching & Mentoring

Training & Development

e-Learning

Teams & Collaboration

OD & Strategic Planning

Human Resources

Consulting

What will you find on pfeiffer.com?

- The best in workplace performance solutions for training and HR professionals

- Downloadable training tools, exercises, and content

- Web-exclusive offers

- Training tips, articles, and news

- Seamless online ordering

- Author guidelines, information on becoming a Pfeiffer Affiliate, and much more

Discover more at www.pfeiffer.com